BETTY PARSONS

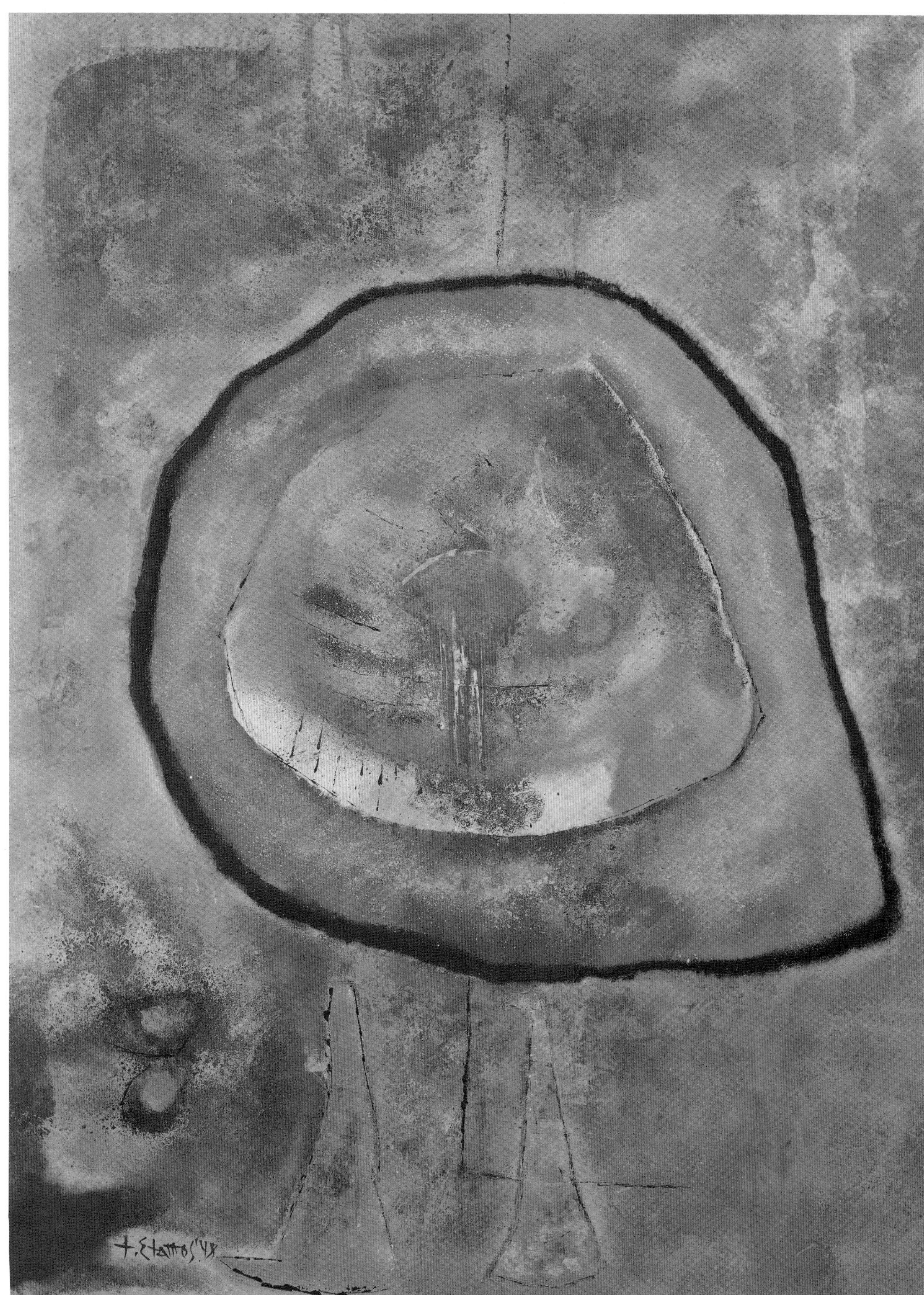

Joseph Cornell, *Untitled (Bébé Marie),* early 1940s. Paper and painted wood box with painted corrugated cardboard floor, containing doll in cloth dress and straw hat with cloth flowers, dried flowers and twigs, flecked with paint, 23½ x 12⅜ x 5¼". Collection, The Museum of Modern Art, New York. Acquired through the Lillie P. Bliss Bequest

Opposite: Theodoros Stamos, *Echo,* 1948. Oil on composition board, 48 x 36." Metropolitan Museum of Art, New York. Albert H. Hearn Fund 1950

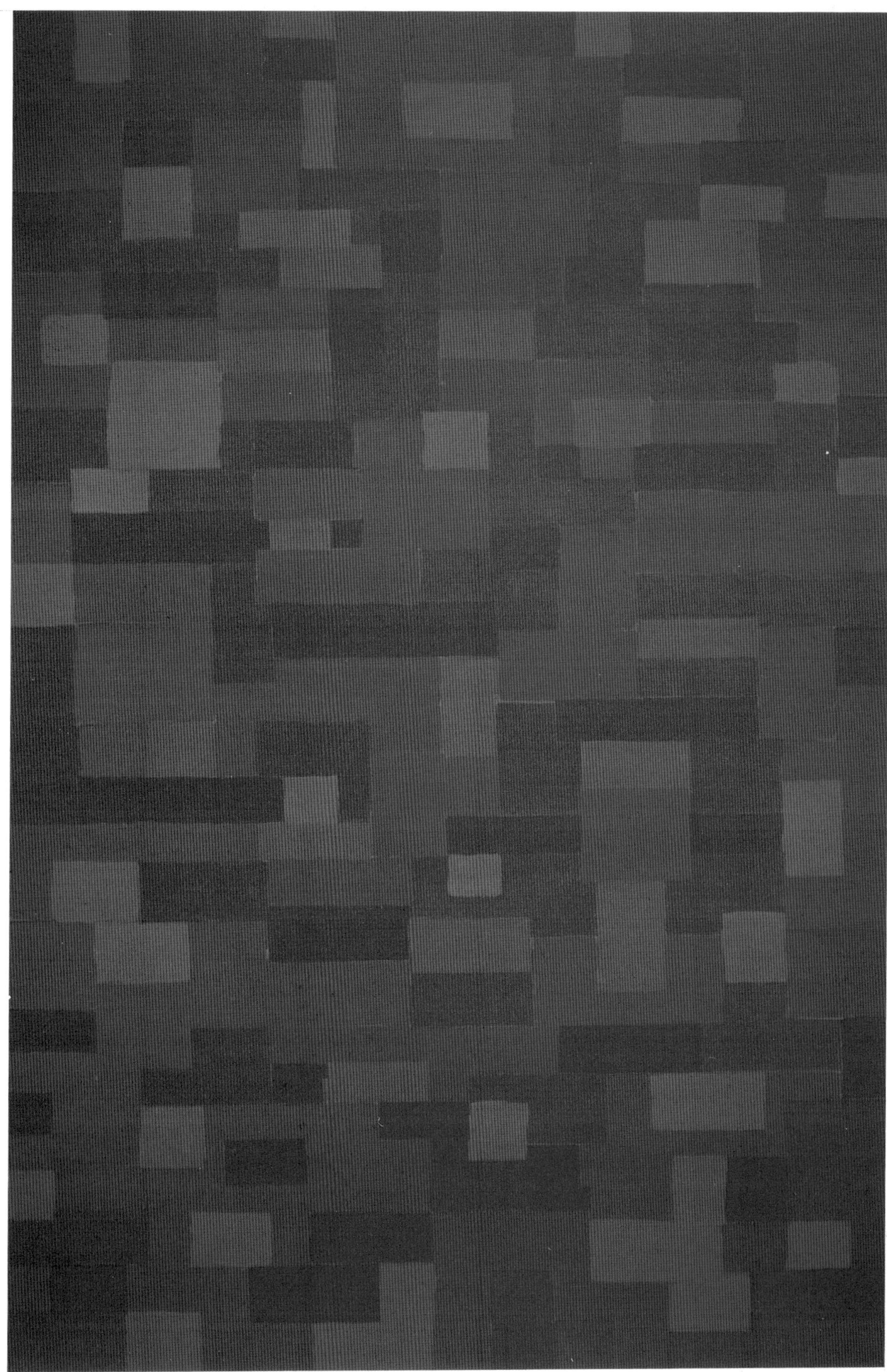

Bradley Walker Tomlin, *Number 20,* 1949. Oil on canvas, 7′ 2″ x 6′ 8¼″. Collection, The Museum of Modern Art, New York. Gift of Philip Johnson

Jackson Pollock, *Alchemy,* 1947. Oil on canvas, 45 x 87″. Peggy Guggenheim Collection, Venice. The Solomon R. Guggenheim Foundation, New York

Opposite: Ad Reinhardt, *No. 114,* 1950. Oil on canvas, 60 x 40⅛″. Collection unknown

Ellsworth Kelly, *Colors for a Large Wall,* 1951. Oil on canvas, mounted on 64 wood panels, overall, 7′ 10¼″ x 7′ 10¼″. Collection, The Museum of Modern Art, New York. Gift of the artist

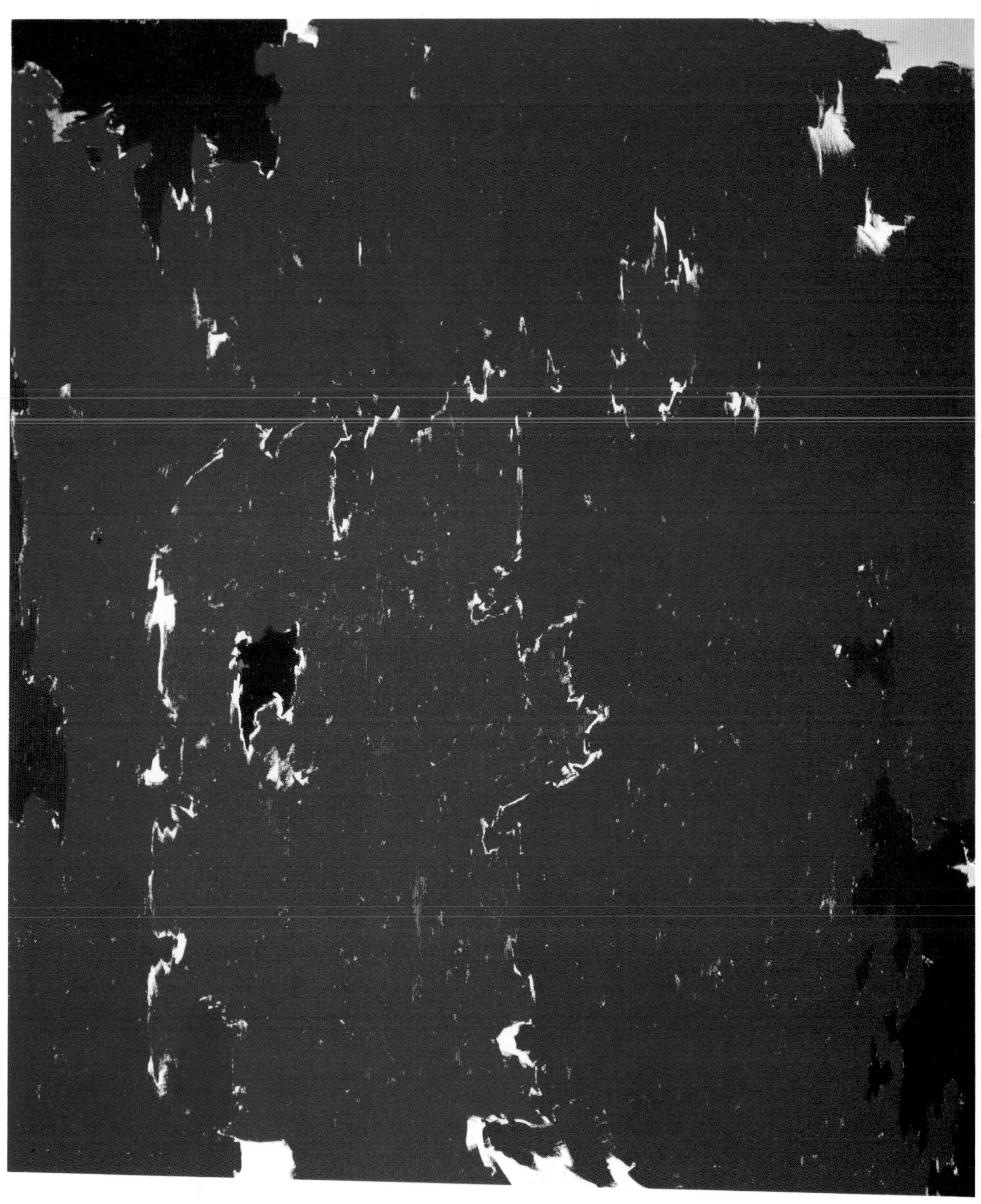

Clyfford Still, *1950-A, No. 2,* 1950. Oil on canvas, 93 x 109″. Hirshhorn Museum and Sculpture Garden, Smithsonian Institution, Washington, D.C. Gift of Joseph H. Hirshhorn, 1972 (72.282)

BETTY PARSONS

Artist · Dealer · Collector

LEE
HALL

HARRY N. ABRAMS, INC., PUBLISHERS, NEW YORK

TO HEDDA STERNE

Page 8, opposite title page: Mark Rothko, *Magenta, Black, Green on Orange,* 1949. Oil on canvas, 7′ 1⅜″ x 65″. Collection, The Museum of Modern Art, New York. Bequest of Mrs. Mark Rothko through The Mark Rothko Foundation, Inc.

Page 1, half-title page: Betty Parsons, *Clocks of Time,* 1968. Oil on canvas, 61 x 49¼″. The Montclair Art Museum, New Jersey. Gift of the Gehrie Foundation, 72.8

Editor: Phyllis Freeman

Designer: Jody Hanson

Photo Research: Barbara Lyons

Library of Congress Cataloging-in-Publication Data

Hall, Lee.
Betty Parsons: artist, dealer, collector / by Lee Hall.
192 p. 21.6 x 27.9 cm.
Includes index.
ISBN 0-8109-3712-3
1. Parsons, Betty. 2. Art dealers—United States—Biography.
3. Sculptors—United States—Biography. I. Title.
N8660.P37H35 1990
709′.2—dc20
[B] 90-45916
CIP

Published in 1991 by Harry N. Abrams, Incorporated, New York
A Times Mirror Company

Printed and bound in Japan

CONTENTS

Betty in her studio, 1979

PROLOGUE

I first knew about the Betty Parsons Gallery in the early fifties when I was a student in North Carolina. Each month, I intercepted the art magazines on their way to the library shelves, lingered over reviews and pictures, and dreamed of New York and the world of art and artists. Betty Parsons's gallery, I soon observed, showed art I hungered to see. As a neophyte painter, I hoped she might show my work someday. The Betty Parsons Gallery, for me, was where painters were born; Betty Parsons was a beacon to aspiring artists.

When I moved to New York, I saw every exhibition Betty Parsons offered. And I saw Betty. Enraged and bellowing abuse at an assistant, she marched from the back room of the gallery; she scowled, muttered, hunched her shoulders, and disappeared into an elevator.

Later, still remembering that Olympian display of temper, I met Betty Parsons at a dinner party at the Central Park West apartment of Hermann and Ruth Vollmer. Ruth was an artist who would later show in the Betty Parsons Gallery; her husband, Hermann, was a German pediatrician who had come to New York after the rise of Hitler. Amid the Vollmer art collection and library, Betty was the essence of courtesy and charm. I liked her and, from then on, talked with her whenever I visited her gallery. She began to look at my work; we became friends and, in the seventies, I began to show my paintings in her gallery.

In 1978, Betty Parsons asked me to write a book about her—"Oh, not so much about me. About the gallery. The gallery is important. Or, at least, some people say so. I'm not so important." Then, dipping her head slightly, peering up and sideways, smiling, she added, "But some people think I'm important, too." Make no mistake about it: the then seventy-eight-year-old Betty Parsons knew she was important; she believed her press, and years before she was publicly acclaimed as the den mother of Abstract Expressionism, she knew herself to be special. Well beyond the age when most people retire, Betty Parsons continued her creation of Betty Parsons: she was eager to have that creation revealed and its story told.

The idea for a biography began with her suggestion to Grove Press that a book about her be written by Lawrence Alloway, a distinguished English critic who was curator at the Guggenheim Museum, in New York. When Grove changed direction and abandoned the book on Parsons, publisher Harry Abrams approached Betty, and the project shifted to his press. Shortly thereafter, Alloway turned his attention to other writing; the book on Betty dropped from sight. But her appetite whetted, Betty wanted a book about her gallery and herself; she turned to me, by then a friend and one of her gallery artists for some years.

I agreed, *on condition* that all of her papers be available, that *she* be available, too, for conversation and, most important, that she answer all questions truthfully and discuss any aspect of her life and career with me. She accepted my conditions; we shook hands gravely. I knew from dealings with Betty in the gallery that her handshake was a contract.

Thus began a series of conversations, some taped and some noted, in which we discussed her life, her artists, her work, people, ideas—anything that seemed to me from reading her journals or sifting through her papers significant. She visited me in New Jersey, New York, Connecticut, and Rhode Island; I visited her on Long Island or in the gallery. We traveled in France one summer. Over lunches, picnics, bottles of wine, we talked; during long drives in automobiles or long walks along beaches, we talked; sitting before her south-facing windows in her New York apartment, we reviewed her journals together, read boxes of letters to Betty from lovers, friends, family, artists, and groupies. Our conversations lasted until 1981 when a stroke made it impossible for Betty to talk easily.

Throughout this book, I have included Betty's comments, and unless otherwise cited, they are taken from these conversations. Similarly, when I have judged that the source is understood within the text, I have not burdened the reader with notation.

In the final phases of shaping thousands of written pages into a book, I cut events and people judged not to be essential to the story of Betty as artist and dealer. In doing so, I have omitted people who know themselves to have been of more than casual significance to Betty; to them, I apologize. Similarly, facing the events that shaped eighty-two years of an extraordinary life, I have not included *all* artists, *all* friends, or *all* activities of that life. I have tried, however, to preserve the integrity of her story and to include the people, journeys, relationships, and happenings that best illuminate the personal and private lives of Betty Parsons.

Many people wanted Betty's story told and generously contibuted to my understanding and knowledge of the woman, the artist, and the dealer. I sought and received excellent advice; I worked with rich material; I owe much gratitude:

Betty's family provided information without any attempt to control my use of it or to edit the contents of the book. William Rayner talked with me, answered questions, opened family albums, and gave me every encouragement to write about his aunt as I understood her. Patiently and lovingly, he recalled his days with Betty and her influence on his life. Her other nephew, Thomas McCarter, provided insight and historical records of the family as he reviewed Betty's contribution to his family and to a larger society: "She was," he reiterated, "truly different and a powerful force. She touched and changed us [the family] all, whether we knew it or not." Arthur Pierson, an artist-cousin who worked in the gallery, recalled Betty from the standpoint of her family's youngest generation as well as from that of an aspiring artist in the trendy sixties.

Marie Hartley, Jock Truman, Jack Tilton, and Gwyn Metz became Betty's chosen family. They assisted Betty in the gallery at different times, spanning the decades from the forties until Betty's death; they typed letters, answered the telephone, balmed temper, dealt with artists and clients, and loved Betty through good and bad times. Each supplied information on the routines of the gallery, on clients and artists and the daily machinations of the Betty Parsons Gallery as it influenced the history of American art.

Artists Richard Francesco, Judith Godwin, Cleve Gray, Ellsworth Kelly, Alexander Liberman, Alfonso Ossorio, Henry Pearson, Aline Porter, Richard Pousette-Dart, and Hedda Sterne talked freely about their association with Betty and her gallery. Elaine de Kooning, though she never showed in the gallery, recalled the reviews of Parsons's artists that she wrote for *Art News* and offered valuable perspective on the role of the gallery from its beginning, on its artists, and on their relationships to Betty. Elaine, speaking as artist and observer of the gallery scene, emphasized: "Betty's gallery was one that we—the de Koonings—could not miss. We saw all of her shows, knew her artists, and knew somehow that whatever Betty did, it was important. She had a way of being at the center of things."

Lawrence Alloway, in an act of extraordinary generosity, gave me the notes and preliminary observations that he had intended to use in writing his book about the Betty Parsons Gallery. Moreover, in extended conversation, he gave perspective to specific artists and shows in the gallery, as well as to Betty's unusual mode of management.

William McNaught, of the Archives of American Art, made available papers related to Betty as an artist and as a dealer. Betty's attorney and friend, Christopher Schwabacher, provided documentation on aspects of the gallery's business and on the friendship of his mother, Ethel Schwabacher, with Betty.

Betty's friends loved her unconditionally. Hope Williams's capricious wit informed her anecdotes about Betty from their years together at Miss Chapin's School until Betty's death. Annie Laurie Witzel's amusement and irritation with Betty enlivened her accounts of a friendship that survived shared journeys and years of gentle adventures. Billie Clarke and Aline Porter examined Betty's emotional importance to themselves.

Rosalind Constable, in her softly sunlit house in Santa Fe, and Hedda Sterne, surrounded by her painting-lit brownstone in Manhattan, won my respect, affection, and gratitude as each, blessed with rich memory and committed to meticulous fact-stating and truth-telling, identified people mentioned in Betty's journals, clarified passages, recalled events, and thereby provided wise guidance as well as a chain of facts on which to build the book. In a just world, Rosalind, I believe, would have written this book, and Hedda, better than anyone else I know, can judge the outcome of my efforts.

In addition to Betty's family and friends, Anne C. Edmonds, head of the Mount Holyoke College Library, and Kathleen Cole, a patient member of its staff, generously made space for me to work in their domain and furnished every assistance requested, even honoring my odd-hour work habits. I thank Ms. Edmonds, Ms. Cole, and Mount Holyoke College for access to a treasure of documents and periodicals pertinent to my research.

To my agent, John Hochmann, I offer gratitude for his unflagging belief in the merits of the project and for his determination to see the book properly published.

Phyllis Freeman, my editor at Abrams, has a perfect ear for biographical nuance and a keen interest in Betty's contribution to American art. Her patient reading of my trials and errors improved this book measurably at every step of its development. I thank her for her lavish application of professional skills to this book and for her friendship.

I thank everyone listed for patience, solicitude, encouragement, information, and assistance; we have shared an uncommon affection for Betty Parsons.

I am grateful, above all, for the good fortune which let me know Betty. She, with boldness and faith, would have called it fate.

—Lee Hall

South Hadley, Massachusetts, 1990

Betty Bierne Pierson at about six

AN AMERICAN GIRLHOOD

•

1900-15

"It all began with the Armory Show. That's where I got on," said Betty Parsons in 1978 as she pointed to several shelves of black notebooks containing "journals" and sketches that, helter-skelter, reflected her life as an artist and as a dealer. Significantly, Betty began her story not with her birth or with her family's history but with the epiphany that, in her mind, identified her as a chosen individual in a universe ordered by spiritual forces. At the age of thirteen, in 1913, along with throngs of other Americans, Betty Bierne Pierson attended the Armory Show, an international exposition of modern art intended to open the eyes of the American public, especially young American artists. Betty, one evidence of its success, said, "I knew then that I wanted to be an artist. That I *was* an artist! It took a long time to get free. But, you see, I've always had this great energy and I believe in the expanding world."

Well before the adolescent Betty's visit to the Armory Show, however, her family's wealth, aristocracy, and attendant values had set the stage for the life of the artist and dealer. She was the second daughter of three born to Suzanne Miles and J. Fred Pierson, Jr., both twenty-eight at the time of her birth. According to her birth certificate, filed in New York City on February 6, 1900, a female child, unnamed at that filing, had been born on January 31, 1900, at 37 East Sixty-ninth Street, in New York—a location actually some blocks north and east of Radio City, where, embellishing her legend, she claimed to have been born. By 1915, however, the family did live at 17 West Forty-ninth Street in a house later destroyed to make way for Rockefeller Center, of which Radio City is a major component. Despite later periods of residence in Paris and Hollywood, Betty remained throughout her life a dedicated New Yorker.

In the interviews she gave in her later years, Betty often told her story as if she were reading from a girls' adventure book, recounting with novelistic dash and romantic whim the influences and events of her life. Typically, she would say:

> *My mother was from the South; she was French from New Orleans.... She was one of nine children and they all had many children. So I have many cousins.... On my father's side, there were intellectuals.... My grandfather was a businessman ... [who] made quite a lot of money. My father spent his life losing money. He had a gift for that.*[1]

On another occasion, she recalled:

> *I was well cared for.... I had everything I needed.... My mother had great taste but didn't care a damn about art. I don't know where I came from or how I got the way I am.*

Though factually true, these simple statements alone do not reveal the woman who emerged from her family to become one of the most important dealers in the history of modern art. William Rayner, Betty's nephew, impishly pleased by his favorite aunt's late-life celebrity, believed that she sprang full-blown into the estate of reigning rebel, that no one and nothing really had influenced Betty very much. Betty encouraged her nephew's viewpoint with stories she told about her life and, perhaps more important, with nods, smiles, winks, and verbal allusions and intimations that, bowing to discretion, she was withholding scandalous anecdotes. In addition, Rayner heard gossip and anecdotes from other members of his family in which the ingredients of Betty's story were often rehearsed: defiant, difficult, rebellious Betty, hell-raising and pleasure-bent, sneered at family values, ignored traditional standards for behavior, and embraced outrageous and revolutionary art; but, talented and beautiful, she triumphed, gaining both fame and fortune.

In actuality, Betty found in the manners and mores of her family and class the building materials that she transformed into a long life of rebellion *against* materialism, *against* conservative politics, *against* social and religious convention, and *against* established art. She also found the ingredients and the style to justify being *for* progress, *for* individual rights and freedoms, and *for* art.

Before Betty's birth, generations on both sides of her family had championed the causes of free enterprise, gathered wealth, enjoyed attaining and exercising power, and honored in practice the form and style of life deemed fitting for the aristocracy of the United States—the rightful leaders and the privileged by birth.

Betty's maternal grandfather, William Porcher Miles, was born in Walterboro, South Carolina, in 1824; after graduation from the College of Charleston, South Carolina, he taught mathematics at his alma mater and won the admiration of the people of Charleston for his selfless services as a volunteer nurse during a yellow-fever epidemic in Norfolk, Virginia. As mayor of Charleston, he reorganized the city's police department and redesigned the tidal drainage system. In 1857, he was elected to the United States Congress; but during the Civil War, he switched to the Confederate Congress. Later, as a senior officer on General Beauregard's staff, Miles assisted in arrangements for the surrender of Fort Sumter, where the first shots of the war had been fired. Betty boasted that he had designed the Confederate flag, to her evidence of artistic talent lurking in the family gene pool.

In 1863, Miles married Betty Bierne, the daughter of a Virginia and Louisiana planter, Oliver Bierne, who owned thirteen plantations and shipped twenty million pounds of sugar annually. After his marriage, and backed by the Bierne wealth, Miles continued his public activities. In 1874, Miles was an unsuccessful candidate for the presidency of The Johns Hopkins University, but in 1880 he was elected president of the University of South Carolina, an all-white university for men. By legislative edict, the university emphasized agricultural and mechanical studies. However, Miles, at odds with the practical curriculum, advocated classical liberal arts scholarship. When he failed to win support for his philosophy of education, he resigned and devoted his remaining years (he died in 1895) to the management of the plantations his wife had inherited, including the handsome Houmas House, in Ascension Parish, Louisiana, a site Betty visited several times. The aging Miles, with the means and leisure to play the country gentleman's role most congenial to him, collected books, entertained distinguished guests, and attracted public attention by delivering polished addresses. "He was," Betty opined, "the only intellectual on my mother's side of the family."

Betty's father sprang from the equally distinguished loins of a rich Northern family. The first Pierson to emigrate (in the first half of the eighteenth century) to the United States came from York, England, and was a noted clergyman, missionary to the Indians, and scholar, who, according to family legend, devised a catechism for the Indians in their own language and wrote a textbook on moral philosophy that was used for several decades in divinity schools. His son, Abraham Pierson, Jr., graduated from Harvard and, after being ordained to the ministry, preached and helped establish parishes in Newark, New Jersey, and in Saybrook and Killingsworth, Connecticut. As one of the founders of Saybrook School, which became Yale College, the Reverend Pierson was elected to the first rectorship of Yale but continued to serve his parish, some twenty miles distant.

Betty's grandfather, John Friederich Pierson, was born in New York on February 19, 1839. At eighteen, he enlisted in the New York National Guard as a private in the socially elite Company K of the Seventh Regiment. At the outbreak of the Civil War, he was attached to the First New York Volunteer Infantry Regiment as first lieutenant, promoted to captain in May, to major in July 1861, to lieutenant colonel in September 1861, to full colonel in October 1862; three years later, for meritorious service, he was breveted a brigadier general. Throughout the Civil War, he was attached to the Army of the Potomac and fought in virtually all the battles associated with that force. As commander of the First Infantry Regiment, he was wounded twice: first, when his horse was shot from under him at Frazier's Farm in Glendale, Virginia, and, second, when two bullets pierced his chest at the Battle of Chancellorsville and he was taken prisoner.

After the Civil War, Pierson did not hang up his spurs; rather, he continued to serve proudly as a life-colonel in the Seventh Regiment, New York National Guard. In civilian life "the General"—the closest his family ever came to a term of endearment—dispatched with military authority and aristocratic probity his responsibilities to his family and community until his death in the 1930s. Blessed with superior moral rectitude trussed in self-certainty, he entered the family business, Ramapo Iron Works, became a partner in the New York office of Josiah G. Pierson and Brothers, and rapidly amassed a fortune.[2] He was the very model of a proper gentleman; let no member of his family forget it.

Betty's father, the General's son, met Suzanne Miles on a business trip to New Orleans. They were the same age; both had been born in 1872. Despite the lingering political hostilities and ideological differences of the Northern and Southern families, young Pierson and Suzanne were encouraged by their families to court and marry, a triumph of aristocracy and wealth over mere political differences. Their lavish wedding in New Orleans inaugurated a strained and tumultuous marriage that ended in divorce ten years before Betty's own marriage collapsed.

Betty's mother, called Susie by intimates, was a spoiled, headstrong, self-centered, and materialistic belle. Diminutive, short-tempered, charming, and beautiful, Susie vaunted her French ancestry as the social life available to her in Charleston and New Orleans bored her. Dreaming of a life of elegance and grandeur, of unending fetes and balls, of lavish wardrobes, of luxurious travel, and of sumptuous houses staffed by perfect servants, Susie married J. Fred Pierson, Jr.

But Susie had consigned her dreams to a frail vessel, for Fred, broker and banker in the family business, the weak son of a strong father, proved to be an inept businessman. "He paid the highest price *ever* for a seat on the Stock Exchange and sold it for the *lowest* price in the world," Betty claimed.

Sandy-haired, mild-mannered, blue-eyed, Fred was prey to insecurities that bred failures which, in turn, provoked the General's searing scorn; and unending failures linked to scorn became the chain that tethered Fred to the family. Alcohol, maintained at steady low levels in his brain, assuaged his pain and protected his dreams. "My father," Betty said, "was charming enough, but he was weak, weak, weak."

Susie and Fred divided their time among houses in New York, Newport, and Palm Beach.[3] Their three daughters, Suzanne, Betty, and Emily, were trundled among the houses, watched over by servants within the nursery life that was the usual pattern for children of that period and class. Their days rolled through a maze of rigidly entrenched care and tutelage intended to prepare them to be wives to rich men, to be flawless hostesses and attractive adornments for their husbands and houses, and to be valuable property to their families—who, as a matter of ritual, would encourage a good marriage.

But the training to make her valuable chattel chafed young Betty, who insisted, from her earliest memories: "They told you what to do. Everything to do. You weren't supposed to think for yourself or make decisions. Eat this. Wear this. Say this. Think that. Don't do that. Rules, rules, rules. There was no appreciation for the creative in anything they did or said or told you to do. I knew it was stupid and wrong, but I didn't know what to do about it."

In her infancy, Betty shared the nursery with Suzanne, but with the birth of Emily, Suzanne ascended to a room of her own and to privileges befitting an older child. Far from feeling deprived, Betty was elated: she had Emily, her adored baby sister, all to herself and she was freed of Suzanne's big-sister bossiness. Betty loved Emily protectively and fiercely and, at every opportunity, pleaded with the nurses to allow her to assist in bathing and feeding and dressing the blue-eyed, delicate baby. Until Emily's death in 1965, Betty loved her more than any other human being. And, in turn, she loved Emily's son, Billy, as she would have loved her own son.

As a child, Betty sulked easily, wept for no apparent reason, hoarded stamps taken from letters and cards that came from distant places, and preferred daydreaming over those stamps or her little box of collected buttons to playing with dolls. As the three sisters grew, Betty's moods and insularity, her tomboyish pranks and games repelled Suzanne, amused Emily, and annoyed her parents.

Betty was marked for life by her parents' squabbling and bickering, and by the tensions that reverberated in their several houses throughout her childhood. By the time of Emily's birth, four-year-old Betty was already aware of the subjects abrading the marriage: Susie and Fred argued over money and social events, disagreed about the management of the houses and the handling of the children. At some point soon after Emily's birth, Betty realized that Fred spent little time at home.

Susie, spoiled and extravagant, was not easily affectionate with her children or her husband. But she was an attractive and popular hostess, busy with her wardrobe, running the family houses, managing the servants, and receiving and providing entertainment. Even by the opulent standards of the day and of her class, Susie insisted on a visibly luxurious life.

Fred lost money as steadily as Susie spent it. Still, under Susie's domination, the Pierson family lived as if their money would be unendingly replenished. Wealth had come to Susie and Fred as an accessory to birth; neither of them had ever worked or contemplated working seriously to earn a living. The General, given to barking commands and expecting obedience as if still on the battlefield, stormed warnings at Fred.

Susie nonetheless insisted on owning and maintaining a fleet of cars painted matching green with initialed family crests painted on the doors. She demanded from Fred—and usually got—additional money for the operation of the houses, for more frequent and extravagant parties, for more lavish wardrobes for herself and the little girls. Fred, in debt and shrinking from the General's endless harangues about the state of his fortune and future, attempted to appease Susie by slicing off capital to meet her demands.

Susie, however, was not satisfied with her life in Newport, New York, and Palm Beach. Everyone she knew there complimented her on her good taste,[4] but she was, after all, French and she believed that only Paris could provide a glitteringly sophisticated and properly cultured life for the deserving rich. She traveled often and sumptuously to France, upon several occasions taking the children with her and leaving them in the care of servants while she shopped and sampled European social life. The children, she insisted, required the cultural influences of France to bring them the social high gloss necessary to attract suitable husbands.

By the time Betty was enrolled in Miss Chapin's School, in 1910—the first formal and outside-the-family step toward establishing her role in society—she was a withdrawn and secretive ten year old; she was inattentive in class and enveloped in daydreaming at home. "It was," Betty said of school, "something they made you do. I wasn't particularly interested."

During her time at Miss Chapin's, Betty was a mediocre student with no apparent interest in the regular curriculum or the special projects and activities the school provided. She left no distinguishing marks on the school's records; her grades were neither good nor bad; her behavior was acceptable; she held no class offices; she won no laurels on the playing fields or in the dance studios or theater. She trudged obediently through the requirements of the school in the same style that she followed the art teacher through the long corridors of The Metropolitan Museum of Art; she was bored and she kept her own counsel. Told to look at the white sculptures and brown paintings, she did; told to feel their beauty and to learn the names of artists and the dates of their creation, she quietly declined to open her mind to experiences urged upon her; she retained, however, gobbets of language applied to art.

But at Miss Chapin's School, Betty made friends, including Hope Williams, Caroline Prentice, and Muriel Ames. These and several other wealthy women who protected and promoted Betty throughout her life were eventually dubbed by Betty and her friend Rosalind Constable "The Katinkas" or, sometimes, "The Powerful Katinkas." When asked the source of meaning of the term Katinka, Betty responded, "Well, it was a name that sounded good. Rosalind and I liked it, and it was the name of little wooden dolls [kachinas] that the Indians have—all alike, except painted different, with different names." Betty apparently forgot, however, that throughout much of her childhood, a cartoon character, Powerful Katrinka, amused American readers with her ability to accomplish difficult feats, seemingly without effort. Later, she combined the two words.

In a photograph from the period in which she attended Miss Chapin's, Betty's prominent rounded forehead—which, later, would catch Saul Steinberg's imagination as he rendered her in line drawing as a beagle—swells above her deep-set, large, rounded eyes that were almost cobalt blue. Her face, as she matured, became more square than oval with a small chin and a surprisingly full mouth. She was blond and tanned easily in the summers to a smooth apricot-brown tone. All of the Pierson girls were beautiful, and according to Betty, "That's all anyone ever said to you. They told you that you were beautiful. They might as well have been talking about a bunch of flowers or a vase. No one ever told you that you were clever. It was all superficial—and that's what all those people thought beauty was, something on the surface."

As a preadolescent, Betty felt unloved and unknown save by Emily; she countered by balancing on an emotional teeter-totter of swaggering tomboyish self-

Betty at thirteen—the year she went to the Armory Show

certainty on one side, and shyness and secretive, sometimes cunning, ways on the other. She did not want to be like her family for she wanted to be happy, but perhaps in the shadow of her family's belief in their own superiority, she felt herself to be special even though she could identify neither the springs nor the attributes of her singularity. Being special, she had no place in the world she knew. She waited, she said, for a sign.

That sign came to Betty at the Armory Show. For the rest of her life, Betty marked her entrance into the Sixty-ninth Infantry Regiment armory as the beginning of her life as an artist. Band music poured from the balcony of the vast enclosure at Lexington Avenue and Twenty-fifth Street in New York, while people looked at works of art by acknowledged masters such as Goya, Ingres, and Courbet as well as by the new and shocking "Cubists" and "Futurists."

Amid the dancing Matisse nudes and the Picasso Cubist figures, near the famous *Nude Descending a Staircase, No. 2*, by Marcel Duchamp, the young Betty saw sculpture by Aristide Maillol and Antoine Bourdelle. Bourdelle's work thrilled her with its strong simplified massiveness, its nobility and ideal forms—all the things that seemed to her to reflect powerful emotion and, moreover, without the encumbrances of obvious arcane skills that she confronted in The Metropolitan Museum's collection of white sculpture and brown paintings. Betty admired Bourdelle's deviation from the strict verisimilitude so extolled by her teachers. "Here," she thought as she looked at his sculpture and longed to touch it, "is an artist; I am in the presence of art."

Sixty years later, she recalled it vividly: "I thought I could do it. I thought I could *make* art and not just look at it. All those sculptures at the Metropolitan looked impossible to do and everyone said that that was why they were good. When I saw Bourdelle, I knew that was just nonsense."

Intrigued by the controversy surrounding the exhibition as much as by her initial aesthetic experience, Betty exulted in Bourdelle's power to shock—didn't everyone say just that? He was shocking, therefore, *modern.* Didn't everyone call him a rebel? She liked the idea.

Despite the ridicule cast in its direction, the Armory Show exhaled a merry and energy-charged atmosphere. Betty was happy in its air of carnival and festivity; her heart thumped to the band music; she moved toward the bustle of art students selling programs at the door and distributing free badges with the emblem of the show painted on them—the American Revolution pine-tree flag with the motto "The New Spirit" written boldly beneath it. Betty adopted the slogan on the spot. Days and weeks later, she recalled, she walked along Fifth Avenue saying over and over in cadence with her steps, "I am The New Spirit."

In the aftermath of her visit to the Armory Show, Betty wanted to know more about art and about the world from which it sprang. Despite her lackluster performance at Miss Chapin's, she begged her family's permission to prepare to enter Bryn Mawr College, where, she believed, she would find her way into the world of art. But, no, her parents ruled, college would make the tomboy Betty still more unfeminine and too independent to be desirable as a wife—her proper estate. She would instead enter Mrs. Randall MacKeever's "finishing school," the next level of predebutante training prescribed by the society that bound her family. Betty pleaded with her parents during her last years at Miss Chapin's School; they remained steadfast in their prescriptions for the proper training for a young woman of Betty's caste.

This failure, however, was not Betty's sole problem at this time. As she entered adolescence knowing that she was an artist, she also confronted sexual ambiguity. Crushes on teachers and on friends had resulted in some fumbling and furtive sexual forays. She knew that lesbianism was an unspeakable aberration, a perversion so awful that she knew of it—but not its name—only through whispered secret talk among the most daring girls at school. But caught in the intense emotional and sexual drives of adolescence, as well as a modicum of pleasure in rebelling, she terrified her parents with her crushes. She quickly learned that by displaying such socially unacceptable behavior, she had the power to cast Susie and Fred into panic.

In 1915, she completed Miss Chapin's five-year curriculum, the total of her formal education. At fifteen, Betty's intelligence had been washed lightly with sedate lessons in history, by well-modulated exhortations to learn sums and math tables, and by cascades of flowery language about art and poetry. She ignored most of it, she admitted, so that she left Miss Chapin's with a pleasant blur of scrambled information, with friends, and with memories of teachers who had been kind and interested in her. She read but could not spell or write with clarity or precision. Classes in literature had stirred her feelings, she admitted, because the teachers responsible for presenting the merits of Shakespeare and the Romantic poets had been objects of her earliest crushes. She knew that paintings and sculptures were expected to be "beautiful" and to be "well executed," that they should call forth tremors of pleasure, states of rapture and reverie, and that the swooning appreciation of art was one of the other duties of women in society.

Until her fifteenth year, as she later reckoned, Betty's resistance to her family had consisted of telling lies, of being inattentive and sloppy and lazy, of crying and sulking to get her way, and of demonstrating occasional flights of temper. When her family denied her ambition to attend college, Betty waged her first calculated rebellion with a tantrum of slamming doors and crying. Escalating her campaign, she locked herself in her room for two days, refusing food and speaking to no one. When she emerged from her solitary resistance, she wore trousers, she had slicked her hair to one side, she dangled a cigarette from her mouth, and without knocking, she entered her father's study to win her war through an apparent offer of compromise. Betty would, she proposed, attend Mrs. Randall MacKeever's finishing classes, as her family insisted, but only on the condition that she would also take art classes. "My father was shocked. He always thought I was meek. He didn't want trouble. My mother was very controlled by what other people thought, and my father was very controlled by my mother."

Without consulting Susie, Fred surrendered unconditionally to Betty's terms, gratefully accepting her promise to return to normal dress and to peace in the home.

Betty, smug and triumphant, began to study art in the studio of Gutzon Borglum, who, many years later, carved the colossal presidential portraits on the side of Mount Rushmore.

COURTSHIP, WEDDING, MARRIAGE

•

1915-23

Betty brought to Mrs. MacKeever's regimen a set of well-honed social skills. Her adroit exercise of good manners included a degree of imperiousness when setting an upstart servant back in his place and ease in captivating someone in conversation. Her charm, duly remarked by the dowager hostesses as well as the young men of Newport and New York, informed her physical grace and agility. After years of lessons in golf, tennis, swimming, and dancing, she carried her flat, broad-shouldered, slim, Egyptian-like body erect, providing an easy frame to drape. Indefatigable at games and dancing, she laughed easily and enjoyed the social life of the wealthy young in New York, Newport, and Palm Beach. Mrs. MacKeever could add little to Betty's arsenal for success in society but, as Betty remembered, "She gave me a little Shakespeare, a bit more French."

Betty, with the same lazy habits she had practiced at Miss Chapin's School, easily languished through Mrs. MacKeever's indoctrination. Daydreaming and bored, she desultorily noted Mrs. MacKeever's strategies and subterfuges, the tricks for triumphant womanhood; she examined and appropriated the games, the mask. Cunning, she already knew, bought freedom; small social deceits seemed a pittance to pay for having one's way.

At nineteen, Betty was "up for auction," as she said, available for marriage, and expected to marry a wealthy man and to live the same kind of life as her parents and their friends. But Betty saw marriage as a trap. She observed the lives of women around her, and without benefit of the "role models" that have buttressed recent feminists, she disliked the prospects offered her by society. She later reflected:

> *I think, in the past, women have been enemies to each other. In the 100% female which I can't stand or understand, every other woman is her enemy because every other woman may be in the way of getting her man. In the 100% male, he is out to seduce every woman he can, without any sense of responsibility about the rest of it. That's the dog . . . the dog and the bitch. In my childhood, I knew there was something about them that made me uncomfortable. The balanced human being has both male and female. If you are born a female you predominate in the sense that you are the one who has to carry the race. Male is the will to power. . . . I have lots of male in me. You see there are a lot of men who have tremendous feeling. A rounded person will have both. I think the world is now become androgynous. . . . I think there are three things we have no control over. We have no control over our birth, we have no control over our death, and if we are sincere, we have no control over our feelings.*[1]

After the First World War ended, Betty and her sisters traveled with their mother several times to Paris, where Susie, now estranged from Fred and in the process of divorcing him, spent several months each year. Betty, remembering her fascination with the sculpture of Bourdelle in the Armory Show, sought out that artist's sturdy and romantic work, made a few sketches of it and of sites that caught her imagination in Paris, and mildly affirmed her interest in art.

Between visits to Paris, Betty continued to study with Gutzon Borglum. "He was a disaster," according to Betty. "He made you draw bones. He was a really terrible teacher. He wouldn't even let you draw *real* bones; you had to draw pictures of the bones he had drawn in his notebooks. Pictures of pictures! Can you imagine? It was utter rubbish."

Betty had no patience with Borglum's urging his students to master the fundamentals of sculpture. She did not learn from Borglum or from subsequent teachers how to build sturdy armatures, to mix and knead clay well, to make workable casts, to design accurate scale models, or to render proposed sculpture well in both drawing and small models. Borglum introduced her to carving that Betty remembered as "stone hacking."

Perhaps, she later admitted, she simply was not ready to settle into the then requisite disciplines of art, but just as likely, Borglum was a rotten teacher. "Who wants to draw bones, bones, bones?" she asked. "Who wants to do someone else's work? That's not why I wanted to study art."

Bourdelle's work in Paris, not Borglum's soporific teaching, nurtured Betty's incipient interest in art. "I was lucky, you see," Betty recalled. "I saw the great works—and Bourdelle's work was great at that time—in Europe when I went to France with my mother. And," she added, "I knew that he was on the beam. He had The New Spirit."

After the betrousered tantrum that had won her art lessons, Betty sustained a polite but distant relationship with her parents, an easy exercise considering that they were preoccupied with their own shattered marriage and with their lost fortune. She avoided them when possible; when necessary, she tossed them tokens of her decorum. She was a suitable daughter, so far as they knew; she had overcome her earlier "growing pains" and accepted the responsibilities of adulthood.

When Fred and Susie dissolved their marriage, Susie and the three girls moved into the General's house. The aged warrior railed against Betty's way of life—even the carefully diluted and masked version she provided for him. "He knew me," Betty thought, "better than my parents did. And he didn't like what he saw at all. He didn't like anything about me. I don't know how I got the way I am and the General didn't know. But he knew that he didn't want anyone like *me*—I was a rebel in my bones—in the family. He was conservative, conservative, conservative; he was as conservative as I was something else." Betty enjoyed baiting her grandfather but could wring only so much fun from casting darts at authority; a bull's-eye too easily achieved offered little reward. Betty was bored by her family and also by her only means of escape from them at that time—her hard-won art lessons with Borglum.

But a new game came to Betty. During the summer of 1919, Schuyler Livingston Parsons, a popular man about New York and Newport, often joined Betty's younger group for tennis. He teased Betty as, with elaborate good manners, he put his name on her dance card; he invited her on sailing parties. He included her in parties given by his family. Betty encouraged Schuyler's attentions, appreciated his exquisite taste, his dark good looks, and his gentle ways.

Schuyler Livingston Parsons, the son of one of New York's oldest and most aristocratic families, had graduated from Harvard in 1914. In spite of his poor eyesight and a medical history of inexplicable headaches, which kept him from being drafted

Betty on the beach in Newport, Rhode Island

into the Army, he volunteered for service in the Red Cross, drove an ambulance through bloody action in France, and won citations for his bravery.

He was ten years older than Betty, better educated by far; he was widely traveled, worldly, and to Betty, a thoroughly romantic figure. She liked him all the more as she collected gossip about his playboy extravagances, his high-stakes gambling on anything that would move or any card that would turn, and about his public drunken capers. For Betty, he was grown up; he was a man at home outside the proper confines of Newport, New York, and Palm Beach. His knowledge of antiques, his poise and self-containment, and his derring-do as an appealing rogue enchanted Betty. Schuyler was not just another youthful suitor; he was a man of the world and a war hero. He enjoyed life and, she remembered smilingly, "He made you laugh. He was very, very witty." And Betty knew she had found another rebel.

The elders smiled on Betty and Schuyler as a courting couple: this, they nodded over their backgammon boards and behind their teacups, was a handsome match; she so beautiful and well bred; he so dashing and rich and aristocratic; both so high-spirited. Betty and Schuyler displayed their courtship to applauding society while cracking jokes between themselves about the clucking vapidity of the onlookers.

Each family also rejoiced in the courtship. Betty's parents and the General thought it a good match on all counts: Schuyler, they calculated, was so rich that money would not matter to him, and for them, perilously close to poverty, money mattered more than anything else. Fred and Susie were middle-aged, divorced, and dependent on the General, who found their profligate ways unacceptable; when he paid their bills or bestowed spending money on them, Betty thought he enjoyed humiliating them by mocking their weaknesses and extravagances.

Fred and Susie would gladly barter a daughter in marriage if they secured their social position and opened access to wealth through a rich son-in-law. Moreover, they reasoned, marriage would tame Betty before she could further embarrass the family with outrageous public behavior; the tomboy would become a radiant bride and all the world would live happily ever after.

The society gossips identified Schuyler as "artistic"—a pejorative suggesting, despite his macho heavy drinking and reckless gambling, an uncertain sexuality. If Betty's unfeminine mien worried her family, Schuyler's faint touch of femininity troubled his family equally. Marriage promised a socially acceptable solution to both family's problems; it was encouraged.[2]

Schuyler and Betty, the charmed young couple of the winter of 1920 in New York, danced and glittered at parties; they shone at concerts and balls; they were attractive and young and adored by everyone who knew them. Schuyler recalled: "The winter of 1919 brought a lovely person into my life and I fell desperately in love and married in the spring."[3]

The young couple married in grand style on May 8, 1920, at the Church of the Heavenly Rest in New York, a production the General gladly financed. Betty wore satin and tulle, a pearl pendant, and carried orange blossoms. Her bridesmaids—her sisters and Caroline Prentice among them—wore buttercup lace over cream dresses. After the six o'clock wedding, guests toasted the golden couple at a formal reception at The Colony Club.[4]

"Yes," Betty thought aloud, years later, "marriage was an escape in a way. Although I was very interested in this man Schuyler Parsons, I didn't love him when I married him. She paused, fingered the rings she wore; a quick sharp glance upward toward her interviewer as she added, "I didn't know much about love at the time. It just didn't work out."

Schuyler and Betty left immediately after the wedding for a nine-month honeymoon through Europe with a chauffeur to drive Schuyler's new Rolls-Royce and a maid to attend Betty. They crossed the Atlantic with the automobile Betty insisted on labeling "the marriage hearse" stowed carefully in the ship's hold, with the servants bunked in lower quarters, and with their fashionable clothing filling several steamer trunks. Betty and Schuyler, good-looking and rich, were the darling couple of first class.

But, the public's view of their marriage was false; Betty and Schuyler quickly knew they had carried their game too far and had made a serious mistake. The capering courtship forgotten, Betty and Schuyler were bound to one another in the bleak knowledge that marriage had not solved their problems. Neither had been set free by the rite, and from Betty's point of view, the honeymoon was an exercise in being lonely and miserable in the company of a *spouse.* "He just couldn't stand my way of doing things. He wanted everything, everything, his way."

On the first day at sea, Schuyler, no longer the carefree suitor, reminded Betty that she was his *wife* and instructed her to change her hair style, to talk with certain passengers and not others; he chose her clothes for the day and for the evening; he adjusted her jewelry. He advised her at bridge in the afternoon. "He placed my bets in the casino. I couldn't even place my own bets," she snarled. "Schuyler wanted to dominate and I didn't like that." At the end of a day that she described as "really dreadful," Schuyler sent Betty to bed while he remained in the ship's bar gambling and drinking until nearly dawn. "I don't know why I even tried to let him dominate me. I thought that was the way it had to be. But it was against my nature."

When they landed in France, Schuyler disclosed the itinerary and the mission of the honeymoon: they would travel to the great sites of culture and he would improve Betty's education in order to make her a suitable wife for himself. He would lecture on the art and culture of Europe; she would learn. "This," thought Betty, "was worse than the family. They at least left you alone." Schuyler, Betty decided, bored her more than school. And marriage—his posh jail—depressed her more than life with her family. Alone, she wept; with Schuyler, she admitted, she tried to annoy him.

Schuyler, possessive and jealous, flew into fits of anger if anyone paid attention to Betty; then, for no reason that she could discern, he would ignore her. She was outraged by his treatment. When Schuyler imagined Betty encouraging the flirtations of strange men, Betty, in retribution, exercised her charm on the most attractive men she saw to initiate real flirtations. Thus goaded, the humiliated and enraged Schuyler scolded Betty abusively and ordered her to behave according to his prescripts. She ignored his commands; he avoided time alone with her.

According to Betty, rankling at the memory, "He was extremely conventional, and of course, I was brought up under a church background, too. But I haven't really got a conventional bone in my body.... I never thought in terms of formulas of behavior. I just did what I felt and, of course, Schuyler was fascinated in one way and very critical in another."

When the couple returned to New York, at the end of their honeymoon, to live in a fashionably decorated Manhattan apartment and in an equally elegant house in Islip on Long Island, they declared a truce. Neither blamed the other for the awfulness of the honeymoon; both wanted the facade of the marriage to succeed; and, behind the protective public mask of the marriage, each wanted a separate life. While both agreed without rancor that, in reality, their marriage was fraudulent, they reasoned together that their courtship had been a successful and amusing piece of theater. Why, then, couldn't the marriage be as artfully enacted for the onlookers? They agreed to transform an impossible private marriage into a convincingly conventional public one; they sought to create a believable charade and enact it for the families, friends, and society as they had played so well their roles through courtship and wedding.

Soon, however, even the guise crumbled. Schuyler gambled and drank excessively; he insisted that Betty, as his wife, wear particular clothes, appear in specific places, charm his friends and adorn his life; he was critical and domineering, abusive and maudlin. For her part in the debacle, Betty admitted that she forgot dinner engagements important to Schuyler, that she failed to instruct servants in preparation for parties, that she neglected his friends, and that she dressed carelessly. The more precisely he defined the duties of a wife, the more effectively Betty rebelled.

As respite from her marriage, Betty decided to study sculpture with Mary Tonetti in a studio on Fortieth Street. In that friendly, vaguely bohemian atmosphere, even when she had no particular sculptural object in mind, Betty liked manipulating the piles of clay, practicing with the tools of the trade and watching other students work. Betty was comfortable in studio grubbiness, amused by student chat. With Mary

Tonetti's encouragement, Betty began again to visit museums and galleries, which, at that time, attracted relatively few visitors. Museum permanent collections were easily accessible; gallery shows changed infrequently; and viewers walked through exhibitions at a leisurely pace. But Betty remembered the excitement of the Armory Show and, looking for "The New Spirit"—which, for her, meant new art, slightly unusual, perhaps outrageous—found Stieglitz's gallery and the paintings of O'Keeffe, Marin, and Dove.

In her later years as a dealer, Betty liked to tell the story of Stieglitz's treatment of her as a potential customer. A Marin watercolor appealed to her; she visited the gallery several times and, each time, found herself standing before the Marin work imagining the brush strokes that generated it. Finally, with three hundred dollars in her purse, she decided to purchase the watercolor. Shy and new to the process of buying works of art, she approached Stieglitz and asked him, "How much is this painting?"

"Two thousand dollars," he replied.

Betty left the gallery, too appalled to continue the conversation. That any painting might cost so much seemed impossible to her. She believed that Stieglitz, noting the value of her fur coat and jewelry and marking her as the wealthy young society matron that she was, asked what he thought he might get.

In October 1922, Betty visited The Brooklyn Museum's exhibition of Negro art, which had been selected by Paul Guillaume of Paris, an art dealer who extolled the merits of African and other non-Western art forms as well as works by major French artists. Negro art, as it was designated at that time, had been generally ignored by museums. Most of the material in the Brooklyn exhibit came from the Belgian Congo, mainly wood sculptures, mainly figures of both sexes. About a thousand pieces were included in the exhibition, some textiles and vessels as well as the exotic sculpture. The presence and force of the work excited Betty and titillated her slightly by its sexual frankness. And she thought this art was all the better because it had not been brought into the sanctity of museums and because it startled and outraged the pious and conservative people who surrounded her.

Betty was not alone in her need for rebellion; in New York in the twenties, rebellion and freedom became chic. Feeling thoroughly modern, Betty and Schuyler agreed to divorce. In discussing the marriage and its conclusion, Betty credited herself with scrupulous faithfulness to Schuyler for the duration of the marriage. Moreover, she insisted, she did not decide to leave Schuyler for another person or even, for that matter, because she believed another marriage at another time might be a happier arrangement for herself. She left marriage for independence, she contended, traded convention for freedom, left the security of an accepted world for an adventure in a larger life in an unprotected but expanding world.

"The world is difficult, cruel, and a very horrid place," she had decided, but, *"Life* is beautiful, extraordinary, has fantastic power in it if you know where to find it, how to get it." And life, she decided, could only be lived alone.

The General, now in his eighties but still the titular and actual head of the family, disapproved of Betty's bohemian interest in art and her unorthodox behavior. Betty considered the General to be consistently both conservative and wrongheaded. Still, knowing the General's sense of honor, Betty trusted him to be chivalrous to a granddaughter and loyal to his family in times of difficulty. She visited the General to ask his permission to divorce Schuyler and to seek his help in securing necessary legal services.

The General's outrage sputtered to an end; he sheathed his temper and commanded, "Wait a year. Stick it out a year." She agreed and shook hands with the General. Grimly, she "stuck it out for a year."

At the end of the year, Betty and Schuyler planned for Betty to file for divorce[5] in Paris, where the laws allowed dissolution of a marriage without the hateful allegations of infidelity required by American law, without the tacky supporting photographs of staged adultery. In Paris, that blissfully civilized city, Betty and Schuyler divorced fastidiously on the grounds of cruelty and incompatibility.

In France in the 1920s

FREEDOM AND PARIS

•

1924-33

Betty married in America in search of freedom; she found it in divorce and in Paris.

At the time she moved to Paris, both "art" and "The New Spirit" connoted pleasure to Betty; both represented a life unrestrained by routine, duty, or ritual obligation. In her way, no less than Schuyler, Betty lived for immediate gratification. By her own admission,[1] she wanted to do what she wanted and when she wanted; she expected servants to care for her needs; and with the assurance of perpetual alimony payments each month, she expected to live in Paris in good style.

As a divorced woman, she had paid her dues to convention; her family[2] need not be embarrassed by an unmarried daughter who, through god knows what antic, might cause gossip. Along with other expatriates, Betty could live outside the conventions of both the United States and France; who would care what an artistic rich divorcee did?

At twenty-four, despite the curriculum of Miss Chapin's School and Schuyler's honeymoon grand tour, Betty remained essentially uneducated. While she spoke French fluently and read about as well in French as she did in English, she had neither the intellectual discipline nor practical need to read deeply or critically in any subject. For Betty, history consisted of a shadowy notion that the classical world, the Middle Ages, and the Renaissance prepared the way for English settlers in the New World; she dealt with three categories: "back then," "the now," and "the great out there," the latter indicating interchangeably the future and the grander spiritual dimension that comprised the cosmos. Though fascinated by technology and her own version of metaphysics, Betty remained unencumbered by knowledge of the sciences, mathematics, or philosophy. Though she might like to *know* many things, she had no interest in the dull process of *learning* those things.

She thought of herself as an artist, not a scholar; artists were free, scholars were shackled by dull ideas and activities somehow tied to the past. Recalling the happy atmosphere of Mrs. Tonetti's Fortieth Street studio, Betty enrolled in art classes at the Grande Chaumière, seeking a sense of accomplishment without an investment of drudgery; she planned to have a good time.

As she settled into the routine of classes in art, Betty began systematically to look up other Americans in Paris, especially other independent women. Shyly and formally, drawing upon connections of connections and friends of friends, she wrote notes to Natalie Barney, Janet Flanner, Sylvia Beach, Gertrude Stein and Alice Toklas, among others. Betty cast her notes in a large untidy handwriting bespeaking her charging energy, tempered neither by syntax nor punctuation other than a series of dashes that indicated pauses. It amused her to think how her teachers at Miss Chapin's would roll their eyes heavenward and moan at the appearance, the language, of such notes; *tant pis,* they could not scold her any more.

As the recipients of notes responded with invitations to drinks, to dinners, to "at homes," or to share evenings in cafés, Betty soon met the nucleus of the expatriate American arts community in Paris. At the salons of Romaine Brooks and Barney, she heard poets read their own or others' works; she applauded dramatic enactments of plays; and fascinated equally by the lives of the women in the groups and by the works sampled, she began to read modern poetry. She liked aphoristic lines and obscurity that permitted considerable latitude in interpretation.

Away from her family's censure, she was free to experiment with sexual relationships as well as poetic expression. On the fringes of the circle that surrounded Brooks, a painter whose subjects were usually solitary upper-class women, Betty observed lesbian relationships. Yes, she later admitted, she had expected her marriage to achieve exactly what her family had expected; that is, to expunge whatever tendencies toward lesbianism lurked in her nature. In Paris, among older women who discussed and practiced sexual freedom in varied forms, Betty remembered, "After years of knowing only people who did what they were supposed to do, did the conventional and correct things, I suddenly knew people who did nothing whatsoever that was conventional. Correct for them but not conventional for the others."

Through her new friends, Betty met Adge Baker.[3] She was drawn immediately to the tall, darkly handsome woman, who was an art student, too, though of decidedly different bent from Betty's. Adge Baker, Betty soon discovered, believed in the reality of spirit over matter and, as they met almost daily for tea, for lunch, for drinks, Betty also discovered that she was in love with Adge Baker.

Betty bought a house on the rue Boulard, behind the Cimetière Montparnasse[4]; Adge moved in with her. Adge called it "a dear little house." Betty called it "home."

Sharp-boned, keen-eyed Adge lavished attention on Betty that she had never experienced; no one, not her parents or Emily or even the teachers she most admired, had ever seemed so piercingly understanding of Betty's thoughts, so concerned to know her feelings, her attitudes, her aspirations. Adge praised Betty and bossed her; instructed her in spiritualism and scoffed at her conventional American materialistic attitudes.

After several months of Adge's conversation, Betty believed that an artist received mystically the knowledge reserved for him or her within the vast universal scheme; an artist must therefore be true to destiny, must keep faith with cosmic forces. For Betty, to whom the intonations of the Episcopal clergy represented religion, this was heady stuff. With neither the intellectual equipment to treat Adge's mysticism critically nor the psychological bent for skepticism about anything Adge professed, Betty fell, bedazzled, even more under Adge's sway. To Betty, Adge seemed infinitely wise. Years later, in her eighties, Betty grinned fondly, and said, "Adge at that time was a better person than I was. She taught me everything I know about the spiritual. She really changed my life. And also," she added, "I loved our little house. It was perfection."

To a cooler eye, the little house might have appeared an agreeable and unpretentious abode for affluent women of bohemian persuasion. Betty remembered every detail and later could describe the rue Boulard house better than she could describe the New York apartment in which she lived. The rue Boulard house consisted of a downstairs comprised of a small kitchen and pantry adjacent to a generously proportioned dining room, which opened into a garden at the rear of the house. In the garden, shadowed and sun-dappled in turn by a flowering nut tree, Betty tended plants purchased from street vendors; until then, she had never touched trowel to earth, never

Adge Baker and Betty in France

planted and tended a flower or herb or shrub. Adge, redolent with English garden lore, annotated every activity in the garden with facts and her own fancy. "It was a miracle," Betty said of the first flower that she "owned," a red geranium. "I put him in the earth and put water—not too much—on him and left him to the sun. He grew and was very happy in my little garden on rue Boulard."

At the front of the house, a small formal foyer led to a large living room with a fireplace, books, paintings, and buoyant masses of flowers that the two women brought home by the armloads. Upstairs, Marie, the maid, lived in the smaller bedroom with its simple bathroom while Betty and Adge shared a large bedroom and a dressing room-bathroom with balky plumbing and large closets. It was magical shelter; it was fun; it was freedom.

Betty, enjoying for the first time the routines of daily life, added a little Scottish terrier, Timmy, to the household. He became her constant companion and sometime model. A black cat, Miss Otis, also found a home at rue Boulard, where, Betty recounted, "She did her nails on the nut tree."

Between the dining room and living room, Betty built an aviary where she placed a pair of yellow canaries and a pair of green parakeets that "sang to each other and tried to increase their families." For eight years, Betty and Adge and their pet family lived in the cozy walled world that they constructed in the midst of Paris.

All the while, Betty and Adge shared their enthusiasm for the study of art, even if their separate studies took them in markedly different directions. Each day, Adge packed her watercolors and went to study painting with a master who venerated the techniques and subjects—animals and landscapes—of English nineteenth-century watercolor painting. As Adge rehearsed the possibilities of traditional painting, Betty alternated between working independently on her sketching, sculpture, and oil painting and taking classes. Betty and Adge disagreed, at that time and until Betty's death in 1982, on almost every point about art save its mystical origin. Adge was conservative in her views and traditional in her own work; she believed the artist's holy vocation was based on keeping alive already understood and accepted symbols of truth; she believed an artist should make icons. Betty, overjoyed at the new freedoms she was finding at the Grande Chaumière, tried to understand Adge's doctrine but she did not want to look back: the future would be better in art as in everything; Betty fixed her eye toward the future.

Early in her studies at the Grande Chaumière, Betty met Constantin Brancusi, who soon invited her to his studio, where they talked about art and its roots, as the sculptor cooked a meal in his studio stove. Betty heartily ate the delicious bread baked in the studio oven and the rich stew; she drank red wine from a clay cup. As she looked about the studio, she saw figures that evoked memories of the exhibition of Negro art at The Brooklyn Museum. For Betty, Brancusi's works, combining the rigors of geometric logic and the mystery of ancient and primitive art, chanted the new spirit in mass and feeling. She saw geometry as a mystical language of absolutes; she recognized mystery in primitive art. If these were the poles of art, separated by continents of ambiguity, Betty had no fear in attempting to grasp both geometry and mystery: both, she believed deeply, held the spirit of art.

During her eleven years in Paris, feasting on the friendships and easily available art of the time and place, Betty also submitted herself on an unrelated and somewhat haphazard basis to three working teachers. She studied with Antoine Bourdelle, Ossip Zadkine, and Arthur Lindsey; each made a lasting impression; each contributed to her growth as an artist and to the "eye" that made her a force among dealers and in the art world of the mid-twentieth century.

Bourdelle, a French sculptor, painter, and designer whose studies with Rodin shadowed his work, taught regularly at the Grande Chaumière. Known principally for his sculpture, Bourdelle gave romantic treatment to classical figures and themes. At the Armory Show, Betty had been drawn to him because of his vision and evident skill; in his class in Paris, she felt a congenial spirit in his emphasis on feeling over technique. Bourdelle, noting the resemblance of Betty's clay figures to pre-Columbian sculpture, encouraged her natural predilection to be suspicious of skill. As she nudged her clay more boldly into geometric compositions which admitted Brancusi's influence, Bourdelle delighted in the simple strength of the work. He teased Betty. "You cannot be an American girl," he said. "You must be Mexican. Here, this work, it is ancient Mexican."

Looking back, Betty frankly thought of Bourdelle as a better teacher than sculptor. In his studio, she learned rudimentary techniques and absorbed attitudes—often grandly expressed—about freedom and creativity, about the singularity and holiness of personal talent. "Find your own way," Bourdelle told Betty, who wanted nothing more than precisely that. "And another thing, don't read too much. It can just get in the way of finding yourself; just read what's really necessary and don't read too much about art." Praising and encouraging Betty, Bourdelle hatched a zealot.

Another fledgling sculptor, Alberto Giacometti, was studying with Bourdelle at the same time. He and Betty, the shy and awkward two in the class, were singled out for the teacher's praise. Betty boasted, "We were the only two in the class looking for something." The rest, Bourdelle told the class, merely restated the past, reissued clichés. According to Betty, "Bourdelle jacked me up so that I never stopped thinking that I have some talent. . . ." And this, of course, is exactly the most nourishing fare for a young artist.

After six years of work with Bourdelle, just before he died, Betty decided to study with Ossip Zadkine, who then worked in a fluid Cubist manner. Fortunately for Betty, she came under Zadkine's influence during a highly charged period in his own development when he struggled between the intellectual rigors of geometry and the romantic urges that he found in his exploitation of the properties of modern materials. By example, if not by harangue, he sharpened Betty's awareness of the conflicts inherent in the creative process. She felt power in the conflict between mind and matter, between idea and object, and, for Betty, such conflicts rightly resolved themselves through chance. She valued spontaneity over plan; after all, freedom—the greatest good—was both discovered and exercised through accident. "But Zadkine imposed Zadkine on you," Betty complained. "So I left. I wanted more freedom."

After she rejected Zadkine's insistence on discipline as he defined it, Adge suggested that Betty meet a fellow Englishman—"a true artist," promised Adge in describing Arthur Lindsey. Betty liked the "Maestro" immediately. Shortly after that, Adge suggested that she and Betty join the Maestro and a group of his regular students on the coast of Brittany and, during the next several summers, the two women painted under his direction, in his informal classes, on the coast. "Arthur Lindsey was not famous," Betty acknowledged. "He had gained a reputation for the miniature portraits of the king painted for the queen's doll house."

Each summer, Betty, Adge, and Timmy, along with baggage and paints, filled the convertible automobile that Betty had bought, and drove with disregard, if not contempt, for the recognized procedures of motorcar operation. Behind the wheel, swearing and shouting at the automobile itself and at the few other motorists that they encountered, Betty sped along the roads of France, giving horn to the bicyclists or pedestrians who slowed her passage. If Adge found travel by Betty-driven automobile frightening and exhausting, she was not the last passenger to recoil from opportunities to travel with Betty. For her part, Betty found driving "a great release."

Once on the English Channel coast, Betty, Adge, and their terrier companion lived in a little hotel; their shuttered windows opened to reveal a long expanse of sea beneath a great and changing vista of sky. In such natural beauty, but without the social constraints of Newport, Betty swam in the sea, played tennis, and painted.

The Maestro's class assembled each morning on the beach or at some other designated spot. Lindsey directed attention toward various features of the day's subject, answered questions, explained the use of a brush or the property of a pigment. As the women worked, he strolled among them, urging them to trust their impulses, to pay attention to a line or plane in their emerging composition. To Betty, he said, "Put down what you feel. Don't copy nature. Capture its essence."

Lindsey taught Betty to paint in an expressionistic mode vaguely reminiscent of styles associated with Dufy or Segonzac. In watercolor, for instance, she learned from Lindsey to paint on a wet surface, applying color so that it would blossom into bright spreading areas adjacent to one another, bleeding into one another; when the flowering patches of color became slightly drier, she would touch them here and there with a darker line to define a structure or semirecognizable shape. In this manner of painting, color does not define form; line does. Color becomes decorative rather than structural or plastic. Betty's work, under Lindsey's guidance, was loosely painted, representational, and stylized; most important, she learned to free paint to move and take form according to natural laws, or as Betty saw it, she learned to quicken paint so as to reflect cosmic order.

Under Lindsey, too, Betty adopted the habit, which became a lifelong preoccupa-

Betty and Timmy in Brittany in the 1920s, while she was studying painting with Arthur Lindsey

tion, of carrying sketchbooks and watercolor paints or pencils with her at all times, of suddenly stopping, pulling a black Winsor & Newton artists' pad from a pocket or bag and making a color note or sketching something interesting, thereby laying claim to an image for future use. Wherever she traveled she carried her watercolors and pads and continuously worked on recording her changing surroundings. Years later, friends who sat beside her in the theater or at a concert while she made drawings and little watercolor paintings, rustling paper and squeaking a too sternly rubbed pencil, cursed the day Arthur Lindsey was born.

The summers' lessons and the sense of euphoria generated by life on the shore followed Betty back to winters in Paris, where she continued to take classes but,

Betty on the beach with Timmy (far right) and an unidentified dog (center)

increasingly, worked on her own in the little studio she shared with Louise Rochester Bove, an American married to a Frenchman.

Janet Flanner, by now a frequent companion and greatly admired "intellectual," urged Betty to see new exhibitions, to go to plays and concerts, to see ballet. Flanner, who became famous for her contributions to *The New Yorker* under the pen name Genet, kept an eye on everything that happened in Paris. Betty thought Janet Flanner knew everybody and understood the volatile and electrifying world of art and intellect in Paris. Flanner, soon cast by Betty in the role of teacher, was a reproving and demanding taskmaster, a strict schoolmarm with a piercing intelligence and no tolerance for the slapdash in the arts, letters, politics, or religion. Many years after their

Landscape in Brittany, ca. 1925

days together in Paris, Janet Flanner, reverting to her former role with Betty, listened to the then aging artist's recital of occult truths. She sighed. "Why," she demanded of Betty, "must you always take up with the holy rollers?"[5]

Through Janet Flanner, Betty met Josephine Baker, the first black person she knew as an individual—an artist who, by accident of skin color, was denied in America a full opportunity to perform. Betty had given little thought to such injustices in the past, but for the rest of her life, Josephine Baker symbolized the suffering of black people. When Betty later wrote checks to Martin Luther King, when she cursed the sheriffs of the South, she remembered Josephine Baker.

Similarly, Betty's education in modern literature was fashioned by Flanner, who directed her to read Hemingway, Fitzgerald, Colette, Proust, Djuna Barnes, Cocteau, and Joyce. She led Betty, too, to the music of Ravel and Satie; she introduced her to dance by Isadora Duncan. In all of these manifestations of the new spirit, Betty found confirmation for her growing faith in mysticism, in the powers of chance and spontaneity, and in art's revelatory nature.

But Betty's interests were not confined to the highest of the fine arts during these years when she found, too, the clothes that Chanel designed. She adopted a Chanel look, particularly suitable to her flat boyish figure and angular articulation of limbs and made it the outward sign of her real self, an emblem of her style; a sense of self and of style matured along with her skill as an artist. Alluring to both men and women, Betty caught the attention of strangers, who sometimes, she noted, stopped on the street to watch her stride past.

By 1926, Betty's experiences in Paris had converted her to modernism in all its aspects. By then confident of the importance of her observations, she began to keep a journal, a practice that she continued throughout her life. Betty's journals, not a conventional handling of the form, are often haphazard and scattered as to chronology, frequently illegibly written, and with numerous sketches, watercolors, and plans for future paintings; the pages are interspersed with pressed flowers, attractive stamps, labels from wine bottles, menus from steamships, programs from concerts or plays, and other items that she encountered and appropriated as tokens of life.

All the while that Betty studied art and enjoyed her life with Adge, she corresponded with Emily and Sukes, her older sister. Emily, a frequent visitor to Paris and Betty, disapproved of Betty's life with Adge. "She believed," Betty explained, "that a woman had to be married. Emily, you see, had been forced to be very, very conventional. My family did that. And then she married a dreadfully conventional man and she had to stay conventional all of her life."

In January of 1926, Emily married Archibald Rayner of Washington[6] without official engagement or announcement. Betty was surprised both by the sudden marriage and by the lack of pomp and ritual.

During Emily's annual visits to Paris, and frequent springtime visits from friends from Miss Chapin's School, Betty customarily suspended her routine to "raise a little hell." Visitors checked into deluxe hotels in Paris but, at Betty's invitation, visited the house on the rue Boulard where Betty proudly displayed Adge, the pets, the garden, and paintings or sculpture that she and Adge brought in from their respective studios.

"No," Betty conceded, "we never talked about life-style. Nobody talked about life-style then." She assumed, however, that Emily—her dearest friend and closest confidante until she met Adge—understood the nature if not the details of her life with Adge. "But we didn't talk. We just didn't. I knew, of course, that Emily disapproved. She loved me but she just couldn't take the unconventional."

Anticipating a visit from Emily and Arch at the end of the summer of 1926, Betty and Adge decided to fortify themselves with a vacation on the shore. They packed Timmy and their painting gear into the automobile; they motored to Dieppe, took a room in a seaside hotel near a restaurant they both liked. Betty noted in her journal her first swim of the year, exulting in its being "cold, delicious, refreshing." Throughout their time on the coast, while Betty swam, played tennis, sailed, took walks, and enjoyed the physical pleasures of outdoor exercise and Adge teased her about her American addiction to physical culture, Betty brooded over troubling letters from Emily, which, Betty remembered, were "full of marriage. Wondering when I'd marry again. You see, it just wasn't done, this being single." Betty's anxiety stained the summer. As she tried to work on her watercolors after the long winter in Paris, she fretted to her journal when the paintings lacked the dash and feeling she wanted, at one point registering disturbance because a heat fog caused "everything to move in and out so rapidly one could not so much as translate a feeling to the mind when outlines had changed." As a consequence she could get neither her mind nor her brush around her work. As the fog hung in along the coast, obliterating outline and mass, Betty did "feeble work in watercolor and found it difficult to look at things and see them." On another day, she was pleased by "cool, hard work all day."[7]

She savored the surroundings of the coast, commented on the shifts in breezes, on "listening to the surf and its musical message." Toward the end of her stay, she jotted into the journal: "musical day, much color, sunshine and you—little work—some tennis."

Betty admitted to her journal that something was not right; her "soul lacked quietness," she observed. Turbulent emotions, at least partly fueled by Emily's letters, filled her days as her anxieties spilled onto the surface of her journal. "To marry or not to marry," she wrote. Would she "live in constant contact with someone," meeting social conventions or would she "try hard, ever so hard [to live] with one one loves seeking nothing from the community. What is the end of such lives?" The socially acceptable union, she observed, would bring "children and the associates convention brings." An unorthodox life would offer, she reckoned, "adventure on the realm of the mind and spirit—uncertainty, a few associates...."

Several days later, Betty speculated: "I think the world is minus some important plan which makes for accord—maybe it is the religious plane...."

In describing to her journals the torment of the summer of 1926, Betty predicted patterns of anguish that would become an emotional sub-theme in her life: was she betraying her own nature? Did her "boredom, impatience, lack of confidence, vanity, selfishness, a desire to be entertained, flattered, spoiled—oh so many ways . . ." doom her to failure as a friend? "I have a goal, dear God," she wrote, "to find the beautiful, the sensitive and put it into something concrete. I wander so far away from it. My life is near someone beautiful, sensitive, far-seeing; strange it does not calm me...."

Betty feared that she would always fail "this dear creature" but noted that "still we find joy in the same things often but our minds rarely meet. In art maybe, but not in life. *Her* wisdom is deeper than mine.... Certain humors visit me when I am fond of anyone. Then I have a frantic desire to go out among strangers, acquaintances, friends, and laugh and talk.... A cloud settles on her then and we are worlds apart."

•

Betty realized that Emily disapproved of Adge, that Adge did not especially like Emily; Betty grieved, wanting the two most important people in her life to love one another. But, before Emily's arrival in the late summer of 1926 and in an effort to avoid strife, Betty and Adge decided that Adge should return to England for a visit. Betty took Adge to the dock and reluctantly said good-bye, wondering if Adge would return, wondering if the little house on rue Boulard would ever be the same again. On her return to Paris, Betty was pleased to find 29 rue Boulard cleaned by Marie, sparkling and cool even though the garden was parched. Her pet birds were waiting. "The green birds find their love for each other inchanting [*sic*] and the canaries are still concentrating on the production of others without success."

Emily would arrive the following day; Emily and her husband and a friend. This friend, Betty asked herself, is this a potential beau? Will this be an attempt by well-meaning Emily to bring about a suitable marriage for her older sister? "I knew," Betty said, "this visit would not be easy."

The next day, Emily and Arch and their friend Bill arrived a little drunk and late for their lunch with Betty at the rue Boulard. Betty observed that "the men look very tall in the small house" and, too, that her intuition had been correct, that Bill had been selected to pay court. She found him "attractive but weak; spoiled by the world—superficial—and useless. Such a pity to waste those long sensitive hands."[8]

Betty examined Arch, her sister's husband, and decided that "he has logic but not high aims—too filled with what money can do." Soon, Betty thought of Arch as a bully who was "not sensitive to Emily." Betty and Arch would fight and argue and compete for attention from Emily for the rest of Arch's life.[9]

Seeing the difference between her own life and Emily's, seeing the pattern for social acceptability that controlled Emily's life, Betty thought, "Well, perhaps I should change my direction, my life."

She tried to like Bill, and her view of his essential weakness notwithstanding, she flirted with him, hoping to please Emily. Fortified by steady drinking and aligned as two couples, the four set out to enjoy Paris and each other. During the week of lunches and dinners at expensive restaurants, golf at Saint-Cloud, dancing every evening in a different bistro, and continual drinking, Betty's manners and chatter echoed Newport, Palm Beach, and New York. "It all came back. The games. The dishonesty. The competition," Betty murmured. "And I was going against my nature. But, you see, I thought Emily might be right about me."

Betty relapsed into mischief, however, when she selected an out-of-the-way bistro that she knew would shock the visiting Americans. There, as Betty anticipated, a drunk and flamboyant lesbian "rushed up to me like a female pirate woman minus the knowledge of danger they have which makes them heroic to the eyes." The pirate woman's attention focused on Betty, as it had in the past and as Betty expected it to this evening. Betty subtly encouraged the pirate woman. Emily, Arch, and Bill, as Betty intended, were shocked.

Bill and Arch quickly removed the party to Harry's Bar for yet another round of drinks. Somehow, at an uncertain and blurry late hour, Betty returned alone to the rue Boulard. Her hangover the next morning, so dulling and painful that Marie's coffee could not dislodge it, depressed her; she wondered if she would be able to keep her date with Emily, Arch, and Bill for lunch.

Before meeting the threesome, Betty decided to visit Bourdelle's sculpture at the Musée de la Ville de Paris. Sitting before the work, alive to its emotional presence, Betty missed Adge, felt out-of-joint, lost and detached. Is this terrible depression, she wondered, the price for family approval and oh, god, is it worth it?

She deferred an answer and, instead, met the other three revelers and tried to obliterate her anguish with more booze and frolic. That evening she "dined in the Bois with Em, Arch and Bill. Cool. Danced with Emily. Heavenly little dancer. Arch is a dear. So is Bill. Very great charm and a natural simple person, Bill." A tentative peace effected, the party continued the next day as if unbroken. They "dined and said farewell. Early to bed."[10]

The time with Emily left sharp little fragments of doubt prickling in Betty's mind, making concentration difficult. She met Adge at the coast and "motered [*sic*] to St. Valery sur Soame [*sic*] to join Maestro Lindsey and the class for two months."[11] Betty tried to return to the hard work that she had known in the past with Adge and Lindsey; though she followed her old routines, the spell had been broken.

At the end of the two months, Betty and Adge and Timmy returned to Paris and to their life on the rue Boulard with their black cat named Miss Otis, the birds, the garden, and the guests who came for drinks and meals. Each woman resumed her schedule of classes and work in her studio. Each, also, expanded a separate social life.

As her relationship with Adge was threatened, Betty turned for attention and affection to a variety of people and indulged in casual sexual affairs, stylish flirtations, and disconcerting and intense friendships—both erotic and platonic and with both women and men. But Betty also found comfort in easy and unfettered companionship with casual chums.

Alexander Calder, such a chum, became a regular companion as he and Betty danced at least once a week in a bistro noted for its dense cigarette smoke, cheap food, bad wine, and loud conversation, as well as jazzy music. Sandy and Betty, soon needing still more activity to burn their excess energies, joined a basketball club for weekly games.

But it was dancing that especially pleased the two young artists. Betty and Sandy, according to Betty, danced from nine o'clock until two in the morning. "And," Betty said admiringly, "he was great fun at dancing because he was free and intense, very creative, very innovative."

Calder, working hard and selling little, had no money at all, Betty knew. She invited him regularly to dinner at the rue Boulard where she experimented with ragouts and casseroles, with big simple dinners of good bread, cheeses, fruits, and salads combined with a main dish. Intense and experimental in cooking, as in dancing, she and Sandy happily shared their feasts and their talk.

One evening after dinner, Betty remembered, "Sandy went upstairs to the john and he stayed for I don't know how long. He finally came down, we had dinner, and he went home. When I went upstairs, I found that he'd made the most beautiful brass fish for my toilet paper. That's what he was doing."[12] The toilet-paper holder, made of string, brass and copper, was a whimsical contrivance, an offering to please Betty and, jokingly, to thank her for her interest in him and for the dinners so often provided. To Betty's lifelong regret, someone stole the toilet-paper holder.

Sandy also made Betty a necklace of hammered and swirling brass, a frequent Calder motif that resembles the wave borders of Minoan frescoes. After her death the necklace was found hidden in a shoe in the back of her Manhattan closet, out of reach of a possible thief.

Betty continued to study art and to enjoy Paris unaware, save for newspaper reports she scarcely read and comments in letters from home, that the Great Depression had gripped America and that her family's fortune, along with other fortunes, was in grave danger. Schuyler skipped a few alimony payments, but after reminders from Betty, sent checks to cover what he owed her. Betty concentrated on her painting and sculpture, which, she felt, now sang with her own voice. She wanted to exhibit her watercolors and to establish herself as an artist, and she set about finding a gallery to represent her.

Even with the security of routine and with confidence in her work, the little verses that Betty began to scribble into her journals recall stylistically some of the experimental writing of the period but, more poignantly, reflect her emotional state:

After days of pondering
and pondrous days
I dwelt upon you and
all your ways to nature.

Later, she wrote:

A thousand orchards shining in the rain
how beautiful will be this harvest.

On March 25, 1932, fleeing from a fight with Adge to the Canary Islands for a solitary holiday, she wrote:

Only a calla lilly with
its open purity could
challenge your snowhite heart.

Shortly after the holiday in the Canary Islands, Betty and Adge parted. Betty was "devastated. Lost. Miserable. This woman Adge Baker, you see," she explained, "had changed my life. She taught me everything. She knew everything."

At the same time, Betty's financial situation altered sharply. Having ignored the Depression, she found it impossible to believe that Schuyler had, as he now claimed, lost his fortune. When the alimony payments stopped without promise of resuming—a possibility she had never entertained—her entire world was threatened. Unable to earn a living in France and unable to remain there without money from Schuyler or her family, she realized that she had to return to the United States. She had no money for passage; neither Schuyler nor her family could provide assistance. She wired Caroline Prentice Cromwell, one of the earliest Katinkas and a girlhood friend from Miss Chapin's School, offering her wedding rings as collateral for a loan. Caroline, refusing the collateral, wired money.

As Betty waited for her bags to be taken to the ship, she sat in the garden at the rue Boulard to read letters from Adge:

> *I was so touched by your lines.... I was so sad, not to have seen you, after my return from London, and my mind has been incessantly full of you through all of this financial and political mess....*
>
> *Paris will be so lonely for me this winter without you. Your presence was always a delight and I valued you the more that if you could not be what I wanted you to be you were still my friend, even more precious than before.... I have so* [sic] *dear recollections of the rue Boulard, the little sitting room when we were together, the books, the burning fire and Timmy and your quiet face with this beautiful forehead....*
>
> *Betty, I loved you much, you were such a beautiful realization, be sure now that my friendship is unchanged. Don't forget me, my friend, I am still with you in spite of time and place.*

Later, Betty unfolded the final letter that she would read at the rue Boulard:

> *Betty, dear, I wanted to know if you were happy and your letter seems to tell the contrary. It grieves me awfully. I am in wreckage now as I stand in life.... You can believe me when I tell you that from the memory of my past love and affection, you are the only being I love still as I loved you when you were there—because your presence was so great, your illumination of each thing so deep that it has left in my heart undying shades. When I think about rue Boulard, I can't help living again these moments I have lived there with you. The silent looks, the fire in the hearth and the shape of your forehead. Shall I ever see you in life?*

That question remained unanswered. Betty's attention fixed on a different question: Would Schuyler be able to resume paying alimony? She was, she realized, without money and without prospects for support for the first time in her life. The General had died and left her nothing; her mother and father could scarcely take care of themselves; Sukes and Emily, though well married, could not be expected to support the sister they considered a black sheep.

On July 12, 1933, Betty sailed with Timmy for New York. She was ready, she thought, to return to the United States.

"You see, [she told an artist later in her life] the American dream did not exist in Europe. And remember, I had been in Europe eleven years. The Italians, the English, the Middle East, they were all dominated by politics. By the male. There was no freedom, and whatever the morals were, the laws were still 200 or 500 years old.... But the American dream was the dream of freedom to do as you please, to do as you risk. Each person must be free.... Well, I tried to be free. In Europe they weren't even struggling to be."[13]

Betty in her habitual beret, California, 1930s

UNSETTLED HOMECOMING

•

1933-35

Betty returned to the United States at the age of thirty-three with the heavy baggage of disintegrated dreams, uncertainty about her future, and immediate anxiety about money. She had never worked; indeed, to her, money was a matter of birthright and work was something that hobbled *other* people with dull routine.

Throughout the summer of 1933, she believed that Schuyler would magically unearth money and resume his alimony payments if only she insisted; she wrote him many letters trying to make him pay the arrears and to agree to continuing payments in the future. Wine, however, could not be pressed from the already-dry *raisin*; Schuyler, too, was destitute and, like Betty, struggling to find a way to earn a living. He assured Betty that he would honor his alimony agreement if only he could; she accepted Schuyler's promises and determined to borrow money to see her through the several months Schuyler would need to achieve financial stability.

Betty first looked to her family. "They had lost everything. Everything," Betty concluded. "And they didn't approve of my life anyway. They never forgave me for divorcing Schuyler. They couldn't understand art. And I was very independent. I wanted to make my own way and live my own life which was very different from theirs."

Next, she turned to her friends, who, delighted to have her in their midst again, soothed her with advice, treats, and psychological support. They offered and Betty accepted their gifts of money, often proffered as "loans" along with their invitations to lunches, dinners, parties, and weekends in the country. Friends from Miss Chapin's—Caroline Prentice Cromwell, Muriel Ames Oaks, and Hope Williams—were soon joined by Dorothy Heydell, a Saint Louisan who came to New York to seek her fortune as a newspaper writer and who, through Betty, met and married Hermann Oehlreichs, a rich and prominent member of Betty's social set in New York and Newport. "Dumpy" Oehlreichs for many years tended to Betty's needs: "She paid my dental bills. She paid my doctor bills. She gave me money. She loaned me money. She bought paintings from my gallery. I don't know what I would have done without Dumpy. Dear Dumpy. She was the *most* generous person in the whole world. But she was very conservative. She hated all the painting that I loved. She hated the Jews. She hated the blacks. But she liked me and she believed in me and she supported me."

Later, other rich friends would join the informal group that watched over Betty and all competed for the privilege of taking care of Betty throughout her life. Rosalind Constable, a Britisher who met Betty in the thirties in New York, was amazed by Betty's ability to attract major survival help from what she and Betty called The Katinkas. "These women," Rosalind recalled, "mostly rich, of course, and all just smitten—for the most part not, I think, in a lesbian way—with Betty. Charmed. Pleased to know Betty, to know someone a little giddy, a little naughty."[1]

Hope Williams with a bear

Over the years, The Katinkas included the early group from Miss Chapin's as well as Margarett McKean, Susan Hilles, and others who became Betty's patrons and supporters. They paid her bills; they bought her clothes or let her have her pick of their not-so-used clothing; they took her on trips to Europe; they invited her to parties; they fed her and encouraged her; and while they generally believed that Betty often promoted crackpot art (what other kind of art was there? they joked among themselves), they bought works by her artists, thus helping the artists while also helping Betty and the art that she championed.

"I told them," Betty smugly recalled, "that they were buying *the* most important art of the century. They didn't care about that and they didn't believe it. When the work got valuable in the commercial sense, they were proud of what they had done. And when they needed money, they sold some of the paintings they had bought for nothing—really *nothing*—and they boasted about that."

Betty decided, with her friends' admiring encouragement if not prudent counsel, that she would be able to earn her living as a portrait painter and as an art teacher offering private lessons in California. She had no experience in either enterprise, but cheered on by her friends, Betty was confident that she could ply her craft through troubled times.

Above, left: Dorothy (Dumpy) Heydell Oehlreichs and Betty

Above, right: Betty with antlers from a moose shot by Hope Williams's brother

On the way to California, however, Betty stopped in Wyoming for a visit with Hope Williams,[2] one of her closest friends from Miss Chapin's and now a successful actress. She traveled by train with Dumpy and Timmy and all of her possessions, intending to stay in Wyoming at Hope's ranch for a week. But the party at Deer Creek Ranch lasted for two months, perhaps a record at that time for Betty. She had come from Paris and New York; her wardrobe—her assortment of skirts and cardigans, blouses and beads, low-heeled shoes and stylish frocks—did not include clothing suitable for a Wyoming ranch. She surveyed the ranch hands, the cooks, and the workmen on the ranch, identifying the smaller men and approaching them for loans of needed garments. She soon effected full ranch regalia: too-large lace-up boots, heavy work pants bulging at the knees but tucked into the tops of the boots, a large warm plaid shirt, and a well-seasoned vest. But, instead of a Stetson, Betty still wore her French beret. "I was a great hit. And I was very comfortable," she recalled.

Hope remembered a horseback trip into the mountains. Betty, totally unfamiliar with American wilderness and with horseback riding, seemed happy to try anything. Unafraid, somewhat wrapped in a daze or in self-absorption, Betty sat astride her horse and trusted it to follow the other horses. She made no effort to guide the horse or control its pace save for an occasional conversational comment to it: "Slower, please,"

Min Luddington, from a 1935 sketchbook

or, "Don't keep watching your feet." So far as Betty was concerned, the horse was an expert in walking in mountains and might as well be in charge. But, at one point on the trail, Betty's horse ducked under a low branch; Betty failed to duck and was knocked from the horse. She smacked the ground, Hope laughingly recalled, but stood up quickly, amused at the incident. "We were simply terrified that something had been broken, but Betty got up, dusted herself off, set her beret straight, and got back on the horse. She was completely unafraid. And she was completely inattentive to possible danger."

Betty's disregard for danger ensured the presence of danger; she moved through the wilderness as she might have strolled through a Parisian park. In an encounter with a mother bear and her cub, Hope remembered, Betty again showed no fear. Ignoring warnings about wandering away from the campsite, Betty faced a great sow bear who, apparently startled by Betty's sudden closeness to her cub, reared up snarling, showing teeth unlike those displayed by a nursery teddy bear.

"Betty may actually have taken one or two steps *toward* the bear; she was enchanted with this great toy teddy and absolutely without fear for her own safety," explained Hope. The camp cook, however, reacted quickly and fired a gun into the air to frighten the bear. As the bear dutifully jogged off with its cub at its side, Betty smiled happily. Asked about the incident, she reconstituted the loopy smile. "Oh, I was very pleased to see that bear and its little one. Very charming, they were. And I think they intended no harm. Animals like me and they know that I like them. I think we could have had a little chat."

Betty's journal contains no mention of either the bear or the horse event.

After the two months in Wyoming's clear air and high mountains, a restored and rested Betty moved on to master her fate in California. She and Timmy arrived in Los

Angeles[3] by train on October 10 and immediately fell into Muriel Oaks's keeping. Muriel, dedicated to organizing the social lives of her friends and acquaintances, launched Betty in California by including her in a party to attend the opening of the great Mae West film *I'm No Angel.* And throughout the next two months, Betty lived with Muriel, who happily orchestrated a fast-paced social whirl for her friend: tennis, swimming, cocktail parties, and dinner. "Muriel wanted everyone to know me. *Everyone*! And she entertained well," Betty remembered. "So I had a terrific time out there. Everyone wanted to know me, too. They were most interested in me because I had been in Paris and knew all the artists and writers there."

But Betty had come to California to *work,* to establish herself as a portrait artist and art teacher. She rented a studio and signed on a few students for instruction in drawing and sculpture: ten dollars a week for three evenings of lessons. It seemed a good idea and ten dollars multiplied by the number of students Betty and her friends optimistically anticipated promised a sumptuous living; alas, their optimism misled them and, after several weeks, Betty realized that she could not earn an adequate living by teaching the few students who joined her classes. "There weren't very many art students in California. The ones who wanted to study wanted to study all of the old ways and I was teaching the new ways, the new art, the art of the spirit and of freedom. They didn't understand what I was about," Betty judged.

In December 1933, Betty's work, left behind for just this purpose, was shown in Paris; it was her first professional exhibition; it was evidence to her friends and to herself of her stature as an artist. She eagerly awaited the reviews and gleefully clipped the *Herald Tribune*'s treatment of her work for her journal, where it remained throughout her life:

> *At the Galerie des Quatre Chemins, 18 Rue Godot de Mauroy, Betty Pierson-Parsons is showing water colors and sculpture. There is a vibrant quality of life and personality in her work, and she states her case with a directness and certainty that is unusual in a woman artist. A skillful adaptation of the medium to her purpose gives a great variety of texture to her water colors.*

Betty's friends celebrated her exhibition and review with a round of all-night drunken parties. "It was drink, drink, drink in California," Betty explained. "Drink in the morning, drink at noon, drink all night. Everyone drank all of the time. And I did, too. And it could have killed me."

Her round of parties expanded when Muriel introduced Betty to Nick and Min Luddington. Nick, with his brother Wright, founded the airline that later formed the basis for Eastern Air Lines. Min and Nick were a glittering couple able to create a party anywhere, anytime. Other revelers included such Hollywood personalities as Robert Benchley, Greta Garbo, Tallulah Bankhead, and Dorothy Parker. But all the California merriment failed to assuage Betty's underlying anguish about the condition of her life. After the parties ended and the hangovers subsided, Betty's troubles remained: she was unable to earn an adequate living, she maintained a marginal existence as a houseguest to rich friends and as recipient of Dumpy's largess. It seemed to her that no one in California was interested in her art. She was lonely, her past abandoned on the other side of an ocean and a continent, her future bleak.

Dumpy, however, offered a practical solution. Already sending money to Betty regularly, she proposed that she fully support Betty for three years so that Betty could establish herself as an artist. "But I couldn't accept that," Betty contended. "I needed to be independent. I had always been independent and I didn't want to give that up."

Self-Portrait, 1935. Done while Betty was giving portrait classes in Hollywood

Nevertheless, between 1933 and 1936, The Katinkas, with social dexterity, did broker a few commissions for portraits by Betty. She, smocked and bereted to connote her French *bona fides,* dutifully painted the heads and shoulders of the sitters but with no marked long-term betterment to her finances. For the most part, the head-and-shoulder portraits were stiff and uninspired, executed usually in gouache with a linear definition of features that tended more toward caricature than toward the expressionist mode intended. (A portrait of herself, typical of the period, remains in her estate.) Neither a technical flair nor a gift for psychological insight informed Betty's portraits; no wonder, then, that sitters did not crowd her appointment book. As the role of famous portrait artist escaped her, Betty had yet to find a reliable means for earning a living.

By now, after years of study, successful exhibition of her work in Paris, and the adulation of her American friends, Betty unequivocally considered herself an artist. But being an artist, itself a mild and glamorous form of rebellion, was another manifestation of life lived for well-styled pleasure. Betty took the tools and practice of art for granted, an old and abiding activity that would not desert her in troubled times, something to do while she fretted over serious problems or waited for the next party to commence or the next invitation to dinner to arrive; if nothing else, the beret and the accoutrements of painting established Betty as an individual and gave her license to behave as she chose. Moreover, as she played the role of artist, she amused her friends.

More out of dependable routine and comfortable role than burning commitment to art, Betty worked desultorily, her attention mired in the private and persistent problems that churned her private life. Reworking the dicta of Arthur Lindsey, she floated watercolor pigment onto wet paper, added lines or brighter defining patches of color, produced agreeable but sometimes technically awkward pictures of architecture, landscape, and flora in California.

Another habit, that of taking lessons in art, reasserted itself in California. Betty studied sporadically with Alexander Archipenko, whose work influenced her sense of pared-down mass enlivened by negative spaces—or holes. Under his sway, she worked regularly on a clay head of Helen Hyde, a friend who succeeded in luring Betty to a few Communist Party meetings that at the time influenced her only slightly.

In later years Betty often suggested that she had regularly attended Communist Party meetings, that she had been approached for membership but had rejected the offer, or that she had been a member with strong feelings for the under classes. The strongest political sentiments in her journal from this time, however, suggest a mild and romantic view of world affairs:

Wars—love—breath of the devil—
everywhere a great negation—
oh god what a wind of action is in
my heart—how can you demand it of me?

and:

With war clouds moving over Europe and poverty pockets encircling America, its [sic] *always a wonder that the sun shines in so many laughing hearts.*

As Betty substituted a circle of fun-chasing friends for her disapproving family, she continued to miss Adge Baker; she worried that she would be identified as a lesbian and, as a consequence, be ostracized from the society on which she depended both emotionally and financially. She explained, "You see, they hate you if you are different; everyone hates you and they will destroy you. I had seen enough of that. I didn't want to be destroyed."

Reviewing her journals from that period, Betty indicated that certain passages were addressed in her mind to Adge:

Strange wild wishes never quite the same.
Desires no mortal man can give a name....

Recollection. Gliding out of the tides
rolling in off the clouds
small house bewitched
by the dusk
those footsteps along
the sand
were they yours
or the memory of your
many ways

Life is a sky that turns out
finally muddy, but underneath
the dew are memories of you

Betty's friends continually expressed concern about her marital state; they stressed the perils that faced a divorced woman, and with awareness born of the ravages of the Depression on their own fortunes, they warned her that she faced poverty unless she remarried. A single woman, they insisted, could not expect a comfortable life; marriage, even a marriage as false as Betty's to Schuyler, provided membership in society; marriage gave a woman identity, and security.

Acceding at least dimly to the importuning of her friends, Betty actively considered marriage twice while in California.

First, she rejected movie actor Dick Cromwell's proposal of marriage even though she enjoyed seeing him and going with him to openings of films—notably to *Lives of a Bengal Lancer,* in which Betty thought him brilliant. Cromwell escorted her to numerous parties and courted her diligently; his attentions were, as she said, "not unwelcome." Cromwell[4] had Muriel Oaks firmly on his side in his attempts to marry Betty. After the opening of *The Lives of a Bengal Lancer,* Muriel gave a dinner party and invited Cromwell's mother. Betty noted in her journal, "He announced to his mother at dinner he wished to marry me. She was very charming about it."[5] While Betty found Cromwell amusing and charming, she thought him "a light weight." She pushed his courtship aside finally and firmly, half regretting her inability to effect what her friends pictured as an advantageous union. "It appealed. It would have been easy in some ways. But," she added, "it just wasn't my way."

At the end of January, partially to cheer Betty up after what she considered the failure of a romance with Cromwell, Min Luddington organized a joint birthday party for Betty and Tallulah Bankhead. "Can you imagine," Betty chortled, "she and I were born on the very same day. The same day, the same month, the same year." Annie Laurie Witzel, one of Betty's later Katinkas, pondered out loud: "Betty, Bankhead, and Jo Carstairs were all born on the same day. God must have been out of his mind. What could he have been thinking to create *three* such women at the *same* time?" Betty visited Jo Carstairs, a well-known yachtswoman and sometime collector of art, on her island off the Florida Coast, Whale Cay, several times in the fifties and sixties.

As was her custom, Betty took the now-aged Timmy to her birthday party and noted gleefully that he, too, was feted with a "hamburger birthday cake and whipped cream. He got the whipped cream all over his face." Timmy's gustatory orgy precipitated a serious illness that resulted in "tyfus," according to Betty's notes in her journal. Betty visited the gray-whiskered little dog daily in his hospital kennel, anxiously eliciting medical briefings from the veterinarian.

Shortly after the grand birthday party, Betty met Greta Garbo, another formidable woman, and soon the two women met regularly to play tennis. Betty, enchanted by Garbo, took casual snapshots of the silent Swede after tennis games or during visits. The nature and intensity of the friendship remains obscured by Betty's game-playing and sense of intrigue. When asked about it, Betty assumed an air of great mystery and spoke in a hushed voice. "She was very beautiful and I was very taken with her," Betty said, "but of course she was very busy and I was very busy. We played tennis. We drank. Everybody drank in Hollywood."

In an interview with Helene Aylon, however, Betty's account of an episode with Garbo, while possibly more fanciful than factual, is significant in that it demonstrates Betty's sense of drama, and her late-in-life desire to be associated with celebrity, as well as her characteristic transmutation of events to fit her dreams:

> *At Christmas, Greta Garbo said, "Come over and we are going to dress the tree." I got there and [Garbo's friend] said, "Go up to the attic and bring down a great big box of Christmas dressings." So I went up there, and Greta and I stared at each other over the top of the box. She was very beautiful. So we dressed the tree. There were candles. The Germans always had candles on their trees.*[6] *I was standing at the mantelpiece with a glass of brandy, and she was coming toward me with a candle she was going to put on the tree. I leaned forward and asked, "Which one of us burns more brightly, me with the brandy or you with the candle?" And she got very serious and said, "You burn much*

Greta Garbo in Hollywood, 1930s. Photographs, from Betty's collection, probably taken by Betty

brighter than I, because you burn from within. I, with the candle, am burning from without." I was fascinated.

She was very shy. Her boyfriend was... very jealous. She liked women very much.[7]

Betty enjoyed the company of other notables in the Hollywood community through Muriel Oaks, who often dedicated her formidable charm and cunning to concocting and dishing up a zesty social life especially for Betty. There were parties and poker games with Monty Woolley, Robert Benchley, Philip Barry, and Dorothy Parker, among others; there were opening nights and small dinner parties; above all, there were artfully arranged encounters with potential husbands.

While Muriel delighted in every opportunity for flagrant matchmaking, she introduced Betty to Robert Benchley, thinking for once, less of romance and more of a probable friendship. "You see, Muriel knew that I liked things of the mind and that," Betty concluded, "was why she knew that I would hit it off with this Robert Benchley." Betty did indeed "hit it off with this Robert Benchley"; they enjoyed a brief affair and long friendship. Betty cherished Benchley without deluding herself that she was in love with him.

Betty noted some of her times with Benchley matter-of-factly in her journal: there were nights spent with him, visits to Mexican restaurants, parties with him at the Luddingtons' beach house. He may have been merely a diversion for her in Hollywood but he became a friend later in New York. More than fifty years later she still professed admiration and affection for him. "He was," she said, "the *most* intelligent man I ever met. Well, *one* of the *most* intelligent men I ever met."

In Hollywood, Benchley bought several paintings from her and encouraged his *New Yorker* and screenwriting colleague Dorothy Parker to buy two, at forty-five dollars each. These and a few other sales, usually precipitated by friends, provided both money and hope for the unrecognized artist.

But she needed more money than the sale of a few paintings or the tuition of a few students in her classes would fetch. Despite Dumpy's checks and Muriel's ceaseless hospitality, Betty admitted to herself that she needed a steady income; she took a job at the Valley Liquor Shop as a wine consultant, part time. "There were all of these people with a lot of money. They wanted to drink the best wines but they didn't know the best wines. I had lived in France and I knew all the best wines. So I recommended wine."

During this time, her fortunes low and her future gloomy, Betty met Stuart Davis, a New York businessman who visited California and the Luddingtons frequently. He left at home a terminally ill wife and a young son. As soon as he met Betty, Davis began to pursue her and, for a while, seemed to have won her. Little is known of him, save for the glimpses of him in Betty's rather haphazard journals. At a time when she often logged into her journal round-the-clock drinking parties and epic hangovers, Betty reckoned Stuart as a heavier-than-most drinker.

Betty accepted money from Stuart regularly, and in at least one emergency, she wired him for funds. Her scruples pinched, however, at her sexual involvement with a married man, and when he pressed her for an agreement to marry him upon the inevitable death of his ailing wife and urged her to return to New York, Betty refused. She insisted that they observe her standards of propriety, as measured in geographic distance at least, so long as he was legally married.[8]

All the while that the affair with Stuart endured, Betty remained partially in love with Adge Baker and, simultaneously, reveled in the sweet pain of a crush on blond, vivacious Min Luddington,[9] who, kindly disposed toward Betty, even loving her as a

Santa Barbara Landscape, ca. 1935

friend, was absorbed in her husband and her children, and her ceaseless parties. Over the years, however, Betty would turn to Min for comforting conversation, for gifts of clothing, and for entertainment in much the manner that she might have depended on the anchoring love of a sister.

The Luddingtons generated their famous parties in town or at their beach house, often hiring Mexican bands to play all night at the poolside. On whim, they swooped up Betty, with or without an escort, and roared off to Mexico for nights of drinking and dancing. Betty joined the Luddington poker parties where she won or lost, often noting the amounts in her journal. In tennis games with Nick and Min, Betty shone as a natural athlete with a well-tuned game and boundless energy. Casually, the Luddingtons and Betty often started an evening with drinks at the Garden of Allah, which soon resulted in forty-eight-hour bashes of heavy drinking followed by forty-eight-hour hangovers.

Abruptly the Luddingtons moved back to Pennsylvania when Nick's business required, halting the parties and the life Betty shared with them. California then lost its salt for Betty. The perpetual parties had left little time for her own work or, perhaps a blessing, for her own thoughts. Stuart's wife had died and he had accelerated his courtship. When lonely, Betty turned to Stuart; he provided money when she needed it; he cared for her, and he seemed to need her. Perhaps, she thought, she was in love with him; at least, she felt *affection* for him. Without Min to comfort and distract her, without the Luddingtons' menu of rich amusements, Betty discovered that California was not for her. She said she was tired of the parties, repelled by the universal drinking and the poisonous hangovers. She felt that her life was moribund. She would, she decided, return to New York and marry Stuart, thereby gaining financial security and reclaiming her social position.

In the week before she departed for New York, Betty wrote in her journal: "Everything in itself has a meaning. It is the privilege of the mind to state it, the heart to understand it, the soul to recognize its importance."

In November, Betty and Timmy returned to New York.[10]

Right: *Mexican Landscape*, ca. 1938

Below: *Newport Harbor, Rhode Island*, 1930s. Signed "Betty B. Parsons"

A DEALER'S APPRENTICESHIP

•

1935-45

In November of 1935, Betty Parsons and Timmy, her aging and now almost continually ailing terrier, crossed the continent in a first-class train compartment provided by Stuart Davis, toward New York and marriage. Suspended in the motion of travel, Betty planned nothing beyond that intended marriage, a legal act that would anchor her in the conformity of a familiar society and a secure future—isn't that what Emily had said? And Muriel and Dumpy and Min? Wasn't that the message preached to her all her life?

As the train rocked and chugged across the United States, Betty sipped gin from a flask that Min had given her for her birthday. Gazing dreamily at the countryside passing her window, she noted in her journal the small events of train travel: walking Timmy at a country stop watched over by "two black cows, three little golden trees, and a blue sky...";[1] she scrawled her poetry in the book:

Through a vision and a dream
we wandered all unseen

and, further along in her journey, she observed in the black book:

a flock of birds
a tuft of grass
a stream of water
no one shall pass.

Breaking her trip in Chicago to rest Timmy, she bundled herself against the autumnal winds and walked him along the streets. He moved slowly, as if to avoid pain, but his enthusiasm for travel and his delight in treats from Betty's meals heartened her. "He was spry. And interested in everything. And, of course, he loved me and I loved him. We had been everywhere together."

Before boarding the train in Chicago for the last leg of her journey home, Betty visited the Art Institute Annual Exhibition of American Painting and Sculpture, which she found "interesting and unsurprising." Why, she wondered, was there so little interest in America in the new painting and sculpture? But art and its condition in the United States only lightly brushed her thinking.

When she arrived in New York, she went directly to Stuart's "pretty, dark, and dull apartment," on Gramercy Square to meet "his son, the monkey, and John." Almost immediately, Betty joined Stuart's household of young Stuart and assorted pets for a weekend trek to Southampton. The weekend on Long Island began with drinks and, as Betty soon discovered, proceeded through more drinks until time for dinner; the next day began with "eye-openers" followed by drinks through the day and morning-after hangovers that seemed to be the standard fare of Stuart's weekends in the country. But, despite the dismal drunkenness of the weekend and Betty's disappointment in Stuart's apartment, she found pleasure in "Stuart's farm—like a little château, cosy and warm."

Betty's life in New York soon almost duplicated her California pattern of parties, drinking, hangovers, and casual working at painting or sculpture around the edges of her social activities. Min and Nick Luddington, now living in Ardmore, Pennsylvania, invited her to frequent houseparties; Caroline Cromwell and Dumpy Oehlreichs saw to it that Betty attended parties, met people, and shared their lunches, dinners, cocktail parties, and wardrobes.

In the name of propriety, Betty hesitated to live outright with Stuart and lived partly with Dumpy, insisting to Stuart that she should not move officially into his apartment until they were married. Stuart accepted Betty's rules of behavior but prodded her to set a date for the wedding. As Stuart grew more insistent, Betty balked at setting an actual date or even formally announcing an engagement, shielding herself against the decision with first one excuse and then another. Stuart argued that an appropriate time had passed since the death of his wife and that Betty should marry him. Betty offered only excuses to wait: Wait, she insisted, until she had herself more settled into New York. Wait until she had spent more time with her family. Wait, she pleaded, until she had given necessary attention to friends. Wait. And wait some more.

"I didn't mind having an affair. That was not like marriage. I didn't belong to Stuart in an affair and I could break it off when I wanted or see anyone I wanted," Betty allowed. "But *marriage*! I had my independence and I just didn't want to give it up for marriage. Yes, I had *promised* Stuart and he had been very helpful to me and I loved him. But I had hesitations."

Betty's adjustment to New York, regardless of her excuses to Stuart, was never at issue. In essence, she had come home and, with her grandfather in his grave, no one dared tell her what to do. As her good times with friends consumed her calendar, Stuart was a burden rather than a companion. "I had had enough of drinking men and men who were jealous," she recognized, "and I thought this Stuart Davis drank too much and resented my independence too much."

Toward the end of her first month back in New York, Timmy again became sick with symptoms similar to those that he had suffered in California. One Friday, before taking the train to Pennsylvania to visit the Luddingtons, Betty took the grizzled old terrier to a veterinarian for treatment and a few days of observation. The veterinarian's calm manner reassured Betty, and she kept her date with Min and Nick. When she returned to New York on Saturday, Timmy's veterinarian told her there was no cause for alarm, but no marked evidence yet of improvement; Timmy needed a bit more time, a bit more medication.

Relieved, Betty met Stuart as planned for an early dinner in a favorite hangout. He was drunk and quarrelsome, resentful of her time with the Luddingtons; he grew tearful. Why, he harangued, wouldn't she marry him? Was there someone else? His drunkenness, his efforts to dominate, his awkward efforts at charm, and finally, his jealousy seemed to Betty to resemble Schuyler's most hateful behavior. Yet, she had accepted his earlier proposal, she had allowed him to help her financially and to bring her back to New York, she had encouraged him as he reshaped his family life after his wife's death to include her.

What was to have been a lovers' dinner turned into angry and tearstained turmoil. Betty, confused and sad, left Stuart after dinner and, spontaneously, decided to stay the night with a friend.[2] Sunday morning, Betty decided not to call the veterinarian, unwilling to disturb him on a day off. But courteously if not contritely, she called Stuart to prevent his worrying about her and to give him her telephone number at her friend's house. She told him, too, that she wanted some time away from him, that she wanted to reconsider her promise to marry him.

On Monday, Betty wrote shakily in her journal:

Timmy is dead. Doctor phoned at 7:30. Had tried to get me all night—a heart attack that started at midnight and took him away at 6:45. I could not sleep from five till seven, was frantically restless. If only I could have been with him when he died. The Dr. called Dumpy. She had my wrong number. She phoned Stuart and he did not phone me. Why I will never know—went to see Timmy's body. He looked so sweet dead.[3]

Stuart, Betty surmised in retrospect, had been too drunk to comprehend the gravity of the situation. Or to care. "He was not," she said, "very interested in what was happening to other people. Especially when he drank. And I don't think he could ever have been very interested in a woman as an equal, as a person. I will never understand how he could not call me about Timmy. How could I think about marrying such a man?"

She wrote:

Bury Timmy beside a picket fence near the water and near the house with the sun up and the sky full of beautiful clouds. Oh Tim be happy with all the wonders of the earth you have found. . . .

Having consigned Timmy to the Long Island earth around Stuart's house, Betty returned to New York to stay with Dumpy who, dependably warm-spirited and solicitous, campaigned to cheer Betty by visiting art galleries with her, arranging dinner parties for her to become reacquainted with Henry Schnakenberg, a painter who was attracting attention for his portraits and romantic landscapes, to see Monty Woolley again and swap tales about Hollywood, to meet the female poet Michael Strange and other people Dumpy thought amusing and likely to distract Betty from her grief. Hope Williams, in town and sparkling with droll mischief, joined Dumpy's operation to dispel Betty's sadness through lunches and lively conversation. Betty's sister Sukes came to town to shop; she took Betty to dinner and the theater, treated her to a new dress at Saks, and commiserated with her about Stuart.

But it was Dumpy, as motherly and generous as she was witty and sophisticated, who fretted over Betty's state of mind and her finances, who sent her to the dentist and paid her dental bills, and who reminded her to get her hair cut or shampooed. Dumpy joked with Betty; she promised better times to come. And Dumpy, recipient of Betty's confidences about Robert Benchley, invited him to dinner at her house.

Benchley, apparently delighted to see Betty again, took her to lunch at The Algonquin Hotel's famous Round Table often during the next few weeks, encouraged her to talk about her life, and alone among her friends at this time, asked out of interest rather than courtesy to see her new watercolors of Southampton. Listening to Betty talk about her sense of spontaneity in watercolors, Benchley encouraged her to show the new work to a New York art dealer. She claimed later to have been terrified but she bundled a sheaf of watercolors into a portfolio and kept the appointment Benchley had insisted she make with Alan Gruskin at the Midtown Galleries.

Alan Gruskin leafed through the portfolio once; then again more slowly. "He told me he liked my work. He signed me up for a show right on the spot," Betty recounted. When the exhibition opened, Betty was elated; people liked her work: fourteen

Landscape with House, ca. 1939

pictures were sold to, among others, Benchley, Dorothy Parker, Wright Luddington, Hope Williams, Wall Street luminary James Forrestal, collector Lee Ault, and Mrs. Hermann Oehlreichs—dependable Dumpy.

Stuart, sober and repentant, celebrated Betty's triumph with dinner at The Algonquin before taking her to a performance of Lillian Hellman's hit play *The Children's Hour.* Bob Benchley honored the occasion with a dinner at Lüchow's for Betty, Min and Nick Luddington, and a group of friends who had begun early to commemorate the holiday season. Other friends joined the party, and after better than two weeks of unflagging celebration and drinking, of dancing all night and nursing hangovers all day, Betty collapsed in Dumpy's house just before Christmas. By Christmas eve, Dumpy's restoration project had succeeded and Betty, dressed in one of Dumpy's expensive new frocks from Paris and treated by Dumpy to a shampoo and hairdo at a salon patronized by the New York chapter of The Katinkas, had lunch with her father, her sister Sukes and her husband Tom McCarter, and their children, Tommy and little Suzanne, "a couple of hellian [*sic*] angels." But the sedate family celebration did not exhaust Betty's bank of holiday cheer. Unerringly heading toward the most grandiose party she could locate, she joined the Luddingtons and Tallulah Bankhead at Ardmore for three days of drinking, cardplaying, and hilarity.

When Betty's merrymaking ended, she surveyed her emotional and financial domain: her affair with Stuart was over but her career as an artist was launched in New York. Not a bad tally, she decided. Moreover, she initiated 1936 with a hopeful heart, a new studio in her former teacher Mary Tonetti's building, and—to her amazement—a *job*!

In December, while Betty's show was up at the Midtown Galleries, Gruskin observed that she attracted a large and lively following among the rich, the famous, and the near famous; he watched her charm people with no interest in art into eager purchasers. He then asked Betty to work for the gallery installing exhibitions and

Reginald Marsh's drawing of the "girls'" triple birthday party at the Luddingtons' house. Left to right: Marsh, Tallulah Bankhead, Jo Carstairs, Henry Schnakenberg, and Betty Parsons, January 3, 1936

selling paintings on commission. Not exactly promising a handsome income, the job nevertheless thrilled Betty with its promise of steady earnings and its proximity to art.

On January 5, in preparation for her new life as an employed person, Betty bought and fiddled with a tiny clock that entertained her "with its hat on one side and a smile" on its face. But a work ethic does not spring full-blown from idleness. The job, no less than other events, required a celebration, a party, a few drinks that flowed through the night before anyone really noticed. When Betty's droll little clock called her to painful attention, she "woke feeling as if clouds and waterfalls had marched over me." As nervous as a teenager on her first job, thirty-six-year-old Betty began work in the Midtown Galleries at two-thirty that afternoon, when the gallery opened. If she could only get up and face the mornings, that schedule would allow her time to work in her studio on her own paintings and sculpture. Independence, she now reckoned, had to be bought with work.

But work also heightened her appetite for nights of drinks and dancing, for more episodes in what might have been the greatest floating gala of the century. The party, its nightly installments seeming to flow smoothly together despite intervals of work in the gallery, lasted the entire month of January. At the end of the month, the Luddingtons, eagerly seizing cause for one more party, organized another birthday bash for three friends born on the same day of the same year: Betty Parsons, Tallulah Bankhead, and Jo Carstairs. The party, launched and generously floated on champagne and music, mixed artists, actors, sports figures, business people, and anyone else the three friends could collect, lure, or kidnap. Reginald Marsh commemorated the event with an ink drawing that he gave to Betty.

Betty emerged from January's parties a little frayed but still a working woman. Euphoria replaced the hangovers: she had a job; she had a studio in New York; she was independent. And, with the money from the December sale of her paintings still in her pocket and expecting a monthly income through commissions on sales for the gallery, she hired a carpenter for four dollars to build a model stand for her studio; she spent nine dollars having some pieces cast in bronze; and she bought a cocktail shaker and tablecloth, noting each expenditure carefully in her journals.

"I loved that studio," she recalled. "It had everything I needed. Space. Light. I didn't mind walking up to it." The fourth-floor walkup, the top of a stable that Mary Tonetti had transformed into her studio and school, became Betty's ideal studio. "I never," she said, "had a better place to work until I built my studio on Long Island. It was perfection. And I loved it."

She also loved her job. As part of her new business-like role, she reminded herself in her journal to "Make contact with decorators," and systematically began to invite the best interior decorators of New York, Palm Beach, Newport, and California to stop by the Midtown Galleries and see the paintings there as possible components in decorating schemes for the houses of rich patrons.[4]

In breaking off her affair with Stuart Davis, Betty finally established in the eyes of her friends and family her right not to remarry, and through her work in the galleries and her success as an artist, she shifted their interest to other aspects of her life. Her declaration of independence from marriage also entailed a shift in her public persona: now she was recognized as a rebel, an independent and feisty woman, an artist with bohemian *bona fides*. Hints by society gossips of interesting stains on her history, she found, created an agreeable atmosphere of mystery that brought more potential clients to the gallery.

When Dumpy took Hermann, her ailing husband, south for the winter, she temporarily abdicated her almost daily routine of taking Betty out for lunches or inviting her to dinners. Missing Dumpy's comforting attentions and stabilizing routines, Betty turned to Gina[5] (not her real name) for, at first, easy companionship. Shortly, however, a love affair developed and continued, with ebbs and swells in intensity, for several years. Early in the relationship, the two women shared more or less public lunches and dinners at restaurants frequented by their social group, but soon, Gina invited Betty to her comfortable apartment, where she cooked sophisticated Italian meals, where her pet parrot squawked in Italian, where fresh flowers made a joke of the winter outside. Betty sprawled on the rug before Gina's fireplace and savored a naughty and thrilling time stolen from the proper world of proper friends and a proper job in an important gallery. "Hurrah for morning flowers," Betty wrote in her journal, "and parrots, no barriers, and ripe carrots." And, a day later, still in Gina's apartment, she extolled "a country-heavy snowstorm . . . a deep voice, a slow fire with logs that melt and ashes that glow are the things that make the spirit flow."[6] Betty, boasting in her journal, "I have loved the illegitimate and the unapplauded," ceased to fret about her sexual interests and, from then on, her prized independence expanded to include guiltless sexual episodes with both men and women.

In the early months of 1936, Alexander Calder and Betty renewed their friendship, invoking the fancy-free spirit of Paris in their New York evenings of dancing and inexpensive Dutch-treat dinners. As Sandy prepared for an exhibition of his recent works, Betty urged her friends to attend, telling them that he possessed a unique vision that he combined with his engineer's skill in remarkable, witty, intelligent pieces.

Buoyed as she was by Calder's high-stepping spirit, she was equally attuned to the different key, the tragic view she found in Chaim Soutine's show at the Valentine Gallery. She saw his work as, "exciting, sincere, vital, heartbreaking, [with] beautiful color." Now that she was an official member of the art world, Betty visited galleries and museums continually to look as an artist at the works on display and, in her new, more professional role as dealer, to learn pragmatically the rudiments of dealing. She not only looked at works of art, she looked at the ways in which they were shown in galleries, checked price lists, talked collegially with other dealers, and picked up the tricks of the trade.

But even exhilarated by her independence and quickened by her role as *working woman,* Betty did not forswear the parties with the Luddingtons, Hope Williams, and her circle of New York friends. Rather, through Gina, who introduced her to numerous theater personalities and international gadabouts, she expanded her circle of partymakers to include Eva Le Gallienne, Katharine Cornell and her secretary, Gertrude Macy[7] (Min Luddington's sister), and actress Peg Murray. Drinking, dancing, joking, and partying were dimmed neither by independence of spirit nor by demands of career; nothing could change the party girl's social habits.

Betty's datebook from these months is packed with engagements with friends, among them Tom Eastman, a businessman and family friend from the South who took her to the theater and bought presents for her as soon as he discovered her interest in something—a radio, a toaster, a sweater, some books. He invited her on trips to escape the New York winter, including a cruise in the Caribbean which gave her visual material for a new clutch of watercolors.[8] He took her flying in his airplane. "He was this fantastic pilot," she remembered fondly, "and he took me up into the sky around New York. We flew all around Long Island. We saw all the bridges and buildings."

Independence continued to mark Betty's social life as it did her entire personality. Dancing, she ignored the music, snapped her fingers to a beat she imagined, and *led.* Painting, she ignored both technique and skill, relegated criteria associated with tradition to the junk heap of sluggish spirits. And driving her second-hand Ford, an adored gift from brother-in-law Tom McCarter, Betty roared forward with reckless disregard for other vehicles. Driving fast, straight down the middle of the road, she gripped the wheel tensely, leaned slightly forward as she barked profane insults at other drivers or inanimate objects that intruded on her territory. As she vituperated the basic courtesies of the road, she challenged the rules for survival. Inevitably, a policeman on Long Island pulled her over and politely insisted that she present a driver's license that she did not possess. She vamped herself free of a ticket, but finally acceded to the state's requirements, and after days of studying and fuming at the totalitarian state that threatened her freedom to drive exactly as she pleased, she got her driver's license. Betty was elated, waving it about as if it were a diploma. But her achievement did not kindle joy among her friends. Rosalind Constable recalls that Dumpy, having ridden in cars with Betty at the wheel and on the accelerator, cried for three days when she learned that Betty acquired the coveted license. "Dumpy knew that Betty simply turned a car on, aimed it more or less, and went as fast as she possibly could," Rosalind mused. "After all, isn't that how she did everything?"

Not everything. To Betty's astonishment, no less than her friends', she found that she "liked working in a gallery. I didn't so much like talking to people. I was very shy. But I liked working with the pictures. And I had a good eye." This recognition registered a change in course for the good-time girl. She worked steadily in the gallery through the spring and, in summer, she spent weekends in the country. After driving to Long Island, and mindful of historic import, she noted in her journal on July 23, 1936, "went over Triborough Bridge for the first time. It was opened this week." Bridges, like tall buildings, signified progress; both, connoting astonishing engineering achievements, belonged especially to Betty's New York, "the most energetic city in the world, the city of the future."

Above, left: Betty with wire-haired terrier, Prides Crossing, Massachusetts, ca. 1938

Above, right: Dumpy Oehlreichs and Betty, Newport, Rhode Island, ca. 1920

When the summer ended, Betty enrolled in drawing classes at the Art Students League to improve her figure drawing and her handling of watercolor paints. At the League, the venerable institution in New York that has succored artists with lessons, opportunities to teach, and facilities for engaging in a variety of activities not easily available to them in their private studios, Betty set her own pace as she balanced her requirements for technical skill against her expressive purposes as an artist.[9] When Betty weighed *the good* in art, independence won over technique and expression over skill.

Although Betty's works had sold well at the Midtown Galleries, several comments about her watercolors had stung her. First, as the exhibition closed, both Calder and Benchley, in differing words and tones, urged Betty to fortify her skills in drawing. Then Hope Williams and Dumpy Oehlreichs decided that Betty's work looked unfinished, amateurish, inept; they offered advice to Betty and admitted that they were skeptical when she insisted that what appeared to them to be "unfinished" was, in fact, stylistic evidence of expressionistic content. Betty embarked on a lecture, her arms waving, on the "new art." With this familiar note, the two friends settled back to enjoy Betty's dramatic espousal of the freedoms of art and the role of the creative mind. As Betty stirred the ashes of Arthur Lindsey's teaching still resident in her memory, she flamed and glowed with excitement for new possibilities and directions in art, for the responsibilities and gifts of the artist. Dumpy and Hope smiled and nodded with the good-humored gentleness of the totally unconvinced who have heard many times the same rigmarole; in turn, Betty dismissed their predictable remarks about her work and about art. What did they know? And she, after all, was a practicing and exhibiting professional artist. In her journal, she took her stand:

Amateur watches nothing
Professional watches everything.

Meanwhile, working at the Midtown Galleries solidified Betty's confidence in her new identity as a professional art dealer: she sold paintings. Sometimes she sold them to strangers; often, actually a more difficult task, she sold pictures to her socialite friends, who recognized no intrinsic worth in a work of art. As clients' resistance and doubts melted under the warmth of Betty's personal charm and the intensity of her persuasion, her air of authority expanded. She had, she believed, a gift for the work, an eye for hanging shows, for placing a picture in such a way that it could best be seen, flanking one painting with congenial partners, grouping pictures so that each could be appreciated. She found that she liked hanging paintings on white walls, that she liked to flood them with strong light; she found that a painting placed an inch lower or higher would become more accessible or more remote for the viewer.

Her work in the gallery—and it was real work in the real world—was compatible to her nature, she discovered to her amazement. First, to her enormous relief, she did not have to rise early, and once in the gallery, she could move about physically and talk to people who came to see works of art—for the most part a self-selecting group of art lovers whose comments she enjoyed; she did not need to record facts or put papers in order. Then, to her astonishment, she earned money. "It suited me. I had this eye. And I knew about painting because I was a painter and I had lived in France," Betty concluded. "I was shy. But I managed. I don't know how."

In December 1936, she had her second exhibition of watercolors at the Midtown Galleries. It consisted of watercolors of Long Island, which she signed "Betty Pierson-Parsons." This show, like the one the previous year, was almost completely sold out. Betty was elated.

Early in 1937, after a brief visit with the Luddingtons in California, Betty began again to study with Ossip Zadkine at his studio in the Hotel Shelton on Lexington Avenue. Sensing that she needed more precision and discipline than that required by the Art Students League and looking for a point of view embodied in a strong personality, Betty turned to her old friend and teacher Zadkine for his clarity of style—his easily recognizable *signature.* Independence, after all, must be evident; an artist must flaunt it. Throughout the spring, still working part-time in the Midtown Galleries, Betty studied clay sculpture steadily, if without specific focus or purpose.

In September, she traveled to Europe with Dumpy, ostensibly to "get over Stuart." In actuality, the trip allowed her to visit Adge Baker in London. Throughout the last few years, Betty had begun to read astrology, to exchange letters with Adge Baker on "spiritual matters," and to explore mysticism and the occult casually but steadily. In Paris, Adge had urged mysticism on the younger Betty, who, despite her ceaseless round of parties, felt a need for something more serious, more stable, and less materialistic in her life. She might have turned to religion or charitable works befitting a rich woman, but in fact, she had surmised that a layer of the spiritual world would reveal meaning to her. "There was no way that I could have belonged to the church,"

Betty remarked. "Of course, I was baptized and all of that. My family supported the church. But I never had any use whatsoever for the church. I always appreciated the religious but not the church. The true religious is very spiritual. It's about the expanding universe. Some of the most religious people are scientists and artists. I don't think religious people like the church very much. I consider myself religious and I don't like the church. All those rules. Too conservative."

While her friends played with Ouija boards and read cards and leaves and palms mock seriously, Betty performed or participated in these "rituals" solemnly. They brushed her with truth, they unveiled the future; they put her in touch with cosmic powers. She reported her wondrous experiences to Adge, who responded with repeated encouragement and "I-told-you-so"s. Ironically, these subjects provided a safer field for conversation between the two friends than did art or shared past experiences.

That fall, Betty began work for Mrs. Cornelius J. Sullivan's Gallery at 460 Park Avenue. Mrs. Sullivan, one of the founders of The Museum of Modern Art in 1929, was a stern taskmaster who demanded that Betty keep strict hours, not tarry over lunch, and work diligently to sell art works that Betty often found boring. She remained with the formidable mentor, however, because "Mrs. Sullivan had this great taste. And I liked her taste. And I learned a lot about silver and antiques and those things that had always interested my family. Mrs. Sullivan also had a great collection of Irish and modern paintings and she was a very great woman." Betty acknowledged the skills of "the Irish artists"—including Jack Yeats, the brother of the Irish poet, and the academic painters Nathaniel Hone and Paul Henry—but she preferred two other artists in Mrs. Sullivan's stable—André Girard and Lyonel Feininger.

Mrs. Sullivan was also clever in the management of her gallery. As an art dealer, she cannily combined her social life with her business, using parties and visits with friends to identify and court clients. Under Mrs. Sullivan's sway, Betty Parsons perfectly blurred the distinctions between work and play. For example, while Betty was employed by Mrs. Sullivan, her Florida holiday combined visits to friends and family with business. Promoting the gallery on such a visit to Rollins College, Betty was introduced as an important representative of the New York and Paris art worlds, a role of authority she enjoyed. Greeted by the president and taken to visit art classes, she noted: "Very discouraging report—the model had to keep on bathing suit and the students were lazy and stupid...."[10]

From Rollins College, Betty traveled to Palm Beach to visit Emily, Arch, and young Billy Rayner, who already showed signs of looking so much like Betty that, as an adult, he would often be taken to be her son. Billy was a treasure upon the earth to Betty's way of thinking. Betty's love for Emily and Billy, however, did not extend to Arch, who remained, in her view, a difficult, sometimes oafish, too often drunken and self-centered man. Betty did little to hide her belief that Arch was not good enough for Emily and did not deserve a son as splendid as Billy.

Bill recalls that, "My father disapproved of simply *everything* about Betty. To his way of thinking, she was an artist and, therefore, not entirely acceptable; she was liberal in her politics and a threat to everything he believed in. She was *bohemian,* he thought, and God only knew what that might mean in terms of her behavior." But Betty valued Arch's disapproval; it further vivified her role as rebel, liberal, and artist. She visited Palm Beach often, where in addition to enjoying Emily and Billy, she dined, drank, and danced. She established herself in Palm Beach as an influential figure from the art world. There, in the role of visiting dignitary, she accepted invitations to view private collections or to exhibit her own work. Her comments were repeated throughout the social community and her opinions valued.

Back in New York after her visit to Florida in 1938, Betty divided her time among her duties for Mrs. Sullivan, her own work, and her parties, noting in her journal the social events she deemed special. In April, for instance, she wrote: "tea with Ford Madox Ford at Dumpy's." She recalled the event years later: "Ford was a very attractive man. He had great charm. I read his books so of course he was very pleased to talk with me. Most Americans, he thought, weren't interested in new writing. Well, they weren't interested in new anything then."[11]

In June, the gallery closed for the summer. Betty again sailed as Dumpy's guest to Ireland, England, and France. In July, after visiting Adge Baker ("looking thin and frail"),[12] she spent August in Brittany working on watercolor paintings and reviewing Arthur Lindsey's teachings. In September, rested and absorbed in her own work, Betty returned to London to visit Adge again. "We talked about things of the spirit," Betty remembered. "Adge of course knew much more than I did and she helped set me on the right path. I had been brought up in the church, which had nothing of 'the spirit' in it. Adge was free from the church. She was free in her spirit and she helped me become that way, too. She just gave me hell when I didn't see things the right way. I learned a lot from Adge Baker."

At the end of 1938, she summarized for her journal her state:

Love, travel, beauty
no money
health good
heart unhappy
mind happy
spirit strong

In 1939, however, Betty's life took a turn for the better. She met Rosalind Constable, who later became known as the "culture scout" for Time-Life Publications, and who would be Betty's lifelong friend. Taller than Betty, but like her blue-eyed and blond, Rosalind viewed life and art from a pole opposite to Betty's. Crisp, obsessively precise in language and manners, ritually rational and pledged to testing ideas and perceptions against the evidence of information, Rosalind Constable fascinated Betty, who still indulged in adolescent sloppiness in her dress and living conditions, who rejected rationality in favor of abstruse mystical cant, and who deified the serendipitous, the accidental, and the romantically chaotic in life and art. For Rosalind's every effort to consider facts, Betty discounted them in favor of expression; for every delight Betty identified as new and "of the expanding world," Rosalind denounced it as harebrained, lacking in authenticity, and possibly fraudulent. The opposing forces of the two women created a strong magnetic field in which they were contained for several years, sometimes in peaceable coexistence, sometimes in emotional combat.

Shortly after they met, Betty and Rosalind decided to share an apartment in order to save expenses. The artist Hedda Sterne recalled, "Betty and Rosalind fought all of the time. Betty, you know, liked to dominate or to be totally dominated. All of her relationships fell into those categories and, with Rosalind as with Adge Baker, she was dominated.... But she adored Rosalind and I think Rosalind loved Betty."

Adge and Rosalind, both British and both strong-minded, buttressed opposite sides of Betty's ideas about art. Adge's insistence on "the spiritual in art" sharpened Betty's vision of what she had earlier thought of as "The New Spirit" and, ironically,

Betty in a beach chair, Saint Thomas, Virgin Islands, ca. 1933–34

encouraged her to champion art quite different from that which Adge herself found even tolerable. Similarly, because Rosalind chided Betty about her slothfulness, challenged her unformed slipshod thinking, urged her toward a more disciplined professional life, Betty gave more attention to her job, soon exulting in her growing success as an art dealer.

Meanwhile, Rosalind's talents were recognized by Henry Luce, who installed her outside his office to review "little magazines," read the latest books, cover art exhibitions, and monitor "cultural matters." In an informal corporate publication, *Rosie's Bugle,* Rosalind trumpeted for Time-Life executives the high moments and best achievements of American arts. Perhaps Rosalind, as Betty later claimed, thought Betty "was on to something." But, whether beguiled by Betty or actually persuaded to her way of looking at art, Rosalind was instrumental in bringing early and very important publicity to Betty's artists and to Betty as a dealer.

Rosalind lamented what she considered to be Mrs. Sullivan's tyranny in requiring Betty to confine her lunch hour, including travel, to a precise sixty minutes. Betty's theater of martyrdom included taking her watch from her wrist and placing it visibly on the table between the lunching friends. Frequently, Rosalind recalled, Betty consulted the watch and counted down her minutes before returning to Mrs. Sullivan's gallery. Encouraged by Rosalind, Betty left Mrs. Sullivan in 1940 to manage the gallery in The Wakefield Bookshop at 64 East Fifty-fifth Street. She was delighted to have reached further independence with this job, which allowed her to run the gallery according to her own style, and to set her own hours.

Betty was eager to take charge of the gallery. Confident in her "eye," she yearned to select artists, to hang their work, to teach viewers to look at the work her way. In

The Wakefield Bookshop, ca. 1941

conversation some years later with Annie Laurie Witzel, Betty portrayed the ideal gallery that she had imagined as she began management of the Wakefield: It would exist on two levels connected by a spiral staircase. This gallery would cater only to the very, very rich. Betty imagined herself, stately and aloof, holding court on the second floor, descending majestically to the first level to meet only the most important clients, preferably Rockefellers or royalty. Annie Laurie Witzel, captivated by the fantasy, encouraged Betty to amplify the shape and substance of the dream: there would be familiar folk from the art world playing various roles to Betty's queen—a joker, a fool, some chivalrous knights to do her bidding, an executioner to rid her of nagging problems, some ladies in waiting. It is significant that Betty held the fantasy gallery in her mind for several decades; it is also significant that, stripped of the fairy-tale trappings, Betty's fantasy gallery proved to be the blueprint for her fame as a dealer.

Delighted by her work at the Wakefield, Betty nonetheless found time to join Rosalind in preparing for the inevitable onset of the Second World War, which had already started in Rosalind's native England. The friends took Red Cross courses in first aid and auto mechanics. "I didn't do very well," Betty confessed. "I thought the engines of autos very beautiful but they were also very mysterious. I was better at bandages and wounds. I volunteered to go to war as a nurse. The officer asked me what I could do and I told him I could speak French. But I wasn't called up."

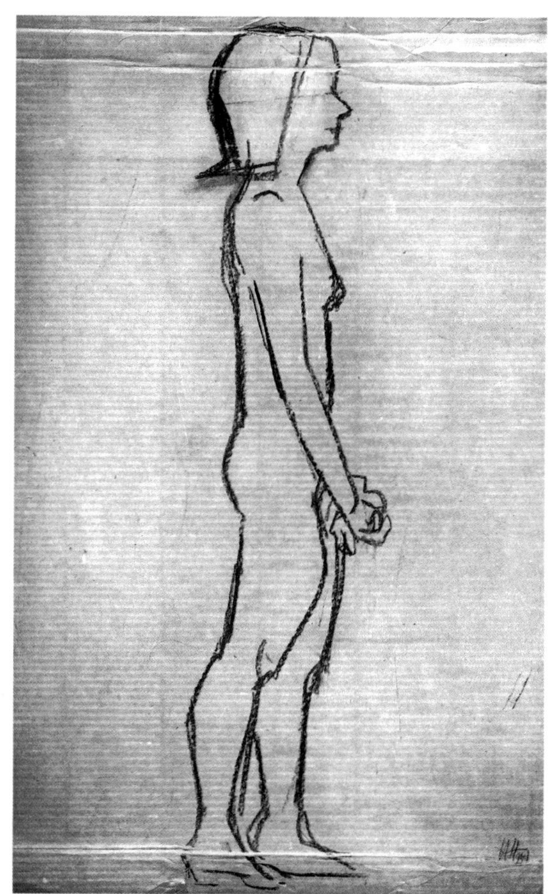

Above, left: Saul Steinberg, 1930s

Above, right: Hedda Sterne, *Portrait of Betty Parsons,* 1935. Collection Lee Hall

Her disappointment in not being called up soon dissolved in her work. Betty's confidence thrived among artists who appreciated her, who liked her; she was, she knew, one of them, an artist first and a dealer only as a means for making a living. She brought clients from her previous gallery associations into the Wakefield; she sold work for her artists, and as her work in the gallery attracted attention in the press and in art world conversation, the seeds of a legend were planted:

> *The remarkable batting average maintained by the Wakefield Gallery is a source of wonder to those who drop in here often. Some of the exhibitions have been fuller packed with interest than others, but there has never been a dull one, never a completely pedestrian painter.... Betty Parsons [is] the Director to whose cultivated taste the Gallery's high score can be attributed....*[13]

Betty developed on her own the gallery's roster of artists which established her as a daring dealer of the time: Saul Steinberg, Theodoros Stamos, Constantine Nivola, Hedda Sterne, Joseph Cornell, and others. As each caught Betty's eye, she identified his or her work as personal, instinct with individual voice and feeling. She quickly formed strong and lasting friendships with these artists; Hedda Sterne remained Betty's lifelong friend; Saul Steinberg, even when his work was handled largely by Sidney Janis, remained loyal to Betty and continued to show regularly in her gallery.

In 1943, Betty spent the summer with Hedda Sterne in Provincetown, where they shared a studio. Nearby, Hedda found a "little room that even has a bathroom"[14] for Betty. They walked on the beach, feasted on lobsters, drank wine, and painted and

Hedda Sterne, *Bedroom*, 1944

sketched all day, every day. Hedda, knowledgeable about European art and interested in the latest theories and practices in psychology as well as in the events marking the progress of the war, encouraged Betty to read books and to talk about her reading. Hedda remembered, "Betty always read in just her own way. She read what she wanted to read. That is, whatever she actually read she discovered the author said what she already thought."[15] Laughing, Hedda added, "How wonderfully like Betty, to be so certain of everything that she discovered everyone agreeing with her."

In the fall, bronzed by the sun and hefting a fat portfolio of summer work, Betty returned to the Wakefield. In February 1944, she showed works by Adolph Gottlieb; his manner of working seemed to her to be driven by his vision of the "secret forces of nature. That was something Stamos had, too, that mysterious knowledge about what went on in nature that you can't see."

With both encouragement and help from Barnett Newman, Betty installed an exhibition of Pre-Columbian stone sculpture at the Wakefield in May of 1944. Newman wrote the introduction to the show, which, as the ensuing decades would show, came close to serving as Betty Parson's personal manifesto. Such works, Newman wrote, reveal their "inner significance...[in the] excitement of the aesthetic experience," a shared emotional experience that promises more success than official diplomatic efforts in establishing community among disparate people, since, Newman argued, "it is by comprehending the spiritual aspirations of human beings that permanent bonds can best be built."

We have no cause, wrote Newman, to identify work as "primitive" and to look condescendingly upon it. "Can we rightfully assume," he asked, "that these works of art are the products of an artless child-like mind? Are they 'the best primitive man could do'? Are not these masterpieces the best any man can do?"

Betty on the beach, photographed by Strelsa van Scriver, Southold, Long Island, June 1951

He wrote of transcending time, of entering the spiritual life of a forgotten people, of touching magic—all themes that gripped Betty's imagination. These sculptures, he said, and others of their mode, compelled modern sculptors "to discard the mock heroic, the voluptuous, the superficial realism that inhibited the medium for so many European centuries. So great is the reciprocal power of this art that while giving us a greater understanding of the people who produced it, it gives meaning to the strivings of our own artists."

Barnett Newman's words exactly reflected the feelings Betty sought to form into thought. In Newman, Betty found an articulate friend who understood her feelings, her interests, and her values in their passionate, sometimes scrambled, amorphous states and who transformed them into language so clear to Betty that, soon, Barney's words became her own. "Barney" became a touchstone in Betty's life, a friend with whom she discussed virtually every aspect of the gallery and of her own progress as an artist; above all, Barney was both the theorist and artist by whom Betty measured all others.

Betty, entering her forties during the Wakefield years, settled into a mature role as art dealer. She also fell deeply in love with Strelsa von Scriver and, by 1944, shared with her a small shingled cottage—Betty nicknamed it "Chips"—on Long Island. Strelsa, an actress-painter from Pennsylvania, wrote letters to Betty attesting to a highly charged love affair, electric with professions of affection and pierced by thunderous quarrels and partings. Betty's friends who knew Strelsa provide sharply differing views of the woman and of her work. "She was," Billie Clarke, a Long Island neighbor, insisted, "the most talented and spiritual person I ever knew. She was a

Betty in her Second Avenue apartment, 1944

totally beautiful and poetic soul."[16] Rosalind Constable, however, dismissed Strelsa as "an animal drunk. A wretched, crazy alcoholic person. I don't know what Betty ever saw in her." Nonetheless, both agree that Strelsa held Betty in emotional thrall for several years. Moreover, Betty's journals, as well as the letters from Strelsa still in her possession in 1978, leave no doubt that Betty was passionately in love with Strelsa and that Strelsa, when separated from Betty for more than a few days at a time, devotedly wrote love letters to her. Betty continued to see Strelsa—though by no means exclusively—for almost a decade.

Toward the end of 1944, Betty learned that the owners of The Wakefield Bookshop planned to close the gallery. Almost at once, Mortimer Brandt invited her to run a section of his gallery on East Fifty-seventh Street and, to her astonishment, he offered her a *salary*—forty dollars a week. In the past, at the Midtown, with Mrs. Sullivan, and at the Wakefield, Betty had subsisted on commissions from sales, which often meant very meager earnings. Indeed, Betty's income scarcely exceeded two thousand dollars a year until she was almost fifty years old. Thus forty *certain* dollars a week promised both wealth, to her way of thinking, and security. And the space—she recalled—the *space* was grand.

Although Mortimer Brandt specialized in Old Master works, he recognized the stirring of energy in the modern movements and anticipated a growth in clients interested in such works. He spotted Betty as the most knowledgeable and most appealing of the dealers interested in contemporary work.

The artists from the Wakefield happily followed Betty Parsons—*their* dealer and champion—to a new venue. She was forty-five years old and, as the director of the Modern Division of the Mortimer Brandt Gallery, ready to extend her role as dealer and champion of contemporary art.

Henry Schnakenberg, *Portrait of Betty Parsons.* Collection Sue Tifft, Marion, Massachusetts

THE BETTY PARSONS GALLERY

•

1946-51

The Betty Parsons Gallery began without a very big bang, but it would quickly occupy the hub of contemporary art's expanding universe. When Mortimer Brandt decided, after the war, to return to England, Betty, urged by her artists and friends, opened a gallery under her own name in Brandt's space at 15 East Fifty-seventh Street, in September 1946.

For financing, she relied on a small group. She scratched together a thousand dollars from her own meager store of money; she borrowed another forty-five hundred dollars from four artists—Hedda Sterne, Saul Steinberg, Hans Hofmann, Henry Schnakenberg—and from two ever-abiding friends—Dumpy Oehlreichs and Hope Williams. With an operating capital of fifty-five hundred dollars, Betty rented space from Brandt, emptied it, stripped it of all architectural embellishment and painted it bone white. She installed strong lights but bought no chairs or rugs to pander to the comfort of visitors. "A gallery isn't a place to rest," she insisted. "It's a place to look at art. You don't come to my gallery to be comfortable." Betty claimed that her gallery was the first in New York to require a degree of physical effort from its visitors, and also the first gallery to provide pure, large, bright open space—exactly what the new abstract artists needed for their gigantic canvases.

By 1947, when Peggy Guggenheim closed her gallery, Art of This Century, and returned to Europe, the Betty Parsons Gallery formally inherited Guggenheim's stable of artists. Art of This Century, housed in Frederick Kiesler's lavishly futuristic space, had presented avant-garde European works, largely Surrealist, with some notable examples of American abstraction, for Peggy Guggenheim's pursuit of the new had led her to several American abstract painters: Clyfford Still, Jackson Pollock, and Mark Rothko. Peggy Guggenheim knew both Betty Parsons and Barnett Newman socially; through Barnett Newman, the artists of Guggenheim's gallery also knew Parsons. Both Peggy Guggenheim and the artists liked Betty. Moreover, they liked the space and location of her new gallery.

"They chose me," Betty said proudly. "The artists wanted to be in my gallery. Barney came to me and said, 'We want to be in your gallery.' And I said, 'Well, that would be fine.'" With the addition of Pollock, Rothko, Newman, and Still to her gallery, the museum directors, curators, and critics looked toward Betty and her shows as a barometer of the storms brewing and fading in the art world. To some, the Betty Parsons Gallery could be expected to dish up fare to feed public appetite for the outrageous, but to many intellectuals and writers seriously interested in the new American art, Betty's gallery provided daily bread.

From the beginning, Betty intended to show the large works of Hofmann, Pollock, Rothko, Still, and other artists who, in forsaking traditional easel painting, made paintings the size of walls in ordinary houses. These new paintings, Betty

Opposite, above: Betty in the office of her first gallery, at 15 East Fifty-seventh Street, ca. 1953–54

Richard Pousette-Dart, *Betty*

believed, should be given "space to breathe," and should be seen in an environment close to the studios in which they were born. The Betty Parsons Gallery, in all of its physical aspects, was soon a favorite of abstract artists.

While working for Brandt, Betty had continued to show the artists she had promoted at the Wakefield: Stamos, Steinberg, Sterne, Gottlieb, Baziotes, Murch, Ossorio, and Cornell. She sold a few paintings and she learned from Brandt the rudiments of running a thoroughly professional art gallery. During her apprentice years, juggling her time among the routines of gallery management, her demanding and sybaritic social life, and her work as an artist, Betty found a rhythm that fitted her needs. She ranged through the terrain of her own work, painting a landscape or sculpting a portrait, as she felt inclined, and when sufficient work had been amassed, she showed at the Midtown Galleries. She handled and sold works of art, pressing her attitudes and ideas about modernism onto what she viewed as the philistine consciousness of friends and strangers alike. Modernism or, specifically, "abstraction" connoted the new, the future, and to Betty's thinking, embodied absolutely the virtues and intellectual power of absolute "good." Art of the past, like events and people of the past, could be abandoned to history's compost pile so far as Betty was concerned; granted, "they"—a wave of the hand indicating anyone and anything before 1900—produced a few notable monuments worthy of scholarly attention but, Betty believed, a miracle was in the making. Artists of the twentieth century, through the mystical powers of art, were in the process of recoding human sensibilities, of opening the human mind and spirit to a paradisiacal new world, shaped and empowered by a creative elite.

Opposite, below: The opening of Jackson Pollock's show at the Betty Parsons Gallery, November 21, 1949. Left to right: Barnett Newman, Pollock, Jimmy Ernst, Charles Egan. On the walls: left, *Number 33, 1945;* right, *Number 3, 1949: Tiger*

Hedda Sterne, *Anthropomorph No. 1*, 1950

All the while Betty espoused her philosophy of the new and preached the doctrine of abstraction, Dumpy and the other Katinkas provided support—outright or in the guise of art purchased—as needed. As a guest of Dumpy or Caroline Cromwell, she traveled to Europe in the summers; she visited the McCarters, now living in Marion, Massachusetts, to play tennis and golf; and recorded her times and places in her journals. She fell in and out of love, collected and abandoned lovers without residual guilt or psychic scars, and she cultivated a public persona, combined of fact and playacting, that maintained her privacy and, simultaneously, gave her an aura of mystery. At forty-six, she was shy and hesitant with strangers when it suited her purposes, but when circumstances dictated, she mustered her aristocratic arrogance in order to dress down a lax railroad porter or impertinent salesperson.

Betty, somewhat like her friend and fellow gallery owner Peggy Guggenheim, used her gallery as a stage on which she played the roles of sexually free socialite, aspiring artist, hellion rebel to conservative family members and darling rebel to the international set of partygoers and party givers who accumulated around the mansions of New York, Newport, and Palm Beach. For those listening, Betty and a few other dealers—notably, Charles Egan and Samuel Kootz—spoke for and as a symbol of the new art: Betty Parsons helped to create, then entered, and then dominated for close to three decades the new American art scene.

At the outset of the Betty Parsons Gallery, its owner and founder, brisk and businesslike, was ensconced in an office between large windows crisscrossed ominously by fire escapes; she added a desk for an assistant. In the beginning, the office, like the public gallery spaces, was white and bare; soon, however, Betty's office became her den, crowded with personal mementos from travels and odd works of art.

In hours of conversation Betty and Barnett Newman explored the instances of resemblance between works of ancient and preliterate artists and modern art; they found parallels in both aspects of style and symbolic potency. To their eye, Picasso, Brancusi, Matisse, and other European artists showed their debt to ancient sources and to primitive forms while extending the reaches of modernist art. They believed, too, that American abstract artists shared an intense and mysterious source of spiritual inspiration with ancient and primitive artists; behind style, behind experimentation and accident, beyond the edges of artistic exploration and personal statement, Betty believed—and Barney corroborated it for her—that chosen human beings, abiding by the laws of the cosmos, could find the wellsprings of art, could draw forth the deepest meaning and most profound spiritual truths as they formed their art. In turn, the works of art, the formations or objectifications of vision, would reveal to the viewer the exact measure of mystical vision and spiritual experience that, in the great scheme of the cosmos, he or she rightfully claimed.

With Barney's wholehearted encouragement, Betty inaugurated her gallery September 30, 1946, with a show of Northwest Coast Indian art; thus at once she would bless the new space and bow to the mysteries and aesthetic forces that in her judgment lay behind all art. Barnett Newman wrote the catalogue which both introduced the works on view and asserted Betty's credo: art, a pure and spiritual quality, appeared in a very potent state in so-called primitive works; similarly, modernist artists—eschewing the phoniness of *fine art,* working outside the limits of understood craft, courting and taming accident—evoked the ancient and mystical spirit that informs the universe.

As in his introduction to the Pre-Columbian exhibition at the Wakefield, Barney stressed the profundity of Northwest Coast Indian artworks, seemingly crude or without reference to human experience, works that—given an honest viewing tempered by critical emotion—would reveal the roots of art and, therefore, the roots of the human psyche.

Betty, reading Barney's words some thirty years after he had written them, nodded and smiled. "Barney," she explained, "really knew everything there was to know about art. Nothing surprised Barney but good things made him smile."

In late October, the first show a success among Betty's friends and a heartening statement of purpose to her artists, Betty aimed to strike a blow for abstraction with work by Ad Reinhardt. She followed that solo exhibition with one by Pietro Lazzari, an artist who showed for several years in the gallery and was among the many who, despite endorsement by the Betty Parsons Gallery, remains relatively unknown. With the first shows, Betty struck chords of excitement; she sent out from the gallery a lure to artists, writers, intellectuals, and museum directors and curators. People came

Portrait photograph of Betty, ca. 1950

to the gallery, she thought, as often on a dare as earnestly seeking experience with the new art.

But it was her group Christmas show that attracted attention beyond the limits of the art world and beyond the drawing rooms of Betty's sphere of friends. Elsa Maxwell, Dumpy Oehlreich's friend as well as a widely read society-gossip columnist and tastemaker of the period, visited the gallery on a tip from Dumpy and wrote that, chancing upon the Christmas show and knowing "Betty Parsons since she married Schuyler, [she]...heaved [herself] into the elevator and arrived on the fifth floor, much to the amazement of Miss Parsons." Maxwell continued:

> *"Betty," I said, "let me see your Christmas show," and she blushed with delight. "These are all mine," she said, waving to the right wall of the gallery. The first picture I saw was one of Hans Hofmann, who is the teacher and prophet of the younger abstractionists."*

Maxwell looked at a cement rearview relief of a horse by Pietro Lazzari, a still life by Walter Murch she considered "absolutely beautiful"; a Newman, an Ossorio, and a "Rathko [*sic*]" called *Heraldic Dreams*.

Overleaf: Betty at her desk, ca. 1953–54

> *Then, [wrote Maxwell] I came across a Hedda Sterne, which was a curious concept called, "The Memories of Aunt Cathy." I would not mind owning it at all if I had a wall to hang it on. Then I remembered that I knew Hedda Sterne quite well as Mrs. Steinberg. She is the wife of the talented artist of the New Yorker, with whom I have occasionally played cards.*
>
> *Now I am not an authority on painting and don't profess to be, particularly on American paintings. But anyone who wants to spend $100 or $150 for a picture by one of the younger American abstractionists may eventually own a masterpiece. Who can tell?*

Finally the widely read and quoted columnist admonished:

> *So don't turn down our own artists, no matter how silly or funny you think them. Their dreams are real and their aspirations pure. Miss Parsons' "Christmas Show" should attract a much larger audience (in numbers) than your old roving reporter.... Some dissenters scream, "Hang the abstractionists!" I echo, "Certainly, but why not on your walls?"*[1]

Reviewing the incident in the last years of her life, Betty repeated Maxwell's closing quip, raising a clenched fist and mock-shouting, "Hang the abstractionists!" After a pause, she giggled and added, "But why not hang them on your walls?" In recounting the event, she ceremonially reenacted her response. "Of course it was exciting. It was wonderful! I knew I was on the beam! I knew I had an eye! I knew, dammit, that *my* artists saw into the future. And that's what interested me. I never looked back."

Elsa Maxwell's article, syndicated in newspapers across the United States, did more than identify Betty as a dealer in avant-garde art; it gave her authenticity. Press attention might converge on a psychopath or fool as readily as on a hero or champion but, aware of the power of publicity from her time in Hollywood, Betty knew that press attention itself in America after the Second World War had the power to persuade. "I read it in the newspaper," was, she knew, a popularly acceptable citation of authority.

Perhaps, as Betty sometimes claimed, her friends were slumming when they visited the gallery, scouting the terrain on the other side of the social tracks in order to report back that they had witnessed outrageous and preposterous paintings and sculpture masquerading as art, but if so, they also kept Betty and her gallery, her artists and their antics, among the livelier topics of social-intellectual conversation. Gossip, a rather haphazard form of communication linked by the social connections that Betty belittled to her artist friends, nourished her growing reputation as a dealer and, by extension, the reputations of the artists she showed. Betty, simply by being herself, attracted attention to her gallery. She knew it, and in any number of guises, she courted attention: fame, she reasoned, rewarded the talented and the chosen; she would be famous.

Betty began the year of 1947 with an exhibition of works by Walter Murch, who seemed to many to be far removed from the splashy abstract paintings publicly identified with her gallery. He was a highly individualistic artist whose impeccable drawing linked him to the masters of the Italian Renaissance and whose compositions of odd elements sharing the same condensed and grayed spaces gave him credentials as a Surrealist. Murch, shown first by Betty at the Wakefield Gallery and then at Mortimer Brandt, was to her a great treasure among her artists. He came from Canada to New York in 1929, and worked as a stained-glass artist. When he shifted to painting,

Betty and Mark Rothko, 1940s

he was soon noted for his love of detail and precision. He was clearly of different grain and persuasion than her other artists, who, often identified as the founders of Abstract Expressionism, traded in high-wire flirtations with risk and accident. Murch, on the other hand, was meticulous, deliberate, and painstaking. He drew imagery from industrial scenes, from fruits and fragments of drapery, from broken dolls; these objects and their shards he reimagined, reformed on the two-dimensional surface of his canvas to produce powerful—almost Photorealist—pieces. Murch suffused his works—both paintings and drawings—with an unearthly light that existed wholly within the tightened spaces he created around objects. "Murch wasn't abstract in the sense that Pollock or Rothko was abstract. Anyone could see that," Betty said. "But he was abstract in a real way. He was abstract in space and he created a totally new and terrific universe. Not everyone could see abstraction that way."

In February of 1947, Betty installed her first solo exhibition of Theodoros Stamos. Stamos, of Greek background and somewhat younger than the other artists of the early years of Abstract Expressionism, was then flamboyantly creating himself as an artist: eccentrically dressed, glib with the jargon of Fifty-seventh Street and the artists' bars, he employed mystical allusions—especially in the titles of his works—and literary or symbolic imagery. Betty, neither impressed nor repelled by Stamos's posturing for the public presentation of his work, believed that his sense of natural forces and his ability to translate that perception into painterly expression made him a significant member of her gallery, and she showed his work enthusiastically for a number of years.

During those years, Stamos was among Betty's closest friends. As neighbors on Long Island, they saw one another there as well as in the cafés, bars, and galleries that artists frequented in New York. Stamos, more than some of her other artists, recognized (or, as Betty later thought, pretended to recognize) her as an artist, too. He encouraged her to work and often talked with her as an equal, as a fellow artist. Later,

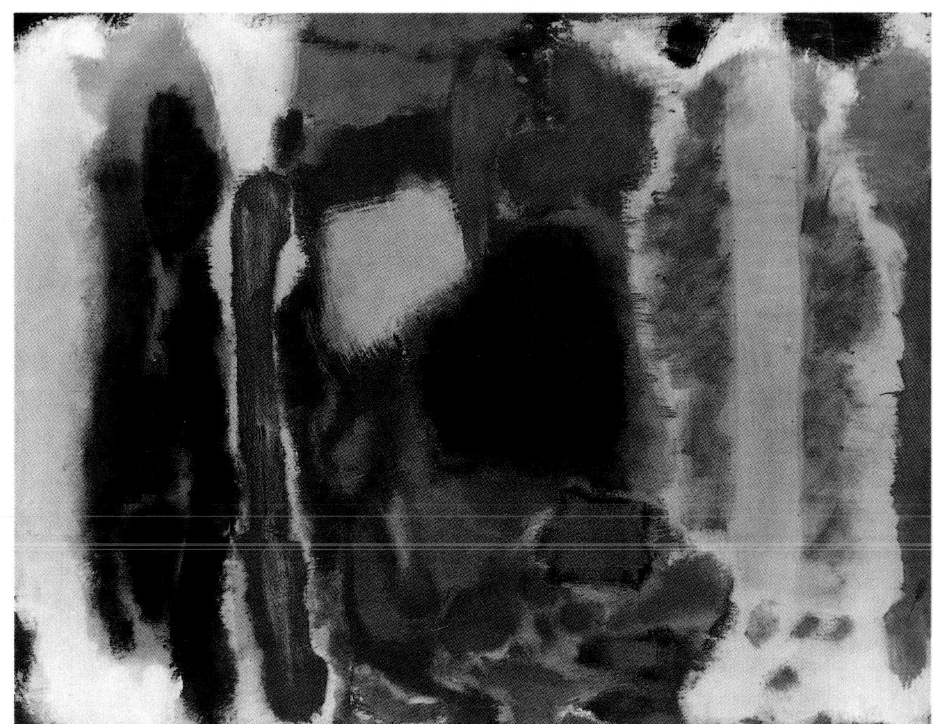

Mark Rothko, *#26,* 1947. Collection the Estate of Betty Parsons

Betty and Stamos had a cataclysmic fight. Several friends speculate that the fight resulted from Stamos's rudeness to Betty's lover at the time, Strelsa van Scriver, but Betty turned aside questions about the fight with the remark, "Well, he was very Greek and he was very dishonest and I just couldn't take that after a while."

In March 1947, Betty also showed new works by Mark Rothko, the Russian-born, Yale-educated artist, who was then exploring tentatively the formal tensions possible between free lines juxtaposed against fields of soft color. He was one of the first of Peggy Guggenheim's artists that Barnett Newman introduced to Betty. "This artist," Barney told Betty, "is one of us. He knows what to know. He refuses to know nothings."

Rothko, in the early years with Betty's gallery, worked through symbolic abstractions in oil, his paintings appearing to come fully finished from a series of decisions made and conclusions drawn that gave them an air of inevitability and, yet, remained disquietingly unresolved. Elaine de Kooning, then writing frequently for *Art News,* recalled those paintings: "Bill [de Kooning] and I used to visit the galleries—Parsons, Willard, Kootz, Egan, Janis, the galleries showing the kind of art that interested us. And, of course, we knew most of the artists. We were both just fascinated by Rothko's *technique*—it looked as if his colors were *breathed* onto the canvas—and the way it became the subject matter of his work."[2]

In his first shows with Betty Parsons, Rothko's works, displayed against the starkly white and—Betty later concluded—often overlit walls of the gallery sometimes appeared clumsy and groping, but they suggested, however faintly, the grander-scaled, luminous style that would gain Rothko recognition as a major artist of the age. "He was an artist, you see. A real artist," according to Betty, "and he was melancholy. He was always melancholy, always working on those terrific pictures of the sky and light and, at the same time, being very, very sad."

In late March, Betty mounted an exhibition of works by Hans Hofmann, known first in America as an extraordinary teacher who could lead even mediocre students into the labyrinths of abstraction with some visible success in their work. His paintings, redolent of virtuosity in displaying the properties of paint, were luxurious compositions of thicker and thinner areas. His visible command of the traditional craft of painting made Hofmann's work attractive to viewers who often winced at the seemingly haphazard, chaotic, and accidental manner in which they imagined some of the other abstract painters worked.

But Betty Parsons denigrated craft for its own sake; indeed, she insisted that too much attention to craft, like too much concern with meaning and with intellectual aspects of art, resulted in stillborn work. Both craft and other "things of the mind" threatened, in Betty's view, to impede the creative act, which, she professed, was the essential subject of all art. Mind, in her view, had a way of diluting spirit.

Betty saw in Hofmann's paintings the record of their genesis: each painting, as she read its richly worked surface, resulted from a series of improvisations or accidents whose character remained on the surface to combine with other improvised passages; at the arbitrary moment when the artist saw that his work was good and decided to let it be, the finished work existed—the result of actions taken to bring it into existence. Moreover, it revealed—but did not *state*—its *being*; a viewer, depending on his own quality of *being*, might see nothing in the work, might find it an affront to his intelligence and values, or might find it revelatory—an iconlike object that symbolized deeply understood and felt order. That is to say, Betty thought of Hofmann as the quintessential Abstract Expressionist.

With the works of Clyfford Still, whose first show at the gallery was in April of 1947, Betty put forward a limited and highly specific facet of abstraction. Still, at that time a young artist who had lived and studied in the Northwest and had studied briefly with Vaclav Vytlacil at the Art Students League, was preoccupied, Betty thought, with an abstract treatment of the figure in landscape. But, she clarified: "Still had no interest at all in the *human* figure; he was interested in the real figure, the essence of spirit. He was painting the unseen." The glyphic "figure" in Still's painting appeared as a reduced vertical passage of jagged-edged paint set against larger vertical planes of color, which, perhaps, could be understood as forces of nature. To refer to "figure" and "nature," however, assigned symbolic portent to the artist's work, advanced concepts which, to the untutored or unimaginative eye, were often unyielding and difficult.

Betty loved Still's large, flat, sometimes chalky or greasy surfaces: loved the awkwardness that proved to her the sincerity of his work; his craftsmanship did not threaten to obfuscate the pure spirit of the paintings. As an artist, Betty learned much from Still and, in later years, often employed the palette knife in a fashion reminiscent of his use of that flexible and hard-edged tool. Moreover, her landscapes or "pure abstractions" frequently called to mind Still's compositions of large areas of flat color broken by smaller, sharply contrasting patches of color and texture that sometimes seemed to have been applied to the surface and sometimes seemed to have been revealed as the surface had been torn away.

Betty's closeness to Still during the early years of the gallery caused later speculation about the possible romantic nature of the relationship. Betty, hearing reports of her alleged love affairs with Still and other of her artists, chortled. "Oh, they always thought that. And I did love them. And they loved me. But I was very honest with them and we always understood each other."[3]

In the summer of 1947, intoxicated with the success of her gallery, Betty closed the gallery and traveled West to visit the Luddingtons and to have an operation which, with characteristic imprecision of language, she identified sometimes as an abortion and sometimes as a hysterectomy. Neither procedure, in the lingering Victorian category of her sensibilities, warranted public discussion. "I was recuperating, you see, from this operation and the illness that followed it. I stayed with Wright Luddington in California and, of course, everyone took very good care of me and entertained me all the time."

One schedule of entertainment for the patient included a day-long trip to a rodeo. Betty remembered the noise and heat of the event; she remembered unquenchable thirst, her mouth and nostrils full of dust; she remembered fading and distorting vision, nausea, and faintness. She sat in what little shade she could find and watched the horses and riders, the livestock; she watched men and women pit their strength and cunning against huge pain-maddened animals; the shouts and bleats of contest rose with the dust throughout the day. From time to time, squinting against the sun-glare on her sketchbook, she attempted to record the events unfolding before her. "But, you see, I just couldn't get it down. There was too much. And everything came from everywhere. Colors. Noise. Horses. Cowboys. Cowgirls. Indians. Little cows and big cows. It was sheer energy."

Later, in the shade of Wright Luddington's garden, she thought about the rodeo, the flash and flurry of colors, the palpable energy, and the tangled emotions in the voices of people and animals. As she set about transcribing her emotional recollections into watercolor paintings, she found that she was painting abstractly. Wright Luddington, happening by, paused and asked, "What is this, Betty?"

And she responded, "It's feeling. It's energy. It's the expanding world."

In that recuperative period, Betty Parsons crossed the frail barrier in her own work between representational and directly presentational painting. From that time forward, she not only showed abstract art in her gallery but, with a zealot's passion born of firsthand encounters, she espoused the causes of abstraction, which, in her mind, were synonymous with "The New Spirit" and "the expanding world."

Betty's second season began in the fall of 1947 with an exhibition by Ad Reinhardt, the abstractionist, who was a former Carl Holty student, former contributor to the newspaper *PM*'s art page, and an instructor at Brooklyn College. Reinhardt would eventually be associated with black paintings, which generated a furor in and around the art world. But in 1947, he showed vividly colored works. Like Barnett Newman, Reinhardt was a talker and a philosophizer; he wrote notes and postcards to Betty as if she were his diary; he dropped by the gallery to talk about his work and about what he saw happening in the art world. Betty was impressed by his command of theory and color, which, with his ability to talk about art and to image precise and vital objectifications of his philosophical discourse, identified him to her as an intellectual.

In the early pictures, Reinhardt, not yet even presaging the minimalist black-on-black paintings, with a barely discernible cross dividing the blackness into quarters, which would earn him the title "The Black Prince," organized tight, intricate pictures with open and closed spaces, straight lines and arcs, and sharply defined colors: from the juxtaposition of complementary colors augmented by countering tensions in line and space, he established complex paintings with very active linear surfaces.

The final show of 1947 consisted of sculpture by Herbert Ferber, whose three previous one-man shows at the Midtown Galleries had established him as a serious sculptor with Abstract Expressionist sympathies. By the time of this first show with Betty, Ferber had devised his dramatic lead and bronze compositions that seemed almost to be figures. But the massive forms and the languid contours overpowered the idea of figure so that, in the end, Ferber's work resisted literary dissection and stood firmly on the Abstract Expressionist platform. Ferber pulled and pushed form to interlace the spaces of his works, often heroic pieces of metal sculpture, into complicated compositions that changed in light and with the viewer's movement around the sculpture.

In 1947, if the artists were clannish, so were the dealers. Compared to the vast array of galleries today throughout sections of midtown, uptown, and downtown New York, there were few galleries, and still fewer of any interest to people who looked for art more demanding than a decorative color swatch to reside above a couch or a sentimental scene to evoke memory or imagination of some emotional place or event. Like her fellow dealers, Betty, not only appraising the competition but also maintaining friends, visited galleries throughout the year; she chatted with other dealers, took an interest in artists in other galleries, and tried to learn all that she could about the workings of her field.

Even though Betty was a recognized authority in the realm of contemporary art, her years in Paris, her visits to museums throughout Europe, and her several programs of formal study in art had done little to introduce her to the major artists included in basic art appreciation courses. Much of what she had learned—what she had been told by artist-teachers—fostered her belief that European art consisted of a series of decadent styles that she and her generation were destined to clarify if not to expunge from history. Reluctantly, at the urging of Hope Williams, she visited The Metropolitan Museum's loan exhibition of Hogarth, Constable, and Turner in the spring of 1947.[4] Despite her fondness for Arthur Lindsey and her interest in his watercolor techniques, she knew very little about the tradition of English landscape painting and the English obsession with nature.

The exhibition, for Betty, was new material. She quickly dismissed Hogarth as coarse and illustrative and turned her gaze upon Constable's quick, rough brushstrokes and Turner's turbulent, sometimes explosive swirls of paint. She saw in these paintings the antecedents of the abstract art that she championed. Here, she thought, were artists who knew the same secrets, who worked to the same drumbeats and took shelter in the same shadows of ambiguity as Stamos, Ossorio, and Sterne. To find similarities between Turner's light-shot color and Rothko's free-floating color patches, to find that both artists employed bits and snatches of line to emphasize a passage of paint, was for Betty a powerful and original discovery. She was exhilarated and naïvely recounted her discovery to friends as if she alone had seen the paintings.

No matter how much an artist from the past interested Betty, her heart belonged to her artists and to the art of her time. Jackson Pollock epitomized the force, scale, and outrageous courtship of accident and failure that, Betty thought, lay at the core of contemporary art. In January of 1948, when she showed Jackson Pollock, Betty noted, "By this time, he was totally free, totally creative. He was making large, expansive paintings. He was the first artist," she added, without full respect for historical accuracy, "to paint large paintings. He exploded the easel painting, the wall painting. His paintings *were* walls—whole worlds, expanding worlds."

Soon after this Pollock show—"It was a sensation. A total sensation. So full of energy and expansion that I needed a change"—Rothko's fifth New York show, which opened March 8, 1949, provided that change of pace. Betty recognized his growing sense of lyricism and a new tenderness that she liked in his work. All the while that he fiddled to find the right tension between line and shape, he remained intellectual, his paintings remained clear. Now, Betty thought, he had resolved all conflicts, and rid his mind of extraneous and diverting concerns in order to paint on a high, rarified, and sublime level.

Without betraying the artists whose works flirted with turmoil, Betty became a strong advocate for Rothko. "Gentle. Strong. He has a strong female component but he's very male, very strong." In the 1947 series, Rothko limited each canvas to one or two patches of muted but luminous color floating horizontally over an almost invisible field of color; he scratched lines onto the surface, thereby adding—but not necessarily integrating—a layer of complexity. The space created, mysterious and perplexing, delighted Betty: "Here is a giant."

These works set the course that Rothko followed to paint the simple bands of color for which he is best known. They sold at prices from two hundred to fifteen hundred dollars and some are now in venerated collections and valued highly. But, as Betty pointed out, not many sold. "They hated my gallery and my artists. All the critics hated what I showed," Betty fumed. "But just look. My artists were the important ones, the creative ones, the ones who believed in an expanding world."

Following Rothko's show, Betty steered the gallery in another direction by showing Richard Pousette-Dart's rugged and fantastic fusions of gesso, ink, and watercolor into brooding and thickly painted linear networks holding barely suggested images. The deep impasto provided a surface from which more thinly painted areas seemed to rise and float free, seemingly poised just in front of the actual surface, an abstract treatment of illusion—the staple of traditional Western painting. Was Pousette-Dart, as some suggested, merely decorative, a latter-day Byzantine mosaicist? Or as Betty insisted, had he sincerely grasped secret domains of order, of cosmic reality that still lay in totally spiritual reaches? Did it matter? Betty enjoyed the confusion that Pousette-Dart's work generated in visitors to the gallery. He was an artist one could talk about. "He caused everyone to ask questions. No one knew what he was about. Everyone asked questions. It was terrific."

Before she closed the gallery for the summer, Betty showed works by Seymour Lipton and Sonia Sekula, continuing her quest for variety of expression and for exploration of three-dimensional as well as two-dimensional forms.

After a lengthy summer visit with Wright Luddington in California, Betty shaped her third season around exhibitions of work by her Boston friend Maud Morgan and by John Little, Ad Reinhardt, and Richard Pousette-Dart. She also mounted an exhibition of works by Hedda Sterne. It was characteristic of Hedda that, having put up money to start the gallery (repaid, according to Betty, "over some years"), she was sensitive about the feelings of other artists and waited what she believed to be a decorous length of time before showing her own work there. "Hedda," explained Betty, "had those beautiful Old World manners. She was always correct. Very correct. Even her work was correct."

Hedda Sterne, a Romanian-born artist who married cartoonist and architect Saul Steinberg, remained a close friend to Betty from the early forties until Betty's death in 1982. Cosmopolitan and chic, Hedda had studied painting in Bucharest, Vienna, and Paris before making New York her home. In 1943, she had her first show in New York City and, for the intervening years, had shown with Betty at the Wakefield Gallery, at Mortimer Brandt, and now at the Betty Parsons Gallery. Intellectual, witty, and propelled by potent ideas that pushed her quickly from one style or manner of working to another, Hedda produced works which refused easy access. Moreover, when other artists were searching for a manner in which to work, a way of working that would be theirs; when they were staking out technical and aesthetic territory that would provide an identifiable (and, therefore, marketable) style, Hedda rejected the whole idea of painting-as-signature. Betty understood her friend's reluctance to travel in only one direction; despite the slowness of critics to recognize Hedda's role in contemporary painting, Betty insisted, "Hedda is a genius. She can do anything in paint. She understands everything from dreams to science."

Some of the works in Hedda Sterne's first show in the Betty Parsons Gallery were done in Paris; most were painted in New York, where she appropriated the Third Avenue El's black and white pillars, strong gridwork patterns, and backdrops of storefronts and houses and reconstituted them in abstract patterns consonant with her intellectual and emotional grasp of reality. Her Parisian scenes, too, grew from her search for abstract patterns in everyday life: here windowed facades and rooftops, painted in warm reds and pinks and pale, cool greens, state Sterne's orderly and often slyly witty view of the world.

During the first years of the gallery, Betty worked long hours and, in her opinion, struggled to represent her artists to an uncomprehending and hostile world. On several occasions, her view of the art public was borne out: holes were punched in paintings, "shit" was penciled onto a surface, and angry shouts were exchanged in the gallery. As visitors to the gallery accused her of knowingly peddling junk, Betty exploded with rage; who dared to question her sincerity or integrity?

Rosalind Constable remembers that a Time-Life executive, in order to play a joke on his wife, bought her a Jackson Pollock painting for a birthday present. He paid $250 for the work, wrapped it up with paper and ribbon. As predicted, his wife was horrified; the couple's smart friends were appropriately amused. The joke was successful. Ironically, according to Rosalind Constable, the painting very quickly increased in value, bringing the couple substantial rewards at the time of its resale.

But despite derogatory slings and arrows from the conservative wing of the art public, the gallery gained stature as a place to see the newest and often the best of American art. Betty, now almost earning a living and enjoying success as a dealer, continued to see her friends, to travel, and to work at painting and sculpture. The Katinkas—Dumpy, Hope, Caroline, Muriel, and others—shared Betty's ascendancy in the art world they did not understand as, simultaneously, they shared their wardrobes, their larders, their vacations, and their purses with Betty.

"Oh," she remembered as she leafed through the journals in 1980, "I was sometimes lonely. I was missing out on a lot of fun. I had had fun out in California, my share of drink and parties. And I knew some quite interesting people. Some of the stars." After a head-tilted pause, she added, "I knew Garbo quite well. Played tennis with her out in California." Pausing as if to review her previous rakehell pursuit of pleasure, Betty grinned. "Well, I finally came to my senses. I finally got on the beam of something very important. I wasn't studying history. I was making history."

Having arrived at that conclusion, Betty was impatient, even infuriated, at any suggestion that every show in her gallery, every artist represented, was not of genius status. When her shows received critical high marks, she was exhilarated, as she was in 1948 when a newspaper critic, Emily Genauer, faintly damned an exhibition of the group, American Abstract Artists, as academic and lacking energy, as formulaic and predictable, but went on to observe that it was not the problem of abstraction per se. As an example of the other side of the coin, she wrote: "Abstract painting dominates the 'Survey of the Season' exhibition in the Betty Parsons Gallery, too [where] . . . the majority of the artists . . . create their strange, unrealistic and generally unrecognizable

Arshile Gorky, *Untitled*, 1940. Page from Betty's sketchbook

patterns not for their own sake alone but, apparently, to plumb the riddles of the universe, of birth and of death, of ancient civilizations and prehistoric origins."

She continued: "There is another difference—most of the artists in [the Parsons] show are much more original.... Some of these paintings may repel you—but you will look at them long, and probably attempt to decode them." So far, so good. But Betty's hackles rose when Genauer concluded, "Jackson Pollock's 'Cathedral,' viewed before, if memory serves, still impresses me as a completely formless, haphazard expression whose violence does not compensate for its lack of discipline. Clifford [*sic*] Still's 'No. 46' is another of the more inchoate canvases."[4]

Ignoring Genauer's praise, Betty fumed at the wrongheadedness of her closing remark about Pollock; she was another of the "critics who didn't know anything at all about the creative world. Why, just think, she absolutely missed the boat on Pollock. A giant. My artists were giants and the critics refused to know it."

Some giants, she admitted, developed and exhibited outside her gallery. In 1948, Betty visited Julien Levy's gallery to see Arshile Gorky's show shortly after the artist, at forty-four, committed suicide. The small paintings and drawings evoked the Armenian-born artist's sense of tragedy and order and wrung Betty's heart. "He was so great. Why couldn't he have stuck around?" she said. Then, she forgave him: "Well, I suppose he just had this tragic component that took him over."

Gorky influenced numerous other artists, including Betty Parsons, who admired his strong draftsmanship and his exquisite small passages within an overall composition. While he had never been a close friend, she had shared her studio with him, allowing him to teach his classes there. In her view, Gorky was an artist, and therefore, he was valuable.

In deep and shared respect for art, Betty and Barney frequently visited The Metropolitan Museum of Art and The American Museum of Natural History, where Barney had studied ornithology for a time. As they looked at ancient and primitive art, they reaffirmed their faith in earlier humankind's possession of knowledge of order and spirit. Why, they pondered, had people traded it away in pursuit of false gods and tawdry goods? Betty and Barney talked continually: the timelessness of art, the eternal qualities of art, the *truthfulness* of art to the human spirit—regardless of the time or place that defined the *art history* of the piece—was the essential fiber in the total fabric of their conversation and friendship over the years. "Barney had all of these terrific ideas. He knew about everything. He was the most intelligent of all of the artists," observed Betty.

During the months of the spring season, Barney helped Betty install exhibitions of Jackson Pollock, Mark Rothko, Theodoros Stamos, and a group of artists, including Betty's friend from San Francisco, Adaline Kent. "The Giants," however, grumbled among themselves, irritated that Betty would bring into the gallery artists they considered minor, trivial, and merely dilettantes who adorned Betty's upper-class social life. She heard their muttering and ignored them, thinking, she said, that these expressions of anger and discontent were no different from the steady stream of complaints that she heard. "They were never satisfied, the artists. They wanted to be famous. They wanted to be rich. They wanted me to buy their pictures. What could I do?" she asked. "I had no money. I had only the gallery. But I was putting them over; they didn't know it but I was putting them over."

She was "putting them over" and, chances are, they *did* know it and wanted more. During the first years of the Betty Parsons Gallery, Betty rarely sold a painting for more than a thousand dollars, the going rate at the time for contemporary American art. Betty, happy to sell a picture at any price, expected the artists to be pleased at the trickle of money she provided. After all, poverty had always been associated with art; why should that change? Betty, who had been both very rich and very poor, but who enjoyed the generosity of rich friends, saw no reason to raise prices or press for sales; she was content to let the initiated find and buy the paintings they deserved; to hell with the rest of the world, an unreliable lot until, somehow, the new world of art would come and save them.

By 1949, The Giants were steadily murmuring discontent. Betty, however, turned a deaf ear to them as she kept her schedule of travel and work. After spending the summer in Europe, she opened the gallery with an exhibition by Pietro Lazzari, followed by a group show. She, as well as The Giants, was dissatisfied with the group show. "It wasn't very alive. I needed new energy," she admitted. Betty, probably unknown to The Giants, equated new energy with new artists.

As The Giants pressed Betty to sell more paintings, give them more frequent and larger shows, get them shows in other galleries and in museums, get museums to buy their works, Betty largely ignored their petitions, preferring not to fight, not to let strife overshadow the life of the gallery. Even in the late forties, when the gallery was still in its infancy—though a precocious infant, by all reckonings—artists were sharply divided as to their loyalties to Betty, to the gallery, and to each other.

And perhaps inevitably as the possibilities for fame and fortune increased, The Giants' competitiveness among themselves threatened the peace. Barnett Newman and Ad Reinhardt had declared enmity that would result in later lawsuits. Clyfford Still, she thought, had decided that he was the only artist in the world. Rothko, ever more melancholy, drank steadily without often being visibly drunk. And all of them, she said, were jealous of Jackson Pollock. Pollock, among the most publicized American avant-garde artists, was generally agreed to be the most daring and either the greatest or the worst. His actions brooked no mediating perceptions: *yes* or *no*; *truth* or *falsity*. "He put himself on the edge," Betty said. "He might be half crazy or even drunk. But he painted like an angel. Yes, he drank too much and he sometimes behaved rudely and roughly. He was from the West," Betty explained, "and he had all of this energy that he was trying to get into those great paintings. In my gallery, he was never drunk. We were great friends."

Betty tired of the "insiders" shambling up to her, eyes glinting with the fires of gossip, to whisper in her ear: "Betty, this Pollock, did you know that he peed in Peggy Guggenheim's fireplace?" Betty had no time or patience for gossip. If it upset these emotional pygmies to think that Jackson had peed in Peggy's fireplace, well, dammit, she hoped he *had*. But she didn't know, she said brusquely, and she didn't care. He was a painter and she was interested in his paintings and not his macho antics.

Pollock's new paintings, swept with movement, were solid networks of thick enamel. Betty rejoiced in the strong pattern and abiding sense of design and structure that suffused Jackson's paintings. "Idiots!" she would shout at or about anyone failing to see Pollock's merits as a painter. "Why can't they see the great, great order here? Why can't they know art when they see it in its purest state?" She believed that Jackson Pollock, in his daring and in his inevitable paean to order, had achieved a higher evolution into the realm of pure art than had most of the artists of the time. His greatness, to her way of thinking, was precisely measured by the anger he engendered in the "fools and conservatives and hypocrites and stupid, stupid materialists. There were only a few who wanted to know what Jackson Pollock knew. Only a few with the creative spirit to face the expanding world."

Barney, agreeing in large measure with her evaluation of Jackson, enjoyed pointing out that Jackson succeeded where Reinhardt merely postured, that Jackson drew his art effortlessly from an inner knowledge (however at odds with the surrounding world) while Reinhardt pumped up his doctrines at the college lectern. Betty refused to listen. Even to Barney. "There is room in the creative world," she emphasized as she slapped a tabletop smartly, "for creative people. I don't give a damn *how* they are creative. Just so long as they're different. Individuals!"

Art, Betty argued, could stem from many experiences. Looking at Stamos's work, she thought that he drew his vision from deep inside the earth, that he accepted a gift from the Oracle. Rothko, on the other hand, seemed to her to pull his paintings from air. She mentioned her theory to Barney, who told her that medieval alchemists had believed all matter to be composed of earth, air, fire, and water. "Well, you see," she said, "so is painting. All painting. The good artists paint from earth or air or fire or water. The great artists paint with all of those." Her sly smile, mischievous and slightly flirtatious, emphasized her pleasure in her observation. "Any one of us knows that. We just *know* it."

Betty's sureness, however, did not cover all aspects of her life. In February of 1949, she wrote:

life is a rapid transit in a vacuum
and meaning that is the scuffle
but ones heart remains high up and
mostly lonely and ones feet
get heavy with nowhere to rest

As she approached her fiftieth birthday, both intimations of mortality and a surge of energy "that came from the creative, that just came," intensified her preoccupation with art, its sources and its processes and, she thought, promised to drive away her loneliness. Later, looking back, Betty concluded, "I was looking for something. I wanted all of life to be one. I wanted the whole creative world."

By 1950, Betty's roster of artists included: Mark Rothko, Barnett Newman, Lee Krasner, Hedda Sterne, Herbert Ferber, Ad Reinhardt, Richard Pousette-Dart, Buffie Johnson, William Congdon, Clyfford Still, Bradley Walker Tomlin, Day Schnabel, Jeanne Miles, Perle Fine, John Stephan, Guitou Knoop, Anne Ryan, Seymour Lipton, Sari Dienes, Boris Margo, Jackson Pollock, and Forrest Bess.

Stuart Preston wrote in *The New York Times* of the group show at the end of the season, pointing out that both admirers and scoffers raised their voices in discussion about artists on "the front line of today's avant garde." Betty's show, he wrote, provided an excellent opportunity to see and appraise the variety of styles and quality.

Not surprisingly, Preston treated the exhibition as a survey of the contemporary art world and dissected it into various camps, or styles. He saw "radical differences between these thirty-three artists. For they have in common only their point of departure, the complete abandonment of representational realism.... Many works here are contrived with deep seriousness. But a great question remains. What meaning or value beyond themselves do these contrivances possess?"

For Preston, Barnett Newman's black bar on an austere blackish background drove a stake into the ground on one edge of the map, near camps already settled by Kazimir Malevich and Piet Mondrian; Clyfford Still, with wide spaces of pigment releasing more feeling than Newman, lived in a nearby camp nonetheless; Ad Reinhardt moved upstream from both Newman and Still but remained aloof from expressionism; Lee Krasner, however, set up her work station at some distance from the formalism of the other artists but it remained for her husband, Jackson Pollock, to claim the extreme edge of expressionism, the opposite stylistic camp from Newman. In addition to the purists and expressionists, Preston identified "the symbolists... who create formal images whose meaning is suggestive but not readily discernible except, perhaps, to the artist," and included in this sect Hedda Sterne, Boris Margo, and Theodoros Stamos. "Their kind of image-making," he wrote, "is particularly favored by the sculptors—Seymour Lipton, Day Schnabel, Herbert Ferber and Guitou Knoop. Their imaginative enrichment of natural forms should certainly enlarge sensibility at the receiving end." Preston admitted, however, that to his "mind and eye the most successfully managed, the most non-discrepant work here is Bradley Tomlin's large canvas. Tomlin is a classicist...an aesthete. He counterpoints his white, ivory and black forms with a beautiful clarity...[which] weave[s] into a delicate and impressive whole; singly they display some spirited feats of draftsmanship."[5]

Betty believed the patently clear purposes and achievements of her artists had been attacked by Stuart Preston. His analysis of style, his attempt to survey the whole map of abstraction, offended her deeply. "He never understood my gallery, never understood my artists. He had no interest in the new and the creative," she insisted despite what many took to be an informed and even enthusiastic review.

Whatever else it achieved, and regardless of his assessment of the individual merits of the artists, Preston's review registered that in its first five years, the Betty Parsons Gallery had become the flagship of modernism.

"The Irascibles," 1951. Seated from left to right: Theodoros Stamos, Jimmy Ernst, Jackson Pollock, Barnett Newman, James Brooks, Mark Rothko. Standing from left to right: Richard Pousette-Dart, William Baziotes, Willem de Kooning, Adolph Gottlieb, Ad Reinhardt, Hedda Sterne, Clyfford Still, Robert Motherwell, Bradley Walker Tomlin. Brooks was the only one of the group who did not show with Betty

BETTY PARSONS SETS THE PACE

•

1951-56

By the mid-fifties in America, public attitudes about art were changing; most people knew enough about "modern art" to make derisory jokes, and (aside from the popular front of combat between "tradition" and "abstraction") the abstract movement had won powerful friends. Post–World War Two American art, specifically the New York School or Abstract Expressionism, had caught the imagination of a fervent group of museum curators, a few collectors, and a small clump of critics—all mostly in and around New York. At The Museum of Modern Art, Dorothy Miller, inspired by its director, Alfred H. Barr, Jr., curated, assembled, and installed a series of exhibitions with names such as *Fifteen Americans* or *New Talent,* names chosen to skirt the issues of theme and subject that often served to anchor museum group shows. By current standards of museum installation and promotion of exhibitions, Miller's shows were plainly presented in unadorned spaces; the accompanying catalogues, square in format and handsomely designed, succinctly set forth the forces and ideas around which the artists worked. And many of the artists included in the exhibitions—Pollock, Rothko, Newman, Still, Reinhardt—were identified with the Betty Parsons Gallery. Betty's sale of paintings reflected The Museum of Modern Art's activities; while her artists were on view at the Modern, collectors—now a growing breed—would visit the gallery and buy a work by an artist who had the MoMA imprimatur.

In addition to the prestige conferred by The Museum of Modern Art's recognition, several commanding writers explored for a larger public the intricacies and meanings of the new art. Harold Rosenberg, Thomas Hess, and Elaine de Kooning wrote regularly for *Art News*; Clement Greenberg wrote for *The Nation.* Critics at *The New York Times* were not, in that period, persuaded that the new art consisted of anything more than a publicity-manipulating maneuver and that newspaper's coverage of gallery—and museum—exhibitions of abstract art often fanned the public's smoldering doubts about the authenticity of Abstract Expressionism.

Even so, abstract art, the avant-garde art of the previous decade, was being absorbed into the American cultural establishment; the large paintings with no identifiable reference to the actual world no longer lurked behind the kitchen door but were now being invited into the parlor. And in the parlor, far from being an embarrassment of poor manners, these strong bright paintings often appeared both beautiful and the essence of civility. They were becoming the required backdrop for informed gracious living in America.

In the earlier days of abstraction, little of that art sold, and when it did, it did so at very modest prices. There were only a few galleries showing contemporary art and still fewer collectors buying it; no one talked seriously of "investing in art." But by the early fifties, collectors had begun to appear, artists were appointed to lucrative jobs teaching in universities, museums organized exhibitions of contemporary art, and the magazines found modern art a consistent good filler, certain to elicit a guffaw or outraged letters from readers. Art, even in its most astonishing forms, began to be seen as a business, and as it did, artists envisioned success—fame and fortune. They saw galleries as the means to those ends.

In 1946, when Betty started her gallery, she virtually manufactured a place and a public for her artists. Before the Betty Parsons Gallery, there had been neither a sympathetic setting—large expanses of pure white wall washed with good light for showing the huge paintings—nor any consistent championing of the artists who made them.

As a consequence of Betty's social connections, she enjoyed the interest and support of rich friends who, in turn, had rich friends who could be enticed into the gallery. Betty claimed always that she had no talent for or interest in "hype." In actuality, she put her gallery in the news and kept it there. For the most part, she attracted attention in a good-mannered fashion, setting out to interest friends in her work and her cause.

One friend, Rosalind Constable, from her influential desk within the Time-Life empire, entered the battle for avant-garde art in the forties; another, Alexander Liberman, creative director of *Vogue* in the 1950s, influenced editorial policy in his domain. Each contributed significantly in their respective magazine empires to the growing reputation of Betty and her gallery. Through *Time, Life, Vogue,* and other popular and taste-setting magazines, as well as through articles such as the one by Elsa Maxwell and critical reviews by Stuart Preston, Thomas Hess, Clement Greenberg, Harold Rosenberg, and others, the Betty Parsons Gallery had become well known. And so had Betty's artists, their anxieties and expectations growing apace with their fame.

Further, the economic circumstances of art galleries were beginning to change perceptibly. Americans' post-World War Two interest in art begot increasingly lucrative business for galleries, and galleries appeared almost overnight to supply the demand. No longer the musty province of European scholars, galleries offered social action, intellectual excitement. Like artists, galleries were identified by points of view; collectors patronized dealers and galleries who served their taste for specific periods or styles: Impressionism, The Eight, social comment or WPA styles, or the avant-garde, which a few daring galleries—the Betty Parsons among them—showed. Along with Parsons, Egan, Willard, Kootz, and a few other dealers put new American art before the public, which often found the work outrageous, unintelligible, symptomatic of a variety of social ills. The communications industry did the rest.

By the fifties, avant-garde art—which in the United States meant Abstract Expressionism—followed a predictable path into the academy where, following an initial fire storm of outrage and a series of lectures and articles defending standards, it settled comfortably into the easy chairs of faculty offices and lounges, infiltrated the meetings of the College Art Association, and saturated curricula. Every freshman art student learned the rudiments of Abstract Expressionism or, at least, learned to extol the values of freedom of expression, of spontaneity, and of accident in producing the great goods of the movement: excitement, newness, and shock. The converts to the new art, as well as the birthright believers, had captured the university and college art departments and, with the GI enrollment tide that swelled higher education in the United States, had begun to repeat in classrooms and studios across the country the words and images that, only the week before, had enlivened conversation in artists' bars in New York or dared the philistine viewer in the Betty Parsons, the Charles

Egan, the Samuel Kootz, the Marian Willard galleries, and a few others. Abstract Expressionism, defanged by popularity, became the new academic art, the new and still lively *institutionalized avant-garde,* an oxymoron destined for still further distillation into the soon widely held notion of art as consumer goods and art galleries as boutiques.

Betty Parsons gave no heed to such trends. While she was known as a dealer, she thought of herself as an artist and she lived as an artist in a large and simple studio over Mary Tonetti's studio at 143 East Fortieth Street. She painted, took occasional classes in figure drawing, worked clay into portrait busts. In her studio, she was an artist. There magazines and journals grew into mounds on the floor, dust balls roamed, and soiled laundry languidly awaited Betty's notice. There, in a space very much her own, Betty entertained her friends in art with special dinners of hearty casseroles, vast salads, breads from local bakeries, jugs of raw wine, cheeses and fruit. Hedda Sterne remembers long nights shortened by talk and booze and high-volume arguments about the art and politics of the time. Betty's studio, the lofts of her artists, and the various apartments and studios of their friends were physically spread about Manhattan, but politically and in spirit, they constituted a ghetto on the fringes of the arts and letters establishment in New York and, thus, in the country.

Marie Hartley, a native Californian who came to New York to teach in a "charm school," developed a passion for the new art of the time and, through friends, met Betty Parsons, who quickly employed Marie as her assistant in the gallery. Marie recalls the fifties as a period of intensity: "Everything was intense. Betty was intense. All the artists were intense. Critics were intense. And Betty was right in the center of all of this tension. Her gallery just attracted intense people and intense ideas and intense paintings."[1]

Early in 1951, in an art world entirely different from the one they had entered as unknown artists, Pollock, Rothko, Newman, and Still had dinner in Betty's studio/apartment to discuss the future of the gallery; they, not Betty, suggested the meeting and set the agenda. Betty, hardly a model for the modern wheeler-dealer gallery director or manager, often discussed gallery operations with her artists, listened to their advice on other artists, and applauded their practice of hanging shows for one another; her gallery resembled a cooperative. Up to a point. She could also spin round on her heel and hurl thunderbolts of authority.

And as the stakes in the art world had risen—as collectors prowled the galleries looking to buy into the excitement of Abstract Expressionism, as museums mounted exhibitions of new work and often profited from the publicity and turmoil that they were able to attract with that work, as other dealers competed for attention and position in the press and the purses of collectors—the knot of "founding fathers" of Abstract Expressionism sought to ensure their almost exclusive ownership of the movement and, whether by design or by accident precipitated by unconscious desire, control of the "product."

Abstract Expressionism was a man's game—a he-man's macho game with a blue-denim uniform borrowed from working men. Women, for the most part, did not need to apply for participation in the world of Abstract Expressionism, save in the role of chicks in the studio game of cocks-and-chicks or in the role of professional mistress/wife/maid—i.e., dealers. It is noteworthy that the early dealers in advanced American art include Betty Parsons, Bertha Schaeffer, Marian Willard, Martha Jackson, and Eleanor Poindexter; Antoinette Kraushaar, heir to her father's gallery, dealt in slightly earlier and more recognized work. Suggestion for pondering: after artists

Barnett Newman and Betty with Newman's *The Wild,* 1951

prospered under the nurturing of the women dealers, did they move on to male dealers who, in the general understanding of roles in society, offered a more businesslike and success-oriented management? To a degree, the history of the Betty Parsons Gallery suggests this possibility.

One thing is certain. Betty resented being cast exclusively in the role of handmaiden to The Giants; she, too, wanted recognition as an artist. Therefore, when The Giants assembled in Betty's studio and proposed that she chuck out all of the other artists in the gallery and concentrate exclusively on them, she was offended. "We will make you the most important dealer in the world," she recalled Barney's telling her. "But that wasn't my way. I need a larger garden. I always liked variety."

Her verdict assured the defection of the artists, one by one. Sidney Janis, now subletting from Betty a section of the floor at 15 East Fifty-seventh Street, "just took them away," Betty recalled. "He could offer them stipends. I couldn't. I had no money.

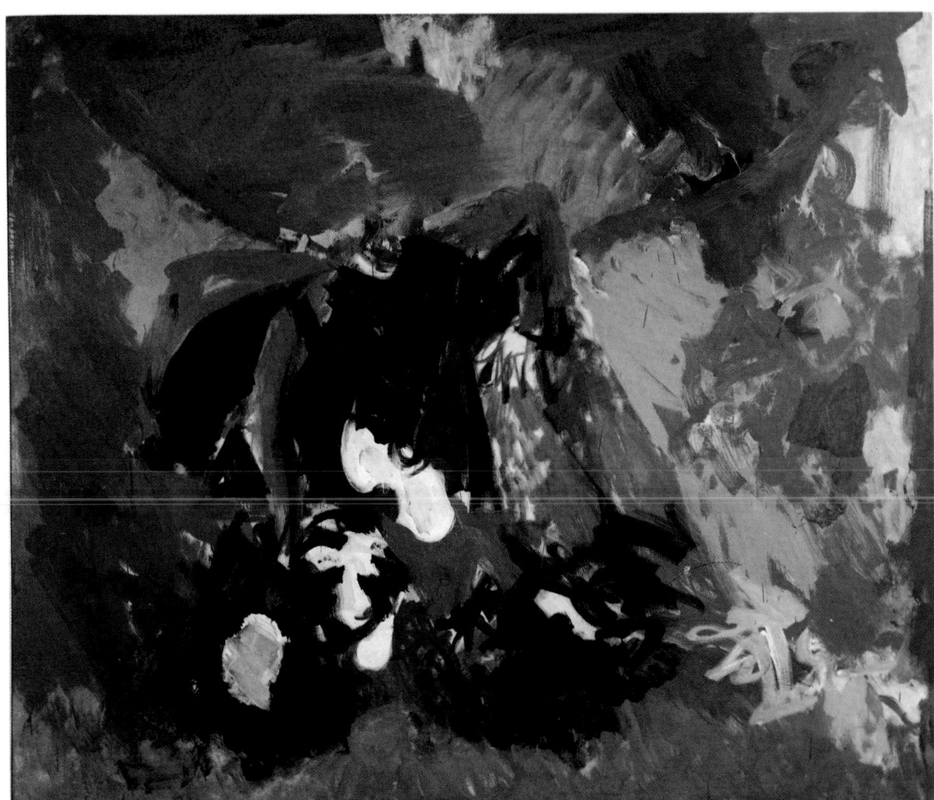

Ethel Schwabacher, *Antigone I,* 1958. Wadsworth Atheneum, Hartford. Study Collection

He offered them money and they went to him. They *needed* money and I couldn't give it to them. I sold some things but they wanted me to sell more."

While Betty made little money as an artist or even as a dealer, she had The Katinkas. And her artists knew it. She seemed to the artists to live well, to dress fashionably, and to travel each summer, to go to swell parties where (at that time) artists would not have been welcomed, and—whether from strength of personality or faith in the benevolence of The Katinkas—Betty appeared to worry very little about the next week or month.

As the artists sighted both fame and the fortune that might be theirs, and measured those potential gains against their status at the time, they thought Betty did little to help them net the trophies they desired and, they believed, they had earned. So, one by one, Betty's artists made arrangements with other dealers.

Betty admitted that she was wounded by the defection of "her" artists. "The funny thing is that my gallery made it possible for them all. Where would they have been if they hadn't been able to show with me? No one would have known about them. Well, I had to go on, you know, I couldn't just sit still and complain."

Indeed, she did not sit still and complain. Betty accepted the inevitability of her loss and transferred her ardor to Stamos, Pousette-Dart, Murch, Ossorio, Steinberg, Reinhardt, Sterne—the predictable group of artist-friends who loyally remained with the Betty Parsons Gallery—as well as a new crop of artists that caught her fancy. Frequently identified now as a "discoverer" of artists, Betty enthusiastically "discovered" and promoted artists—some who had only peripheral membership in the gallery when it was dominated by The Giants; she discovered the talents of some old friends. Some new acquaintances, she found, were artists. Soon she added to the gallery's roster Marie Taylor, Robert Rauschenberg, Calvert Coggeshall, Kenzo Okada, Marjorie Liebman, Dorothy Sturm, Ethel Schwabacher, Lyman Kipp, and Richard Lindner; she sang their praises in the same key she had used when she lauded The Giants. Not everyone agreed that her gallery consistently provided the same quality of excitement and excellence in all its shows, in all its artists.

But most critics and other artists agreed that one artist, Walter Murch, was also a giant. Murch, one of the first artists that Betty showed at the Wakefield and then took with her to Mortimer Brandt's modern section, remained with the Betty Parsons Gallery. Consistently, Betty pointed out, he was appreciated by people who otherwise disliked abstract art; he seemed to many of Betty's friends and clients to be an anomaly in the gallery. Murch's paintings, the result of his patently skillful draftsmanship and his arbitrary takeover of identifiable objects from the real world, seemed to the enemies of abstraction an oasis of intellectual calm in a sea of chaos. Those same features, interpreted as existential masking of reality by the fragmented trappings of actuality, won Murch respect from the purest of the abstract artists—Newman, Reinhardt, and Betty herself.

Other artists were not so widely applauded, Betty acknowledged. In May of 1954, she exhibited Sari Dienes's huge (eight- and nine-feet-high) works on paper that could roll and unroll like Japanese screens. Covered with inks and pigments applied with rollers, stamps, and sponges, these works seemed to Betty to radiate some of the same allover surface energy as Pollock's but in a muted and subtle—possibly decorative—manner. Betty saw in the works numerous almost hidden little dramatic activities of pigment, squirming and sparkling close up or merging and blurring softly into slight suggestions of texture when seen from a distance. To Betty, these were serious works by a talented artist. As the show proceeded, however, Betty was dismayed that others—critics and collectors and casual visitors to the gallery—seemed not to see in Dienes's work the same searching and free spirit that Betty admired.

Betty was similarly perplexed at the end of the season when she showed paintings, drawings, and sculpture for the first time in New York by Hugo Weber, a Swiss-born professor at the Institute of Design in Chicago. His highly energetic work rang with the doctrines of Abstract Expressionism as he assiduously both avoided recognizable imagery and retained in the finished work the traces of his manipulation of materials, whether paint or bronze. Betty's applause for his work, however, was not matched in the art world. When Weber's show did not generate the excitement that earlier abstractionists in the gallery had enjoyed, Betty was convinced that fame was fickle and that quality had nothing to do with recognition.

Her response to such situations—to the reception of Dienes and Weber—was to stiffen her determination to find and put forth the new, newer, newest thing in art. She added artists to the gallery stable. Her garden, indeed large and still growing, contained haphazardly attended exotic flora as well as weeds, perfect examples of certain species and strange hybrids.

As the star system and the clustering of star artists within a particular gallery set the stage for art as business, ambitious artists often took a swashbuckling stance and daringly pursued fame. Ad Reinhardt, detached enough to see the changes occurring in the art world, designed a cartoon-satire in 1954 on the emerging art establishment and spread it across the pages of *Art News.*

Reinhardt composed his gadfly message in a dangling section of type set at an angle, combining it with drawings and type. He aimed to prick smartly some of the most visible art world hides. In part, it read:

ParsongiftShoppe
antiquesjewelry
workesofarte
forthe
upperlowbrow

Reinhardt did not confine his mocking view, his twitting and teasing to Betty and her gallery but, to her delight, included Sidney Janis in a passage of satire:

Wholesale&Retail
JanissButcherBakers
&Candyschtickmaker
fakedupHistory
fortheTrade
museums&missionaries[2]

Betty laughed at Ad Reinhardt's humorous jibes. Not stung by references to gift shops and antique jewelry, Betty saw no threats in the developing art world establishment. As she traveled, she proselytized unapologetically for the new art, preaching the same sermon to the converted and to the heathen and, more significantly, preaching the same message in 1954 that she bannered in 1934 and 1944. For her, art remained the mystical means for entering and claiming a new world, a re-created world that was both unfettered by the past and mounted on the eternal nature of the human spirit.

In a program that was to become, in one form or another, an annual ritual, Betty visited the South and Midwest in the summer of 1954, armed with a film about Seymour Lipton and his work and a collection of slides of work by other artists in the gallery. Betty arranged to visit museums in Cleveland, Toledo, Chicago, and Saint Louis to show the Lipton film to directors and curators in an unabashed and for her unprecedented effort at selling.

Pausing in her promotional work for her artists, Betty visited Marie Taylor in Saint Louis, and then traveled by train to New Orleans, where she was met by Dusti Bongé, an artist who lived and worked on the Gulf Coast. The two women flew the following morning to Miami where they were met by Jo Carstairs, who had bought from Betty several paintings by Walter Murch.

Jo Carstairs shepherded her friends onto a plane that flew through "black clouds and bumps to start" and arrived in "Nassau in sunshine...go to Prince St. George Hotel as Jo's guests—spend afternoon on beach swimming...dine at 8:30...write letters." During the next few days, luxuriating in Carstairs's hospitality, Betty enjoyed Nassau's sunshine, swimming, massages, and shopping to "buy skirts, shorts and dress from Madras and pair of espadrills [*sic*]—$130.00 worth." After a few days at the Nassau hotel, the women boarded a small seaplane that took them to Jo Carstairs's island, Whale Cay. During the next two weeks on the island, Betty swam "in incredible blue green and amber water...observing undersea fish life," walked, played poker (which, consistently, Betty spells "poka") and Scrabble with the other guests, and painted. Over the coming years, Betty frequently accepted Jo Carstairs's hospitality and, according to Rosalind Constable, allowed herself to be regimented thoroughly by Jo Carstairs, "this Little Admiral," who dictated the events and all aspects of the mode of life on her island. "Why," Rosalind said, "this Little Admiral—I always admired her neatness and the sharp nautical dress that she affected—*insisted,* absolutely *insisted,* that all her guests swim nude. I never understood why Betty would

Above, left: Dusti Bongé, *Recollections*

Above, right: Dorothy Sturm, *#2*, 1957

stand for all of that nonsense. But she did buy some paintings from the gallery and I suppose it was worth it to Betty."

After the visit to Whale Cay, Betty spent several weeks with Dusti on the Gulf Coast, but by the first week in August, Betty and Dusti, accompanied by two men who were Dusti's friends, departed for Mexico and traveled through Tampico, Mexico City, Xochimilco, and Cuernavaca, until the end of August, when they reentered the United States at the Texas border.

Soon after her return, Betty resumed her campaign to interest museum directors in cities other than New York in the work of her artists. In Memphis, artist Marjorie Liebman met her, and Betty, as if changing summer frocks or interchanging one friend for another, resumed a pattern akin to the one she had shared with Dusti. She and Marjorie painted and picnicked, walked along the Mississippi River, visited other artists around Memphis, and talked about their own work.

Dorothy Sturm, another artist-friend in Memphis who was soon to show in Betty's gallery, joined Marjorie Liebman in orchestrating a public relations campaign for Betty—and themselves—in Memphis. They arranged to have Betty interviewed on the local television station where a reproduction of a Rembrandt—an artist, after all, of impeccable *bona fides*—was flanked on camera by works by Dorothy Sturm and Marjorie Liebman. A local newspaper, following a tip from Dorothy Sturm and Marjorie Liebman, informed the Memphis readers that "The name Betty Parsons is synonymous with contemporary art in New York City.... She is one of the leaders in the bitter rivalry to discover new talent.... To an artist, it is an honor to have the prestige of her name behind him. He becomes 'of the Betty Parsons group.'" After mentioning Stamos and Pollock as two such group members, the writer added, "Marjorie Liebman and Dorothy Sturm of Memphis are two more."

According to the writer, "[Betty Parsons] does not mouth trite phrases about modern art, or abstraction, or non-objectivism. She does talk incessantly of 'contemporary' art. Surprisingly enough, she has helped make many 'moderns' popular by removing the stigma of the word 'modern.'"

The writer concluded, "Mrs. Parsons made it plain she does not think of abstract art as non-objective. Artists of our time, she has found, are deeply concerned with the saga and the mystery of life and death. Have they not been so always?"[3]

Betty's celebrity as a dealer accorded her a degree of social power which she sometimes consciously manipulated. But if she understood her own arsenal of power, she did not fully recognize that she was courted and waylaid continually by artists interested in joining the gallery. Rather, she believed that her fame as a "discoverer" was spreading and her public growing consequently, a notion that was corroborated by the warm hospitality and effusive greetings she met in her travels.

Betty, the patron of change, did not adjust her sails to the shifting winds in the art world; indeed she registered no differences in direction or velocity. While abstract painting became more widely practiced, as various mannered versions of the several modes of New York School painting were rehashed in colleges and universities and small town art clubs across the country, Betty continued to believe that the mysteries of abstraction were reserved for the few initiates. Thus, as she traveled across the country, she often "discovered" artists who were, in one degree or another, copying artists she already represented.

To the dismay of some of the artists in her gallery, Betty began to discover artists at an alarming rate, which some suspected exactly paralleled the pace of her social life and the warmth of hospitality she received. She admitted to her gallery a large group of artists (too large, said some of the artists themselves, for the space and calendar available in any gallery) with a surprising variety of styles and points of view. Such variety necessarily included some weak artists, plying feeble talents to lay claim to a seat among the avant-garde. If Betty's stable of artists seemed uneven to outside observers, she herself had no trouble separating the sheep from the goats.

Her gallery, as she saw and operated it, was cohesive and highly focused: it dealt in the new, in abstraction, and in the spiritual aspects of art.

In October of 1954, Paul Mocsanyi, a critic who later became the Director of the New School Gallery, wrote in an article that was sent over the United Press wires to newspapers around the country, that Betty Parsons, widely known as a champion of abstract art, had entered a business agreement with a newcomer on the New York art scene touted by press releases as "a youthful woman of beauty and charm, an accomplished golf player and deep sea angler who studied art history and painting on her Wisconsin silver fox farm." The business partner, according to the flack sheet, "had lived long enough in Paris to acquire, together with a slight French accent, a penchant for French modern art."

The business venture revolved around Betty's selecting paintings for her wealthy partner to show in her "swanky town house in the...heart of Manhattan's 'silk stocking district.'" Abstract painting with Betty's imprimatur, available only by appointment, would free "important collectors" from the hateful possibility of mingling "with hungry looking young men and violently intellectual young women. Purchasing abstract expressionism will become an elegant affair. The actual selling," concluded Mocsanyi, would be effected by the partner and "Betty Parsons will lend the venture her name. It is hoped that this will serve as a sort of assurance for excellence of product, and that the name built up in years of sacrificial devotion will finally pay off."[4]

Betty, soon realizing that she had been snared in a public relations program, pulled free and swam in her own currents. She later explained her foray into the partnership: "I tried to make money. At least some of the time. I was never very good at it," Betty said, "But everyone said I should be a better businesswoman and do public relations. So I tried. But it wasn't my way."

If the partnership had threatened Betty's sense of integrity, she regained self-esteem through the gallery. She turned immediately to preparation of an exhibition of new pristine work of Hedda Sterne. The result of two years of intense work, Sterne's black grid-shafts loomed like trees against a mysterious sky implied but not explicitly painted. "Oh, Hedda always painted the sources of mystery," Betty exclaimed. "She was so intelligent and so sensitive. But she changed all the time, and the damn critics thought she wasn't serious. Maybe they thought that because she was a woman. And beautiful. Beautiful women, you know, have a difficult life. Hedda was always searching, never satisfied. She had many ways; most artists just have one way to go."

In December, Betty exhibited simultaneously the work of Dorothy Sturm and a group show of drawings that *The New York Times* treated under the headline, "Dorothy Sturm's Collages of Lingerie and Towels Bring Quilting Up to Date."[5] The review infuriated Betty; years later, frowning and pointing to an offending paragraph, she reiterated her belief that "The critics never understood my gallery. They never understood my artists. They hated the abstract and the new," Betty raged. "It was terrible. The critics were such fools. They didn't understand at all what Dorothy Sturm did. Her work had nothing at all to do with lingerie or towels or quilting: it was art."

Following the Sturm show, Betty installed the precisely crafted bas-relief work of Boris Margo; at the same time, Charles Egan showed Reuben Nakian's terra-cotta reliefs based on the story of *Leda*. Betty recalled, "I was fascinated because there were some similarities. They were very different artists. Nakian was very ancient. His work was from the oldest past. Boris Margo worked in the future." Margo adventured into the complexities of innovative printmaking, building up complicated raised surfaces with a variety of materials, plowing directly into metal with engraving tools, or furrowing the field of a plate with metal-biting acids. For Betty, Margo's cut metal images suggested geological surfaces covering mysterious deep-earth events. He, along with Stamos, extracted the secrets of the earth, Betty said.

Following the show of Margo's work, Betty installed Kenzo Okada's softly surfaced and serene paintings. For Betty, Kenzo Okada's work sometimes resembled gardens but his spirit, she insisted, was pure light. In the late forties, Okada, newly arrived in the United States, adopted the prerogatives of Abstract Expressionism to induce paint to assume *being*; in consequence, his work glowed with enlivened surfaces as well as subdued soft colors. If he was, as Betty insisted, a "painter's painter," he was also a "collector's painter," for his paintings sold steadily, enriching the coffers of the Betty Parsons Gallery for decades. His work soon appeared in the collections of The Museum of Modern Art, the Guggenheim Museum, and the Whitney Museum, as well as in numerous private collections known for their high quality. Okada's work, as well as the loyalty of his following, led Betty over three decades to anticipate a major one-man museum exhibition for the Japanese-born artist. But, however well his work sold, Okada was never accorded a major solo museum show.

Okada's new work, larger and including more decisive shapes and more definition in color than his prior work, was, Betty thought, "devastatingly beautiful." Skillfully combining Oriental spatial concerns with the courting of accident favored by American abstractionists, Okada effected a shimmering surface as delicate as silk flowers. Betty recalled, "They were the most beautiful things I had ever seen. For Okada, beauty had energy and force; energy said something to him. What does an American know about beauty?" she roared. "We call everything beautiful. Film stars. Motor cars. Clothes. I don't trust *beautiful* paintings unless they are *truly* beautiful. Okada's paintings are *pure* beauty."

Betty's anger at the unsympathetic critics and museum curators only intensified as they virtually ignored Calvert Coggeshall's scrupulously painted version of Chinese symbols and fragments of geometry. "Coggie" suspended figures on the canvas ground in a style that Betty found "perfectly amazing," a meshing of spiritual and physical properties. Coggeshall's very simple, very serene paintings shadowed Betty's memory many years later. "They were like dreams. They had this intensity; they were so powerful I've never forgotten them."

While still loyal to Rothko and his luminous vision, Betty observed that Rothko had left no room for Coggeshall in the public's eye. It was as if the world could absorb only *one* artist working in any given direction. "I thought that was strange, of course. In earlier times that was one thing that was better than now: there could be two or three or several artists working on the same thing and each one would still be seen. There was more room. Of course, there weren't as many artists in the older world. We were beginning to get a lot of artists."

When the Midtown Galleries showed Betty's latest work in 1955, a reviewer wrote:

> *Betty Parsons works whenever she can, which isn't often except in the summer when her fantastically busy gallery closes. She paints wherever she happens to be, and wherever that is gets into her work. In New Orleans, it was pink color, windows, ironwork; in Venice, columns, arcades; in other parts of Italy, bits of stone, plaster, sgraffito. She works in a deliberately rough, almost discourteous way. (No paint, even quick-drying-Permalba, is going to boss her around!) She tends to build frames of darker colors around her abstractions through which she enters to discover, in the larger paintings, forms like vegetables. The small pictures from her sketchbook are better. They are souvenirs of a journey expressed in a symbolist's shorthand—pigeonholes into which are stuffed little pieces of places. Her color, always expressive, has a burnt-in quality.* [6]

"Oh," she remembered, "I was pleased by the review. I always got reviews. They liked me some of the time. I don't know why. I don't think they understood what I was getting at." While Betty continued to think of herself primarily as an artist, she also continued to exact more attention as a dealer.

She showed the keenly intellectual but fragile collages of Anne Ryan; then the decorative pieces by a friend from Boston, Maud Morgan, whose work took shape ambiguously between abstract-geometric formalism and naturalism. Betty believed ambiguity could "be energy. Who can be sure of anything? The problem was that Maud's paintings were *too* beautiful. I told her that."

"Beautiful," a term spattered over the pages of art history, became incessantly ambiguous in Betty's lexicon. When Betty employed the term, she could mean "pretty" and, therefore, unacceptable as, presumably, she meant in the case of Maud's paintings in the fall of 1955. At other times, she intoned "beautiful," breathing deeply and flinging her arms back to expose her bosom to imagined forces in the universe, and she intended to evoke images of the sublime, the perfect—as, for example, when she spoke of Okada's work. Beauty, for Betty, was either meat or poison for an artist; and she made the judgment from the recesses of her own intuition as to which it was for a particular artist.

Originality, not beauty, was the quality Betty sought in her artists. Original voice, Betty argued, did not issue always from intellectual rigor any more than from aesthetic theories about beauty. Consistently, Betty showed together or sequentially artists who were different, not similar, in the belief that distinction served to define. While she thought of Sari Dienes and Stamos as sharing such a degree of sensibility that she would not show them together for fear of detracting from the originality of either artist, she, contrarily, emphasized stylistic contrast between Richard Lindner and Lyman Kipp by showing their work together. Lindner combined brightly colored stylized images of decadence with features from Surrealism, from Cubism, and from Expressionism. Most visitors to the gallery regarded Lindner as a Germanic aberration in the art world, as a highly skilled artist exorcising the horrors of war lingering in his own psyche. Betty thought otherwise. "He was," she said, "an original. People said he was like George Grosz but he wasn't. Later they said he was the first Pop artist. He wasn't that either but that helped sell his paintings later. When I showed him, I couldn't do anything at all for him. Nobody understood his work and everybody hated what it was about. Later, when everybody got interested in Pop art, they thought Lindner was a Pop artist and then he sold very well and got a lot of attention. But he was no longer with me then."

"At that time," she explained, "Kipp was much better understood. People liked his sculpture and wondered if they were looking at toys."

But few, according to Betty, found Ellsworth Kelly's work either easy or playful. For Betty, his work exuded life; it shone with positive force and implied the intellectual existence of a sheer pure joy. At the end of the spring season of 1956, Betty enthusiastically organized and opened an exhibition of Kelly's work, his introduction to New York. He had been living in Paris, where he had evolved a strong geometric style using black, white, and simple colors. As a constructionist in metal, he worked with similar ingenious and mathematically rooted shapes. From the first time that Betty saw his work, she knew that "Kelly had this strong ability to put everything together. There was never too much. And everything fit. He saw the universe expanding and he captured that in simple shapes that were really terrifically complicated. And," she added, "he could draw better than anybody. I have one of his drawings. One of his very best, I think. He gave it to me."

Kelly's uncompromising search for purity delighted Betty. "He was," she said, "a very smart guy. And in a serious way he was a very happy artist. Even when he worked in black and white—just black and white—he made the sun shine on you."

Betty's old friend Henry Schnakenberg visited her during the Kelly show and while his own work was on exhibit at the Kraushaar Gallery. Schnakenberg worked on the other side of the world from Kelly. He guided thin, often dark-toned oils into paintings of scenes and people, including a portrait of Betty (painted in the early forties). He had invested in Betty's gallery even though she found his work too literal and old-fashioned for her stable. "Well, you see, I loved Henry Schnakenberg. He was a very amusing man. But his work was about the past and was completely opposite to everything that I stood for. He was full of old attitudes and too much technique. He was not the slightest bit interested in the new or the expanding," Betty said with a sniff.

William Congdon, *Piazza San Marco, Venice, #10,* 1952

"And he decided that I was mad, mad, mad. He never could take my artists. He thought Ellsworth Kelly was just the end—total madness. And he thought Kenzo Okada was just decorative."

If art took many forms, so did artists; Betty listened for the original voice and championed it when she heard it, defending artists on personal as well as aesthetic grounds. William Congdon was such an artist. His subjects—sometimes religious, more often references to such famous sites as Athens, Istanbul, Indian temples, French cathedrals, Italian and Ceylonese landscapes, Positano, the Eiffel Tower, the Sahara—were set by the artist's singular hand. His stylized mixture of drawing and painting, sometimes moving perilously close to overworked or dead-looking paint, avoided the doctrines and dicta of Abstract Expressionism. According to Betty, Congdon's work caught "the feeling. Congdon had the feeling. He didn't give a damn for pretty pictures. He wanted to capture the feeling."

A maverick in the art world, William Congdon showed with Betty Parsons for many years but chose to live in Europe rather than New York, to work in a semiabstract vein rather than in the avant-garde, and to convert to Catholicism. "A lot of people thought Congdon was all technique or all subject," Betty recollected, "but I found him *very* abstract. Very free and very, very spiritual. You know he became a Catholic and went to live in Italy because he just couldn't stand the material nature of America and the material nature of his background. It is simply killing. You have to escape. He escaped to the Church. I don't approve of the Church but I do for Congdon because I think it has kept him alive. I think he would have died, just died, if he hadn't joined the Church and moved to Italy." Frowning, she added, "I could never have escaped my conservative background that way. I was too much of a rebel, too independent. I could never swallow the Church's teachings, all those don't do's and do's, all that hypocrisy."

Right: Marie Taylor, *Big Beetle*, 1969. Collection Mr. and Mrs. Joseph Pulitzer, Jr., Saint Louis

Below: Forrest Bess, *#31*, 1951

THE SECOND DECADE OF THE GALLERY

•

1956-66

Betty's gallery, during the first ten years of its existence, presented some of the most exciting and innovative artists of the era and largely defined avant-garde art in America. In the increasingly competitive commercial world of art, a dealer had to be able to exploit an artist, to build a public image of his or her work, to create a demand for that work, and to control the supply so as to increase the prices steadily. Betty had shown herself to have a gift for attracting attention and for proselytizing on behalf of the new art, but she spurned any suggestion that she should systematically develop and ply the skills of advertising and promotion for her gallery and its artists.

By her reckoning, she remained interested in the intangible qualities of art, in art as a search and seizure of spiritual experience. "Well, you see," Betty explained, "I had learned that Americans liked the physical, not the spiritual. And they didn't like anything very new. I would not please everybody. I knew that. I was interested in the spiritual and in the new. I was interested in art that showed the spiritual and showed the new and I knew that Americans just wouldn't care for that very much."

When The Giants defected and Betty had cobbled her wounds, she continued to run the gallery exactly as she always had—as an extension of herself as an artist. She continued to celebrate the new, to extol originality, and to operate without reflecting on past mistakes and on future strategies. Each show in the gallery was a particular and specific event; Betty saw no need to fit artists or exhibitions into an overall pattern or point of view for the gallery. In the Betty Parsons Gallery, Betty Parsons's eye reigned; what was seen in the gallery had been selected by Betty Parsons. It was of no concern to Betty that her criteria were not readily apprehended by visitors.

At the beginning of 1957, *Art News* selected the exhibition of Ad Reinhardt's uncompromisingly difficult and intellectual paintings at the Betty Parsons Gallery as one of the ten best shows of the previous year.[1] "*All* of my shows were interesting. They were important shows. I didn't show entertaining things or easy things. I showed the work of artists who had their eyes on the other world," Betty pontificated. "But Ad was a very great artist. One of the best. He and Barney were the most intelligent of all the artists. That's why they could never get along. They hated each other. But both of them could paint and think and talk. I loved them both."

Early in 1958, after ten years in postwar Paris and extensive work in the theater there, Jack Youngerman had his first New York show with Betty Parsons. His oil paintings were composed of richly applied paint in crisply defined patterns. "Jack and Ellsworth Kelly were friends. That's how I found them both," Betty recollected. "I discovered them both. They were working in Paris and I told them to come back to New York and I would show their work." Kelly's recollection is different, and the discrepancy amuses him. "How like Betty," he says. "The story of Paris just got away from her."[2]

Emily Rayner and Betty on board the S.S. *United States,* June 10, 1956

According to Betty, *all* of her artists at that time were "great! The artists—every one of them—had something to say. And that's what I was after." As this article of faith led Betty to take risks with unknown artists, it resulted in an uneven quality in exhibitions and, for some viewers, a confusion of styles. For instance, Day Schnabel, the Austrian-born American who had shown her work in New York since 1947, installed a seven-foot work, *The Sphere,* alone in a room in the gallery. The enormous piece of sculpture, the major piece in this first solo exhibition in the Betty Parsons Gallery, consisted of an outer pineapple or pine cone shape with perforations; another form occupied the interior spaces thus defined. "It was a tremendous work," Betty declared. Baffled, she added, "Why don't they understand Schnabel's work?"

If Schnabel's work was offputting in its seriousness, the opposite characterized Marie Taylor's fish, birds, and beasts, works that she pulled from the hard stones she collected from the Maine coast or country fields. Her diminutive creatures, coming cozily to the human hand, suggested rather than depicted zoological specimens. "Marie has such fantasy and charm," Betty contended. "Who cared if she wasn't the latest thing, wasn't making the largest and most serious work in the world? She *was* serious, you know. That's why she was so playful. I always knew that play—what children do before we ruin them with all those hypocritical do's and don'ts—was very serious."

Marie Taylor, Betty's long-standing friend from Saint Louis, brought her hand-sized stone carvings of animals to town for a show in the gallery. As Betty fondled the simple masses of stone, incised shallowly and shaped only slightly so that the original stone as well as the beast discovered in it were equally evident, she exclaimed, "Just look what Marie Taylor can do with almost nothing. Isn't this amazing? Aren't these perfect? They're like very, very ancient works—Pre-Columbian or Egyptian or those early Greeks. They're really massive. It doesn't matter that they're small." Then, stroking a reclining beast, she added, "And they're alive. When we turn the lights off in the gallery, I can hear them dance and leap. I think they must have festivals in the night when we are not here. Look at him. And him. And him. Marie has great vision."

In addition to Marie Taylor, Betty handled the work of several other friends, including Aline Porter. Married to photographer Eliot Porter and living with him in

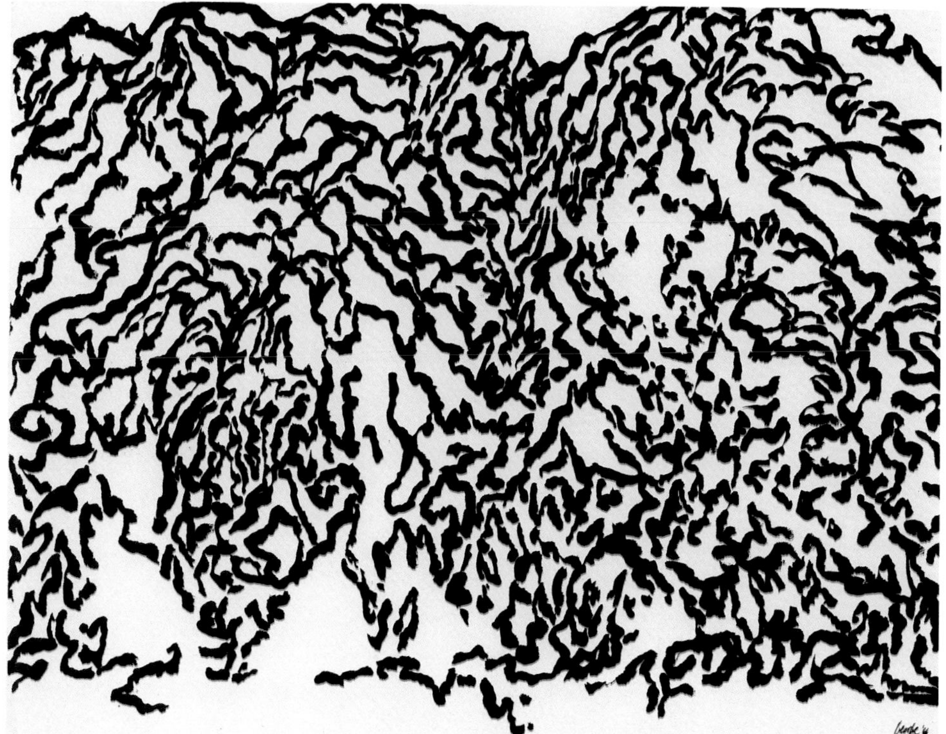

Above, left: *Boat,* 1956. Saint-Jean-Cap-Ferrat

Above, right. Bradley Walker Tomlin, *No. 9,* 1952. © The Phillips Collection, Washington, D.C.

Left: Thomas George, *Norway Series, #20 Telemark,* 1966. Brush and ink, 20 x 26¼". Collection, The Museum of Modern Art, New York. Gift of F. M. Supper

New Mexico, Aline came to New York, spent long periods in the gallery looking at the work of other artists and talking to Betty about her own interests in painting. She invited Betty to lunch and dinner and, in a short time, Betty accepted Aline's invitation to visit the adobe house she shared with her family in Teseque, New Mexico, near Santa Fe, the following summer. By the time Betty returned from New Mexico and her visit to Aline Porter's white studio, Betty had made another discovery; she planned to show Aline's stylized and sometimes oddly composed still-life paintings. "Aline is very sensitive and very, very alive to nature. She sees into flowers and knows all of their names. Her work shows the essence of flowers and all of her paintings are very abstract. Those are not real flowers and that is not real space."

At about this time, Betty recalled, she felt that she was going mad trying to show and give attention to too many artists; moreover, the artists under her wing were clamoring for time on the exhibition calendar, nagging for greater exposure to press and collectors, and chiding Betty for not furthering their careers more visibly and rapidly. She was facing the onerous prospect of weeding her garden when, early in the year, she met and formed a strong friendship with Susan Morse Hilles.

The sandy-gray-haired, blue-eyed, and ceaselessly energetic Betty, in the last half of her fifth decade, fascinated Susan Hilles, who soon became a Katinka. Susan began to visit the gallery as a part of her weekly visits to New York City when she escaped from the routine of being a faculty wife in the Yale University community. At Betty's urging, she began to collect contemporary art.

Betty enjoyed visiting Susan Hilles and her husband, Fred, in New Haven on weekends. She talked with them about her gallery. More and more artists had begun to seek her out and beg space in her stable; often, she turned away a young artist with authentic vision and extraordinary talent, she told her friends.

"Susan Hilles came to have lunch with me one day," Betty remembered, "and I knew that she had something on her mind.

"She said, 'I hate the idea that you are turning away young artists. You have always discovered artists. I think you must open another gallery so that you can go on discovering artists.'

"Just like that, she told me what I should do. And before I could say a thing she said that I should find some space and that she'd pay the rent for two years. Such generosity. I was overcome."

Betty agreed on the spot to find space and to open another gallery, a subsidiary gallery, in which she would show the work of new and undiscovered artists and, throughout the spring, looked at available spaces. Betty discussed the project with other friends, especially with Natika Waterbury, a friend who worked as Betty's assistant in the gallery. Agnes Martin, in town from New Mexico, encouraged Betty in the project; Barnett Newman, Annie Laurie Witzel, and Hope Williams, too, thought it a good idea. Even her sister and brother-in-law, Sukes and Tom, believed that Betty Parsons's success in art should be extended and amplified. Of course, Hedda Sterne and Saul Steinberg, her unfailingly staunch supporters, cheered her toward new frontiers. Betty talked the idea over with everyone she met, both casual friends and new acquaintances. Everyone—from Jane Bowles, visiting from Morocco, and Henry Schnakenberg, who took her to the theater, to Margarett McKean, John Singer Sargent's grandniece who lived on the coast north of Boston, grew carnations, bred Afghan hounds, and counted Betty among her closest friends (thus becoming a ranking member of The Katinkas). Leon Polk Smith, who showed with Betty—until friction with Ellsworth Kelly over who first shaped canvas before painting on it drove him from the gallery—told her that she owed it to artists as well as to her reputation to extend the reach of the gallery.

By March, Betty was convinced that it was both her duty and her destiny to open another gallery. When she went to Baltimore for the opening of the Boris Margo exhibition, she had already decided to accept Susan Hilles's invitation but she wanted Adelyn Breeskin's blessing. Adelyn, the director of the Baltimore Museum, welcomed Betty to her "small but cozy house with small old collie." Betty admired Adelyn, one of the few female museum directors in the United States at the time, and eagerly recounted her plans for the new gallery to well-received applause. "Adelyn is very intellectual and dedicated to art. She's not a politician. She's like me. She thinks about art and about artists. It was a great, great honor to have Adelyn approve of Section 11 [as the new gallery would be known]."

On March 20, 1958, Betty wrote to Susan Hilles:

Dear Sue:
In confirmation of our telephone conversation, the rent of the gallery at 11 East 57 Street is $450 a month or $5,400 yearly. In addition it is necessary to pay half-monthly rent between April 1st and August 1st or the sum of $900. As you have guaranteed me two years' rent, it would be better for me if I could have this in one lump sum—$11,700.

Would there be any advantage to us if we set it up as a corporation? I am hoping that you will be able to supervise the keeping of the books on the gallery.

Looking forward to seeing you soon.

Ever,
Betty Parsons

While Betty often visited her sisters, Sukes and Emily, who, in maturity as in childhood, were "very different, very much a part of another world," Emily's son, Billy Rayner and his wife, Chessy, became the center of her family in New York. They invited Betty frequently to join them for dinner, to accompany them to the theater, or to stroll with them through galleries and museums. Betty was "damned glad that Billy married Chessy, who loves art as much as Billy does. She is terribly shy but she took one look at Billy—she called him 'that blond boy'—and decided to marry him. Just like that. And they were married and I approved absolutely."

But Betty's social life, as always, centered not so much around family as around the old friends she met for drinks, for lunches, for dinners: Janet Flanner, Jeanne Reynal, Hedda Sterne, Rosalind Constable, Muriel Oaks, Hope Williams, Annie Laurie Witzel, and Sandy Calder appear often in her daybook. She saw, too, her artists: there were lunches and studio visits with Ellsworth Kelly, Enrico Donati, Calvert Coggeshall; there were special treats, such as a Segovia concert with Hedda Sterne, where "Betty stared straight ahead. You couldn't imagine what she was hearing or if she liked it or not," Hedda remembered. "But later, when she talked about it, she was enthusiastic and I understood that she heard music the way she read books. That is, she heard what she wanted to hear. She said of Segovia, 'He plays nature.'"[3]

Betty, who felt throughout her life that she had been deprived of an education and was therefore handicapped, both denigrated the role of rationality in creativity and extolled "the intellectuals." Her admiration of those she thought intellectual bordered on the comic. For no apparent reason, Betty once decided that "the intellectuals" ate at an East Side diner near Annie Laurie Witzel's New York apartment. "She would insist," Annie Laurie recalled, "on going to dine at the 'intellectuals' diner.' I don't know who or what she thought an intellectual might be, but there we sat, Betty

Saul Steinberg, *Betty Parsons,* 1958. Private collection, New York

picking at her food and looking around to spot the intellectuals." Admiration for "the intellectuals," coupled with her sense of being deprived of membership in that elite class, increased her pleasure in visiting college campuses, the natural habitat of intellectuals. The intellectuals found Betty's artists and invited them to exhibit in college and university galleries. Invitations to exhibit at a college were, in Betty's judgment, high accolades, and when possible, she visited campuses and attended openings of the shows.

Betty's success, visible in the gallery and applauded by friends and associates, brought her a modicum of financial security if not wealth. Betty was ebullient and restless, she had energy in need of spending. As in the past, she invested some of her spillover energy in travel. Annie Laurie Witzel recalled, "Betty and I were flying from Boston where we had been visiting Betty's friend, Margarett McKean, and Betty just turned to me and said, 'I'd like to travel with you. Let's go somewhere.' And I said, 'Well, if we're going to travel, let's go around the world.' And Betty said, 'That would be fine.' She had just come into some money." Betty said, "I've always thought about this world being round. I thought I should go around it and see it all. And so I did."

After a brief visit to Annie Laurie's ranch in Wyoming, the two women flew over the Rockies to San Francisco, where Betty visited Jesse Reichek, one of her artists who lived in Berkeley. When Betty admired Reichek's new paintings, Annie Laurie observed Betty's pleasure in the artist's recent work and bought one as a gift for Betty. "People gave me the most amazing treasures," Betty recounted. "I never could afford to buy anything."

Margarett McKean, Prides Crossing, Massachusetts, with some of her Afghans

Another gift in San Francisco, however, changed Betty's life. A casual friend, Adaline Kent, had studied with Bourdelle in Paris during Betty's time there. In March 1957, at fifty-seven (Betty's age, too), Adaline Kent was killed in an automobile accident. Her devastated family asked Betty to handle her sculpture. Kent, who had exhibited in New York and Paris, as well as in San Francisco, worked in hydra stone or terra-cotta; sometimes she embedded small stones in cement. But, despite a commission to represent Polynesia with a gigantic statue, *Musician,* at the San Francisco World's Fair in 1939, Kent was unknown.

As Betty worked in Adaline Kent's studio to catalogue her sculpture, Kent's daughter gave Betty a book on Subud, an Oriental mode of contemplation and meditation; Betty described the book in her journal as "Terrific." This gift, like her visit to the Armory Show, marked a born-again experience for Betty. She studied Subud as arduously as she pursued anything, found the spiritual discipline to parallel art and, eventually, joined—"was opened to"—Subud. After she had accepted the Subud teachings and submitted to the "opening," the ritual that included her in the community of practitioners, Betty followed the teachings and seldom talked about Subud. In one official instance, however, she described it: "Well, that's from the Far East, that's from Jakarta, Java actually. And I just found that out in California accidentally. Ten years ago. I've been in it. It's sympathetic to me because it's not a contemplation or meditation. It's a surrender. And what you do is you throw the rot of the brain out and you throw your emotions with it, and you empty yourself. And that's exciting to me and I've been able to do that—not always, but sometimes. And it always helps."[4]

Betty and Annie Laurie sailed for Japan on the S.S. *President Wilson,* but Betty's real journey took her through a slow and thoughtful reading of Subud, an inner journey that could not be mapped in nautical miles. As she physically crossed the

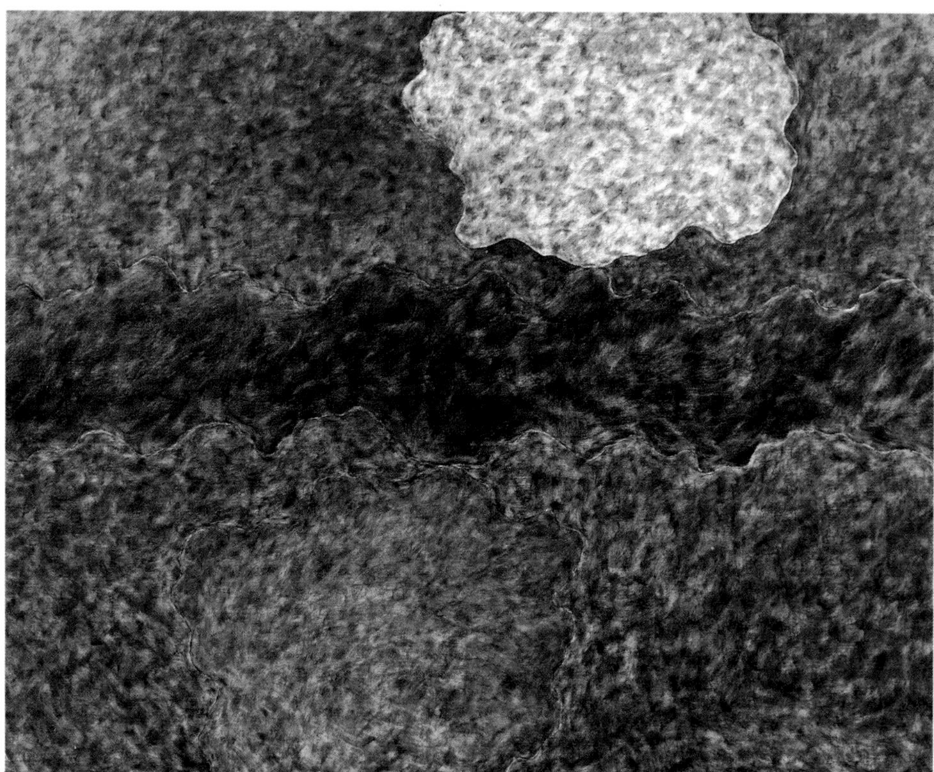

Jesse Reichek, *December 3*, 1958

Pacific, so Betty mentally and spiritually ventured into Eastern thinking; she began a journey that would last the remainder of her days on earth.

By the time they docked in Honolulu and spent a day ashore, exploring the island, "Betty was more preoccupied and self-absorbed than usual—and that's saying a lot," according to Annie Laurie. Back on the ship, Betty continued to explore the book on Subud, interjecting references to it in her journals: "The further you are from somewhere the nearer you are to forever." Subud brought to mind many of the homilies Adge Baker had offered on the life of the spirit. Haunted by the feelings and ideas of Subud, Betty "painted in rather a low grieving mood." Nearing Japan, she stayed up all night to finish reading the book on Subud. She noted: "a tantra with 7 levels depicted ... Subud's 499 qualities."[5]

In Tokyo, Kimi and Kenzo Okada enfolded Betty and Annie Laurie in a program of tea ceremonies, visits to museums and Zen temples—an immersion in Japanese life. At Kenzo's brother's house, Betty "had a big beautiful Japanese bath—dinner extraordinary and slept in guest house in a wood by the sea." She attended a No play and Kabuki theater; she met geishas; she shopped: "bought Kamona [*sic*] black ... ordered clothes to be made."

Even an injury to her foot, efficiently diagnosed as a slight fracture necessitating splints, did not mar Betty's time in Japan. Hobbling on the damaged foot, she accompanied Annie Laurie to the opening of an exhibition of Kenzo Okada's twenty-two large paintings at the Takashimaya (which she identified in her journal as "Tocashima") Department Store.

From Japan, the two women traveled to Hong Kong, Bangkok, Angkor Wat, and Bombay. On visiting the Taj Mahal, Betty found it "so creamy—so perfect—so too full of detail—what a fasace [*sic*]—what a moat—charming and unreal—a city of people restless. The architecture incredible."[6]

She found New Delhi "large [with] expansive population indifferent to foreigners except for sales. The New US Embassy very beautiful in scale and design." And, with reference to Le Corbusier's city, Chandigarh: "Shangralai. An extraordinary city and the wings of justice—such a reach toward the future may it be allowed to happen."[7]

Traveling on to Greece, Betty sketched "Pyreas [*sic*]," walked through the small streets of ancient Athens, visited museums and the Acropolis. She visited the Greek Islands and recorded, "Just came back from the Island of Crete where the clouds are all pleated and the donkeys grey and nobody anywhere gets in the way. Mikinos [*sic*] more white and delicious. The boat trip there was a nite [*sic*] mare everybody ill the boat dansed [*sic*] like a dervish. Returning at nite was calmer but both ways very crowded."[8] She and Annie Laurie "Arrive Delphi 4:30. that devine [*sic*] shrine where oracle spoke to the sun and the moon, the echo was heard in the ears of some men."

The Oracle spoke to Betty, she remembered. "It told me to release my mind and let the powers of the universe flow into me. Everywhere in the world—and it is a big round world—the spiritual forces are just waiting to get free. They wait until people have the freedom to let them out," she explained.

From Greece, Betty and Annie Laurie traveled by ship to Venice, where William Congdon waited to escort them on gondola rides, for leisurely drinks before San Marco, and on twilight walks about the city. Betty found time, too, to "visit Scola St. Roco [*sic*] marvelous Tintorettos and 2 Tiepolos ... with Titian Asumption [*sic*] and other Donatello very marvelous. Stroll through a beautiful pink glow along the canals." She mentions in her journals, too, long walks on the Lido, "green mint" in a street café, dinner at Harry's, drinks at Ciro's, endless walking and sketching, and "the Academia [*sic*] to see the Bellinis, Tiepolos, and Tinterettos [*sic*]. Marvelous ... Doges Palace."[9]

After Venice, Annie Laurie returned to the United States and Betty went to visit her beloved Dumpy, now married to Ferdinand, prince of Liechtenstein, and living opulently on the French Riviera. Betty wrote in her journal, "Very happy to see Dumpy again. She is looking wonderful." In the warm sphere of Dumpy's attention, Betty settled quickly into a routine of long late breakfasts on a terrace overlooking "the slate green blue grey Mediterranean ... and red flowers reaching all around and the weather marvelous. A pine tree rising before me on my right and two stone lions on my left." Following a breakfast of pears, peaches, grapes, and figs "on a platter that looked like Nero's table," Betty and Dumpy sunbathed and swam until time for lunch on the terrace. An afternoon rest, painting "till 6:30 on balcony near my room," kept Betty occupied until time to dress for late dinner.

When Betty left Dumpy, after two weeks of perfect sunshine and civilized parties, she journeyed to England to visit Adge Baker and other friends there. Adge, Betty recalled, "had introduced me to the spiritual things of the world. And I was beginning to understand Subud, this Eastern way of emptying yourself and letting positive forces into your being, and I wanted to introduce her to Subud, too. Well, of course, she was very much interested. I think I taught Adge something."

In September, as Betty headed home by ship, she noted in her journal, "all our freedom is in the necessity within us." Back in New York City, Betty immediately resumed her usual social patterns: dinner with Barney and Annalee Newman, lunch with Clyfford Still, Alfonso Ossorio, and other artists; dinner with Rosalind Constable, The Katinkas, and other friends. Enjoying the little events and occasions that brought her friends around her, Betty observed, "Such a sweet strange thing is love ... time walks with change."

Her summer journey over, her life with friends reaffirmed, Betty concentrated on Section 11. Following a series of discussions on business practices, bookkeeping, and daily operation of the gallery, Susan Hilles discreetly consulted her attorney and, on October 16, 1958, to establish at least a veneer of businesslike organization and understanding, wrote a letter to Betty:

> *I am writing to outline the arrangements which I have discussed with you for helping you out with your new BETTY PARSONS GALLERY, SECTION 11 which you have opened at 11 East 57 Street, New York, New York.*
>
> *I have already advanced or given to you some amounts for your expenses, and I expect to continue to do this sort of thing in the future from time to time to the extent that I feel able and willing to do so. I wish to make it clear, however, as we both understand, that I have no proprietary interest in the Gallery, that there is no partnership between us, and that I have no interest in the profits and no liability for the losses or expenses of the Gallery.*
>
> *I am enclosing an extra copy of this letter and if it correctly states your understanding of the situation, I should appreciate it if you would sign the copy and return it to me so that our respective positions will be clear.*
>
> *Yours sincerely,*
> *Susan Morse Hilles*

Section 11 proved an administrative nightmare for Betty for the next four years. She could not be in both galleries at once. Artists in Section 11 complained if Betty did not tend that gallery, investing her full attention in them and their works; artists in her regular gallery, the established stable of the Betty Parsons Gallery, complained if she dimmed her attention to them in order to serve the newcomers at Section 11. The sibling rivalry was exasperating. Betty closed Section 11. Susan Hilles said, "I was always sorry about Section 11 because it didn't come out the way I had visions of it."

But Betty could, and did, discover artists without Section 11. She offered, toward the end of the 1958 season, a collection of paintings by Theora Hamblett, a retired schoolteacher from Oxford, Mississippi. Although she had a painting in the collection of The Museum of Modern Art, Hamblett claimed no formal training save for a few study guides from a correspondence school that she discovered, Betty thought, as a result of a "draw-me" contest advertised on the cover of a matchbook. Hamblett deftly combined fantasies and materials in images that might otherwise be merely a folk form. "She was a very intelligent woman," Betty said.

Betty looked for originality above everything else in art, which led her to show the calm, post-Mondrian works of Leon Polk Smith and, on the other side of the stylistic map, Alfonso Ossorio's compositions of snarled and raging materials brought to control against an implied grid.

Boasting that she had been the first dealer to show really large paintings, Betty installed an exhibition of "Paintings for Unlimited Space" in 1958, including mural-sized works by Ad Reinhardt, Hugo Weber, Hedda Sterne, Richard Pousette-Dart, Ellsworth Kelly, and Kenzo Okada.

Somewhat earlier, Betty had discovered Forrest Bess, a Texas shrimp fisherman whose visionary small works convinced her that he had grasped and captured the symbology of Jung. She was furious when the show elicited a critic's snipe: "Devoid of any primitive charms as a painter, Bess must be quite a character personally."[10] "Who the hell do you suppose thought that one up?" Betty asked, her anger still near the flash point thirty years later. "Isn't that the most ridiculous statement you ever read about an artist? Well, of course, Annie Laurie Witzel thought it was aimed at *me.* She thought the critic was saying that I showed Forrest Bess because of a personal relationship. I don't care, of course, about that kind of gossipy thing. I've heard it all my life and I hate it. But, can you imagine treating an *artist* with that rudeness? An artist deserves *respect.*"

At this point in the history of the gallery, Betty showed—and respected—the works of such diverse artists as Sari Dienes, Jeanne Reynal, Ellsworth Kelly, Kenzo Okada, Alfonso Ossorio, Agnes Martin, Jack Youngerman, Wallace Putnam, Ethel Schwabacher, Leon Polk Smith, Boris Margo, Eduardo Paolozzi, Minoru Kawabata, Alexander Liberman, Lyman Kipp, Paul Feeley, Ruth Vollmer, Ad Reinhardt, José Guerrero, and Enrico Donati.

In 1959, Betty unexpectedly inherited money from her family. "My uncle," she said, "who had inherited from my grandfather, the General, felt guilty, I think, that the General had disinherited me. So he left me some money. I was very grateful. I bought my land on Long Island. I built my studio out there. I was able to travel."

Tony Smith, not yet famous for his massive black sculpture, was the architect Betty selected. She handed over the forty-thousand-dollar check from her uncle's estate to Smith with instructions to build her a studio by the time she returned from Europe at the end of the summer. She and Smith settled on no plans, set forth no specifications; she laid down no limitations or restrictions or instructions but, rather, handed Smith her trust along with her check. When she returned from her travels, she told him, she expected a perfect studio.

Her incessant travels had long before 1959 become the stuff of family amusement; her nephew Tom McCarter recalled a family joke: "When my father saw a train or ship or bus—or even heard one at some distance—he would remark, 'Well, there goes Betty,' and everyone would laugh. She was always on the move. No one ever knew where she was or where she was going or where she had been."

Betty's journals are studded with fragments of itineraries, stamps, ticket stubs, labels from wine bottles, addresses scrawled on envelopes, pressed flowers or dried leaves, written or drawn notations of places, clippings from foreign newspapers, menus from restaurants in Europe, picture postcards, foreign stamps, train schedules, airline tickets, baggage markers for a steamship, or exotic words printed with the care of a usually reluctant schoolgirl. The written passages erupt with phrases dealing with travel plans, schedules, names of places, lists of food eaten and wine drunk; Betty mapped her journeys into the pages of her journals, factually noting the route out and the return. In kinship with ancient travelers, Betty planted *facts* like flags throughout her records; should she want to return to a place or to a memory, the marker was there for her. No form of transportation repelled her; no trip was too short or too long, over too-familiar or too-strange terrain. She learned to travel light and, in her own fashion, to live off the land. When she could not afford the price of passage, someone seemed always to miraculously appear and invite Betty for a weekend in the country, a week in the West, a month in Europe.

Not all of Betty's travels were totally successful, however. When she sailed for Europe with Susan and Fred Hilles, Annie Laurie Witzel, Lyman Kipp, and Tony Smith took Betty to the dock and helped her with her bags. In Betty's stateroom, Annie Laurie realized that Betty was crying—an uncommon occurrence in her experience with Betty. "She didn't want to talk at first but I insisted because I loved Betty and I just couldn't stand the thought of her traveling across all those waves and going to foreign places and being *sad,*" Laurie recalled. "Well, it turned out that when Susan Hilles had invited her on the trip, Betty assumed, of course, that she was to be a

Whale Cay, Florida. Page from a sketchbook

guest, and she was accustomed to being treated very well indeed as a guest. All those women friends of hers took her places in the grandest possible style, you know. Well," Annie Laurie said with a sigh, "that's not how things were to be with Susan Hilles. *She* paid for Betty's ticket but she took Betty along as sort of a personal secretary or assistant. She put Betty in a small inside stateroom—the kind of thing that might be reserved for a nanny. And Betty knew that this was happening. She knew that Susan thought of her as an *amanuensis.* Susan hurt Betty's feelings."

Susan Hilles and Betty began their chauffeur-driven visit to the great monuments of art in western France and Spain. Susan Hilles, in preparation for the trip, had steeped herself in art history; she sought access to great aesthetic treasure houses; she fancied that Betty would unlock the mysteries of art for her, would guide her through the inventories of history and human achievement. If Betty was unclear about her role, Susan was not. "I thought," Susan admitted, "that Betty would be better than a *hired* guide; after all, art was her *business,* her *life.* I thought she would tell us things we wouldn't read about or hear from a simple *guide.* But," Susan haughtily recounted, "that certainly wasn't the way it was. It turned out that Betty really didn't know very much at all. She looked at things and commented, all right, but she just had everything mixed up. *All* the dates wrong. *Even* wrong artists with *wrong* works. And she didn't know marble from glass. It could have been a disaster"—Susan exhaled—"if I hadn't brought along plenty of guidebooks and if I hadn't been to Europe many times before. One day with Betty, and I knew I had made a colossal mistake. Here she was, this famous gallery dealer in New York—a gallery so famous and important, I believed, that I had financed an extension of it—and she didn't know the first thing about art.

Not a thing. So far as Betty was concerned, everything that existed before 1950 was dead and she was really only interested in the art and artists *she* showed."

Betty, never claiming potential to be an art history teacher, recorded the trip in her journals with characteristic misspellings and misinformation as well as mundane observations on places, schedules, menus. After "Bayeuyx and its tapestries very beautiful...[and] lunch at Mont St. Michel marvelous—watched the omelets made they beat the eggs like a riveter.... Romanesque church on top of mountain," she and Sue arrived in Bordeaux, where "Sue had els specialty. delicious." In Spain, Betty noted, "lunch Burgos... museum of 18th-century sculpture & marvelous cloister 15th-century and restored." After "Ascorial," she arrived in "Madrid @ 6 o'clock...beautiful hotel rooms & service, dinner in garden of Hotel. Fair." Things improved "at Prado—fabulous the dream, passion, and majesty of man's paintings—Prado in afternoon lunch at Ritz—dinner Plaza Maria." But, she noted, "Sue feeling poorly in room last two days." Fred, who had been in England for ten days, joined Betty and Susan, however, and rescued Susan from her vapors. Betty parted to visit Mark Rudkin in Paris and Beatrice Monti, a dealer, in Milan.

Betty's summers typically passed in movement, ricocheting among contacts with friends, exotic dinners and odd-hour schedules, and glasses of wine or cups of coffee in restaurants or cafés in Italy, France, Spain, or England. In addition, she often went West to visit friends; she went to New England; occasionally she went South. If pressed for a reason for travel in general or for a particular journey, Betty averted her eyes, frowned slightly and muttered, "I'm always looking for new artists."[11]

Betty accepted happily invitations to visit acquaintances or associates. According to Hope Williams, Betty and her sisters were often guests in grand houses and were grateful for both the attention and the actual lodging and meals. "They were," Hope iterated, "very poor and unlikely to be anything else. Their mother insisted on living in grand style but they hadn't a farthing. So, very early on, young Betty learned to sleep in any bed, to be pleased with the simple comforts of three meals a day, and to be a *guest*. She rather specialized in being a *guest*. Some do, you know. And Betty quite liked that. She liked being taken care of. She liked attention. And she liked comfort very much—not opulence, not what her mother thought of as comfort; Betty liked the simple comfort of being fed, of being warm, of being clothed, and of being entertained. She was like a child. She wanted those things done for her. And there were always people around Betty just dying to take care of her. She had a pretty good life."

Some believe that Betty's good life was constructed at the expense of others. Often her hosts divide between those who found her charm repayment for any amount of hospitality offered and those who grew weary of her self-centeredness. Betty knew that many invitations carried the requirement that she put her imprimatur on the artist of the household. One artist in the gallery who was dissatisfied with her promotion of his work regularly mustered his wife to entertain Betty as a houseguest. The artist concentrated on manipulating Betty toward more assertive handling of his work; the wife did duty in the kitchen, the scullery, the automobile, and with the social calendar. She complained bitterly about Betty's selfishness in requiring special attention ("a little egg" for breakfast, just-so tea in the afternoon) regardless of family activities. She lamented Betty's lack of consideration and her stinginess: Betty rarely helped with household chores; she even more infrequently invited her hosts out to dinner. Still, the put-upon hostess said, "You wanted to take care of Betty. She was so like a child." Finally, she admitted that, even when Betty invited herself for a weekend or longer, "Who could turn Betty down?"

Betty painting, ca. 1969

FAME

•

1962-69

Betty felt that she had been turned down by the art world. Hungry to be accorded full recognition as an artist, sometimes confusing celebrity with identity, she required attention to a degree that became an addiction; it drove her social and professional activities. When Jock Truman, product of an architectural education and gallery experience with an antique dealer, began his long association with Betty in 1961, he understood her needs and her frustration. "I will make you a star," he told her. "You can't show your work in your gallery and you can't ask dealers to show your work, but I can. You can't call up critics and writers and tell them about your own work, but I can. And," he promised, "I will."

Later, Jock would boast self-mockingly of his instincts for peddling. But at the time he joined Betty, he wanted to be associated with someone significant, with good taste, and with excitement that bordered on outrage. He believed, he confessed,[1] that Betty, if sufficiently absorbed in her work as an artist and if publicly applauded for that work, would turn the Betty Parsons Gallery over to him. On that count, Jock Truman sorely misjudged Betty Parsons: she wanted it all—power as a dealer, popularity as a celebrity, and importance as an artist.

Jock's efforts to establish Betty as a star soon resulted in exhibitions, like that in April 1962, at the New Art Gallery in Atlanta, which disseminated catalogue and press materials emphasizing Betty's remarkable creativity and energy: "Mrs. Parsons is ultimately a creator," according to the catalogue. "Her dual interest in painting and the fostering of contemporary art are in no sense contradictory. Her creativity, her profound sense of discovery and its presence in her paintings reflects the core of her being, expressed both in her paintings and her gallery...."

In 1962, she was planning with Tony Smith the addition of a guest house to her Southold compound to accommodate visiting friends and to protect both her privacy and her schedule for her own work. Her major concern, however, was a lawsuit she had initiated against Sidney Janis, the dealer who occupied a portion of the same floor as the Betty Parsons Gallery. Betty, who leased the entire floor, chose earlier to sublet half of the space to Janis in order to cut costs. As the lease became due for renegotiation, Sidney Janis—whether, as Betty claimed, by subterfuge or as Janis claimed, at the owner's behest—acquired the lease and notified Betty that she would have to move.

"Sidney Janis did this unspeakable thing to me. How would I know that new leases had to be settled before old leases were used up? I didn't. I thought I would *renew* that lease—it was *my* space; I had rented it to Sidney Janis. I hadn't given it to him. My gallery was there first," Betty argued. "And it was known in *that* space. I was in that space—The Mortimer Brandt Gallery, you know—even before my gallery was there. Janis," Betty opined, "went sneaking off behind my back and talked to the landlord. I don't know what kind of promises he made. I don't know how much money he offered.

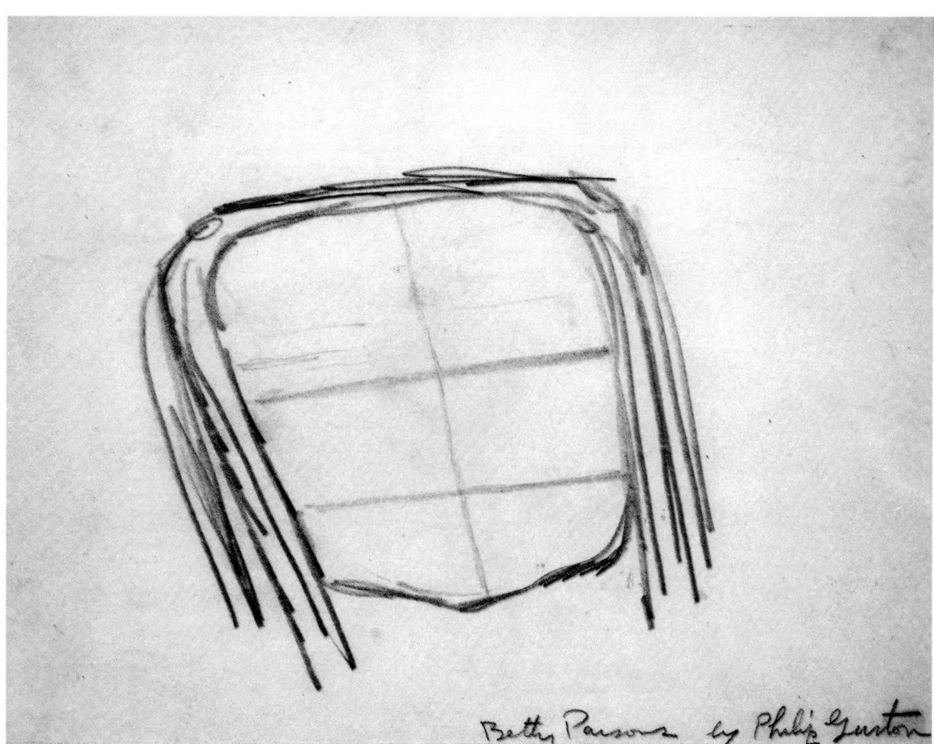

Philip Guston, *Portrait of Betty*, date unknown. Private collection, New York

I just know that he *stole* my lease. A gentleman," she added, "even if the law allowed, would not *do* such a thing. And I've always hated Sidney Janis and I've always thought that he had very, very bad morals."[2]

When the court hearing was postponed, after an emotionally charged period of waiting, Betty was disgusted: "I was sick and tired of it all. I couldn't stand another minute of it. I had to get away." Taking her own advice, she spent the remainder of the summer traveling and visiting friends: the Porters in Santa Fe; to Santa Barbara to see an exhibition of Clyfford Still's work; Marie Taylor in Saint Louis.

In November 1962, soon after she reopened the gallery (still in the contested space) for the fall season, *Time* carried an article about the state of contemporary art and, ironically, directed attention toward both Betty and Janis without alluding to their pitched battle. A picture of Betty Parsons in her gallery with works by Minoru Kawabata, Ellsworth Kelly, Kenzo Okada, Seymour Lipton, and Pousette-Dart, was captioned: "Betty Parsons ... one of the first to champion postwar abstract art, presides over barnlike gallery on East 57th Street." The article, entitled "The Modernists," stated:

> *More than any other dealer, Betty Parsons is credited with bringing abstract art to its present status. She opened in 1946 with about 13 artists, including the even then venerable Hans Hofmann and Ad Reinhardt. She gave one-man shows to Mark Rothko, Jackson Pollock, Clyfford Still and Barnett Newman.*

Commenting on initial public indifference, even hostility, to the new work, *Time* reported the "unexpected boost" Betty received "her first year from a most unlikely source," and quoted Elsa Maxwell's titillating tip to "spend $100 or $150 for a picture by one of the younger American abstractionists (and maybe) ... eventually own a masterpiece." *Time* also revived Maxwell's by then famous quip, "Some dissenters scream, 'Hang the abstractionists!' I echo, 'Certainly, but why not on your walls?'"

Above, left: *Emily's Garden, Florida,* 1961

Above, right: Page from a sketchbook

The article continued:

> *Sidney Janis, the onetime shirt manufacturer who also turned to writing about art . . . is not known among his colleagues as a discoverer, but he has a good eye for properties that others have already started on their way. It was to Janis that Pollock finally went, and so did Gottlieb, Motherwell and Willem de Kooning. Last week Janis was the cause of a good deal of speculation with his big new show of 'pop art.'. . . Janis has apparently spotted a new bandwagon—but he did not discover pop art.*[3]

In Betty's judgment, the *Time* article "put Janis in his place. He *never* discovered anyone or anything. He took, took, took. He even took my gallery away from me."

During February 1963, Jock's handiwork resulted in Betty's showing her work in Miami while, with Jock's help, running a full schedule of exhibitions in the gallery, including works by Thomas George, Minoru Kawabata, Jesse Reichek, Marie Taylor, and Ruth Vollmer. The gallery sparkled with activity and Betty felt that she was gaining ground as an artist.

But the spring of 1963 heaped unhappiness on Betty: first, she lost the lawsuit against Janis and had to give up her gallery space at 15 East Fifty-seventh Street. Chafing beneath the defeat and feeling herself publicly humiliated, she faced a second defeat: Ellsworth Kelly decided, after a series of minor disagreements with Betty about insurance claims and commissions, to leave the gallery and seek more vigorous promotion of his work. At that time, Betty told him that he was free to go to any gallery he liked but that she would never speak to him if he chose Sidney Janis as his dealer. Ellsworth Kelly, one of Betty's prized artists and one she considered a personal friend of long standing, did just that: he joined Janis's stable. She was hurt and she was furious. (In later years, Betty and Kelly were reconciled, and again became good friends and traveling companions.)

Finally, she remarked the third loss in the privacy of her journal:

> *Thursday night, April 18, 1963: My most darling Friend, Strelsa van Scriver died of Cancer at the age of 48.*

Betty tucked Strelsa's mother's briefest possible note into the journal:

> *Dear Betty,*
> *George and I appreciate sincerely your expression of sympathy and the beautiful flowers.*
> *Ruth van Scriver.*

Turning the note over in her beringed and age-gnarled hand in 1980, Betty muttered, "Strelsa. I loved her and, of course, her parents and her awful brother hated me—just hated me. I think they hated Strelsa, too. This note," she said, waving Ruth van Scriver's letter before her visitor's eyes, "isn't that the coldest and stupidest thing you ever read? Some people are born dead and stay that way. Strelsa lived and Strelsa died."[4]

These several defeats cast Betty into gloom; she briefly considered closing her gallery and retiring to her studio on Long Island. Her friends and artists rallied to her side, however, and persuaded her to find new space and new energy to continue the gallery. The horrors of searching for affordable real estate kept Betty in a state of near agony. When the space was selected, Betty turned what might have been considered adversity into another token of triumph. "You see," she explained, "I was the first gallery to move across Fifth Avenue. I was a pioneer. Until I crossed Fifth Avenue, galleries were all on the *east* side. I opened up the *west* side."

In the early fall of 1963, as she opened her gallery in its new address, 24 West Fifty-seventh Street, Betty boldly asserted her ambition for her own work. Lawrence Alloway remembered "an amazing and painful lunch that Barney [Newman], Betty, and I had. Betty announced that the gallery, her own gallery, soon after she moved to its present quarters . . . was going to show her own work. She said, 'It had nothing to do with me. It's Jock's idea. I won't touch it.' Barney and I looked at each other and took her out to lunch and we forced her not to do it. She was furious, really mad. She hated to be opposed. And, then, a little while after that, she showed at Sachs and I think that was better."[5]

Jock Truman recalled the crisis somewhat differently. "Betty was so eager to show her work. She felt that she was being left out. Felt that she was an artist first and foremost, you see, and that no one really respected her work, that no one really understood her as an artist. She asked me if she should show in her own gallery and I didn't see why she shouldn't. But it was her idea. And it was her idea because she felt left out." Jock, learning of the lunch and sensing Betty's bitter disappointment, and knowing that she had had few opportunities to exhibit her work since the early shows at the Midtown, let fellow dealer Abe Sachs know that Betty wanted a Fifty-seventh Street gallery; Sachs telephoned Betty immediately to invite her into his stable and to set a date for an exhibition of her work. That exhibition in the Sachs gallery elicited reviews; works sold; Betty was pleased but not satisfied.

In the fall of 1963, honoring the tradition that she had made, she opened her new space with an Amlash sculpture show introduced by Barnett Newman. Her new space thus blessed by a reaffirmation of the timelessness of art, Betty showed new works by Hedda Sterne and a Christmas group show, which, like the showing of old works in new spaces, had become a tradition in the Betty Parsons Gallery.

Meanwhile, marking the opening of the new space, Lawrence Alloway wrote an article on Betty for *Vogue* magazine. The widely read piece established Betty's biography-for-public-consumption; she found the stuff of celebrity. Alloway told the success story, riches to riches, of an American aristocrat who, in her own words, "always managed to be in the right place at the right time." He praised Betty for daring to show artists "between fame and oblivion" as well as those "destined for success."

Alloway charted a typical week in Betty's life. In addition to hanging exhibitions and waiting for clients, he described Betty attending an opening at The Museum of Modern Art of *Americans 1963*, which included Ad Reinhardt as well as two former artists from the gallery, Chryssa and Richard Lindner; there, she talked with Dorothy Miller, curator of the exhibition, and courted some collectors. Alloway noted that "she lunched with Rosalind Constable, from Time-Life, and dined with a client for whom she had arranged the sale of a de Kooning." Midweek, Alloway followed Betty as she consumed a sandwich in the gallery for lunch and traveled to New Haven with Richard Pousette-Dart, one of her artists. There, Alloway reported, she attended a dinner for a hundred people at Yale University to celebrate the exhibition of two collections—those of Richard Brown Baker and Susan Morse Hilles, the backer of Section 11. At the dinner, Betty sat on the right of Andrew Ritchie, director of the Yale Art Gallery. Such social contacts, noted Alloway, are the means by "which paintings are sold and artists remembered," and they "arise from or are maintained by such a round, parade, or schedule."

Alloway described Betty's typical day in the gallery, where, on arriving, she wrote letters to the Milwaukee Art Center to request that institution to send a painting by Ellsworth Kelly, on loan for exhibition, to the San Francisco Museum of Art, for another exhibition. She wrote the Walker Art Center in Minneapolis to arrange substitution of one sculpture by Lyman Kipp for another in the São Paulo Biennale, that year being curated by the Walker. She also telephoned the Whitney Museum of American Art to determine attendance at the retrospective exhibition of works by Pousette-Dart. Satisfied that his work was attracting viewers, she had cause to telephone such collectors as Mrs. Albert List and Ben Heller to remind them of the show and to report its success. She also put in a call to Robert Hale in The American Department of The Metropolitan Museum of Art. She telephoned an architect about a sculpture and a sculptor about a possible architectural commission.

On this typical day, Betty decided she was too busy to keep a lunch date with an artist downtown so she invited him to bring his work to the gallery instead; he did and they shared a sandwich. In the early afternoon, *Saturday Review* art critic Katherine Kuh dropped in with a collector to see sculpture by one of the gallery artists. Adelyn Breeskin, formerly at the Baltimore Museum and now director of the Washington Gallery of Modern Art, telephoned to discuss changes in the choice of Ellsworth Kelly paintings in a show she was arranging called *The Formalists*. Betty made more telephone calls to the Whitney Museum, one concerning a Pousette-Dart purchase, one concerning the gift by an anonymous donor of a sculpture to the museum. Then she wrote to Adelyn Breeskin confirming the availability of the Kellys. She asked Jock to prepare a shipping invoice for a summer exhibition in New Mexico at the Roswell

Museum and another for an exhibition at Parke-Bernet's auction rooms arranged by the Art Dealers Association.

Toward the end of the day, Betty telephoned Hedda Sterne to discuss a symposium on art and industry at which Hedda was to speak. Bradley Walker Tomlin's brother and sister arrived in the gallery for the annual accounting of his sales.

Alloway's article spread Betty's fame outside the art world; after the appearance of the *Vogue* article around the country, she may have been the most widely recognized art dealer in America. From that time forward, regional publications often accorded her the treatment generally associated with a personality from the entertainment world.

Betty's fame, as she well knew, rode on her history of discovering artists who seemed outrageous and in championing them until time and taste proved her early sighting of talent correct. Richard Tuttle, a young artist who worked in the gallery as Betty's "busboy"—i.e., helping with the hanging of shows, crating and uncrating paintings and sculpture, and performing whatever tasks, menial or intellectual, were requested by Betty or by Jock Truman—soon amassed a body of related objects he had made that he wanted to see displayed together. In 1965 he requested permission from Betty to install his things in the gallery during the summer months when, by tradition, the gallery was closed. Betty agreed. Tuttle asked Betty to look at "his show." She did and, in the following season, Tuttle had his first one-man show in New York. Betty Parsons, now sixty-five, logged another discovery.

With Richard Tuttle's exhibition, Betty believed that she pointed up the gallery as she steered it beyond the tides and eddies of Abstract Expressionism's giants, who, in the middle sixties, were strongly challenged by younger artists and by new schools of art that sought attention or—as some would have it—by new "schools" of art that were cynically invented by critics who sought attention and fortune for themselves as much as for the artists they lauded. But Betty dismissed such arguments. Self-conscious now about her position as an avant-garde dealer and jealous of her role as discoverer, she was also aware that the challenges by younger artists and by new critics were often directed at her and her gallery. Rising to the competition, Betty kept her eyes and gallery open to manifestations of "the new spirit," including Minimalism and Conceptualism. She had, after all, always included in the gallery a berth for hard-edge abstraction, a precursor if not antecedent, of Minimalism and Conceptualism and, without shifting aesthetic positions, she regarded both Minimalism and Conceptualism as further reductions in ingredients, a fated and proper progression of more implied by less—often with spoken or written reference to the writings of Clement Greenberg.

Betty saw the Minimalists as an extension of a tradition that she appreciated in the works of such gallery old hands as Calvert Coggeshall, Jack Youngerman, and Ruth Vollmer. Each artist, in his or her own way, pushed his imagery toward ultimate ends, toward logical conclusions that escaped logic to burgeon into a realm of romanticized rationality that neatly illustrated for Betty her own blend of Eastern mysticism and Victorian poesy.

Betty loved artists, however, more than she loved ideas about art; moreover, she often loved and defended odd works of art with as much determination as she lavished on masterpieces, and by the same token, she sometimes opened her eyes to artists who might otherwise have been ignored. Two such artists, Emil Hess and Thomas Stokes, showed in the gallery during this period.

Emil Hess attracted attention in the early fifties with his toylike wooden sculptures. "Everyone liked those things," Betty reminisced, "and they were fascinating.

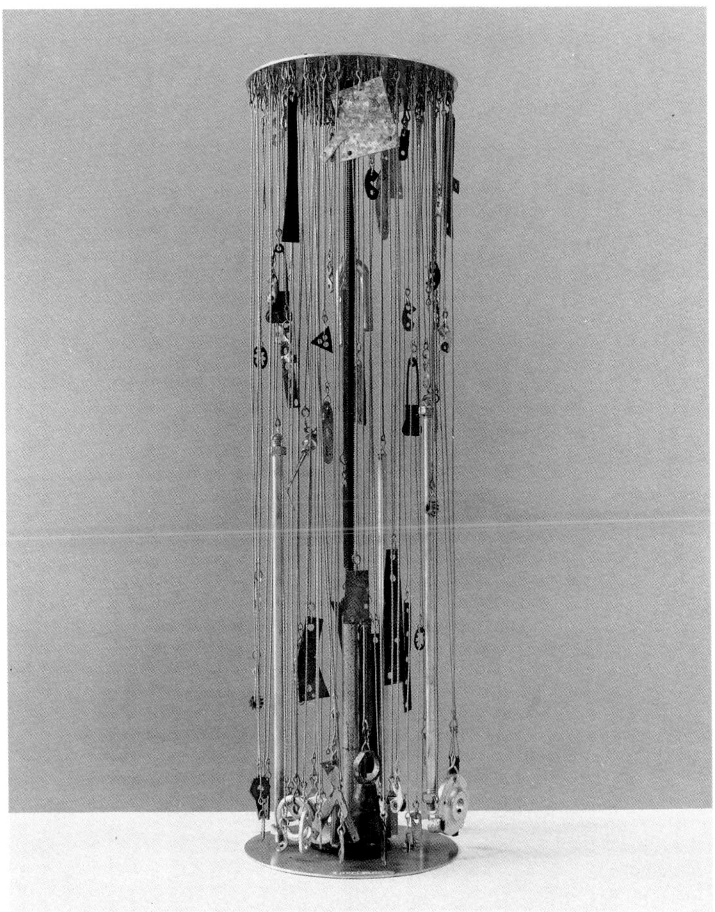

Emil Hess, *Silver Tunes*, 1968

But Hess didn't like people liking them. He was after the new, you see, and it worried him that his work might be popular. But he was—and is—an artist." In 1968, after years of hibernation, Hess reappeared with columns composed of suspended metal particles that, when jiggled, responded with agreeable albeit not very musical plinking and tinkling sounds. Betty poked them into song; she peered closely at the assorted screws, bolts, metal cuttings, chains, and wires of which they were made.

While others might have viewed Hess's works as some personal form of Constructivism, or, if they seemed too romantic for that, as an eccentric treatment of kinetic sculpture, Betty refused to label it, insisting that Hess's work, like the work of any other serious artist, dwelt outside labels. "Look," she argued, "you can name something but that doesn't *explain* it. Nothing explains it. You have to get to know it just as it is. Just as if it were a real person."

Betty expressed affection, too, for the softly poetic work of Thomas Stokes. "It's absolutely beautiful," she urged a gallery visitor to acknowledge. The paintings on view, thinly washed with luminous colors, contained barely visible suggestions of shapes within shapes within shapes—all only slightly defined by delicate modulations of color. The atmospheric nature of the work appealed to Betty, who had cherished the gentler possibilities of abstraction along with the more accepted and more applauded macho works of Abstract Expressionism; her vision encompassed both intellectual and expressive works. "There are many voices to be heard," Betty explained, "and Tommy's is pure poetry." She cared only that an artist *have* a voice, a particular and singular and truthful voice.

Toko Shinoda, *#4*

Betty believed that underneath the stylistic differences of East and West a common thread of spirituality awaited discovery. Her attraction to Eastern sensibilities grew in the presence of her Oriental artists—Okada, Kawabata, and Shinoda. Of all of them, Toko Shinoda remained the most rooted in the traditions of the East. Her traditional references and techniques yielded compositions including calligraphic elements in ink, areas of silver leaf and white paint on Sumi grounds. Working in large, wet flowing strokes, Shinoda covered vast spaces—acknowledging her familiarity and comfort with Abstract Expressionism, but arriving on different shores. Instead of excitement, she offered quietude; instead of fragmentation, synthesis; instead of flirtations with chaos and personal expression, order and control.

When asked to comment on the works, Betty held out a clenched fist which, slowly, she opened palm upward. "They give and they receive," she replied.

Minoru Kawabata's shows cheered Betty regardless of her mood or the weather. Working on a theme, a simple shape or fragment of a shape, Kawabata produced paintings that explored the possibilities of changing color and mutable shapes. In the winter of 1969, for instance, as if to dispel slush and murk, Kawabata showed vibrant high-key paintings of arching shapes held on a white ground; sometimes the arches interacted and appeared to catch and bounce the color that crossed their paths. Sometimes they rested quietly, surrounded by sparkling color. "When I come in this gallery," Betty said, "I can feel flowers come up all over the world." When others expressed similar happy sensations, she was pleased, a bit smug. "I've always told

Ruth Vollmer, *Spherical Tetrahedron,* 1969. Courtesy Jack Tilton Gallery, New York

them that Kawabata has the power of the spirit. He has the spirit of the East and the power of the West. He can turn on lights no one has ever seen before."

Betty explained her views about order, about mysteries that lay beneath the surface of experience, to cosmopolitan Ruth Vollmer, who agreed with her. Ruth had learned the rudiments of clay sculpture in her native Germany before fleeing with her husband to escape Hitler's persecution of the Jews. Settled in the United States at a time when the art world was rousing to the works of other Europeans—de Kooning, Albers, Hofmann, among them—Vollmer began to study art again and to read art magazines and to frequent galleries. She soon pared down her gallery list to the few that showed contemporary—largely abstract—works; among these, she especially admired the shows at the Betty Parsons Gallery.

When Betty and Ruth met in the gallery, they found conversation easy; they agreed on everything important. Soon Betty was a regular guest at the Vollmers' dinner parties in their Central Park West apartment. There, amid furniture handmade by Bauhaus craftsmen, Ruth gathered artists, scientists, students, medical doctors, and musicians to talk about politics, art, science, or archaeology. With excellent food and fine wines, the evenings extended into the morning hours; arguments started at one dinner party were concluded at another; friendships developed; books and addresses were exchanged.

In the Vollmer apartment, Betty saw small pieces of ancient Greek and Cycladic sculpture sharing space with extensive and sagging shelves of books in many languages and small works by Grosz, Klee, and other artists Ruth and Hermann had known in Europe. She saw framed music manuscripts by Bach and Mozart and stacks of recent issues of scientific journals and monographs on classical archaeology.

Ruth's squarish studio, at the end of a small octagonal-tiled corridor with rows of opaque-glass-and-metal doors with chipping black lettering, was in the old S. Klein building on Union Square. An immense table held her tools and materials, her works in progress and her bucket of soapy water for making soap bubbles on copper forms that she constructed. When Betty first visited the studio, she sat with her back to a sunny window, ate a picnic lunch that Ruth had prepared, and played with the soap-bubble apparatus.

"Ruth Vollmer," she told a friend, "understands science. She knows *why* soap bubbles happen. And she knows about the ancient world as well. She is both old and modern."

Ruth showed her work first in Section 11 but, after its closing, remained in the Betty Parsons stable. Ruth's show in 1968 consisted of work compressed into simple, pure shapes that she believed illustrative of mathematical principles. Moving from clay to bronze and now including spun aluminum, Ruth usually worked on a small scale. An adult hand could rest comfortably on one of Vollmer's spheres. But recently fascinated with large-scale sculpture, she produced two spun aluminum pieces, one a waist-high piece that rocked at the gentlest touch on its well-conceived point of balance, the other a piece filled with polyurethane and designed to float and to be seen surrounded by water.

Ruth sniffed the beginnings of Conceptualism and Minimalism on the winds of the art world at about the same time that Betty did, and she was an immediate convert. She believed Minimalism to be based on mathematical precision and concept and, with Betty's blessing, began to search for and use new materials with a highly technological and nonart quality—plastics, screening, spun aluminum. Ruth made endless drawings on graph paper, measuring dimensions and plotting curves with protractor and 4H pencils. Both Ruth and Betty found the amplitude of the new work wondrous.

As Betty trusted Ruth Vollmer to direct her toward books, ideas about science and art, and art of the ancient world that corroborated her belief in the timelessness of art, she looked to Alexander Liberman to open a path for her in the sophisticated and worldly spheres of New York and Europe. Liberman's worldliness intrigued Betty almost as much as his protean energies. She was grateful, too, for Liberman's powerful support of the gallery.

In the fifties, affected strongly by the force and creativity of the artists in Betty's gallery, Liberman, under the auspices of *Vogue,* hosted a luncheon party-roundtable discussion with the artists and Betty. The meeting, photographed and recorded in *Vogue,* according to Betty, "helped put over the gallery. It helped me get the word to people. It helped the artists. People thought, well, if it's in *Vogue,* you see, it had to be all right. And a lot of people started coming to the gallery to see things that were approved by *Vogue.* That's what I call the fashion group. But, after a few shows, a lot of people were on the beam, too, and they came back because they knew something terribly important was happening in my gallery. Alex was like that. He knew what was important—what was going to be important. And that's why he has that important job at *Vogue* magazine."

During the sixties, Alexander Liberman's astonishing rate of production fascinated Betty. "I don't believe he sleeps," she confided. "I've never seen such energy. It comes from the creative. He's very creative." In the winter of 1969, Liberman showed a series of paintings in which a dominant color was set resonating by the position of contrasting slashes of color in a triangular motif. Each of Liberman's shows with Betty had explored another dimension, another area of art; sometimes lyrical, sometimes

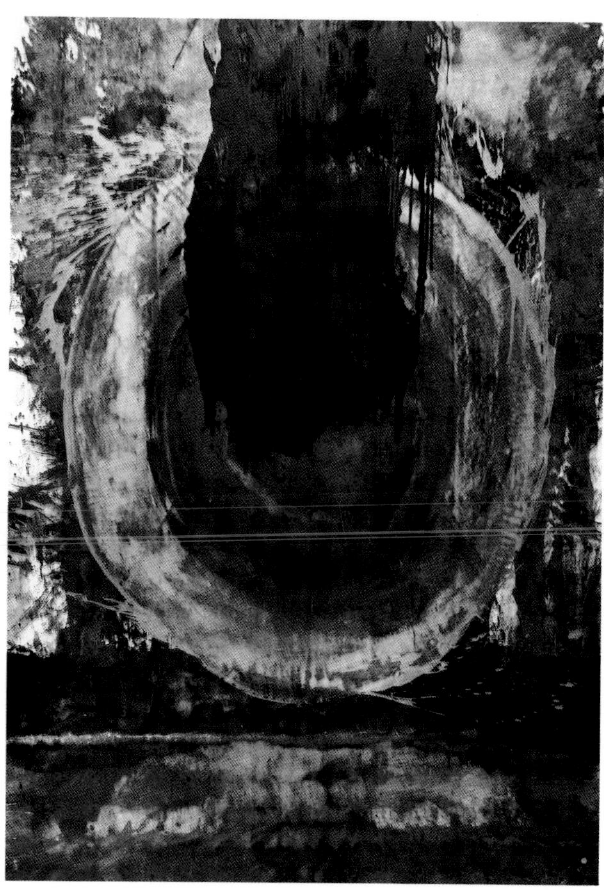

Alexander Liberman, *Black into Pink,* 1964

powerful and almost strident, sometimes cool and hard-edged. "He's very clever," Betty said. "I call him the Russian Fox. He's very sly and very quick and very Russian. He has perfect taste—perfect taste in wine and food, in clothes and places; he knows the world and he knows everyone in the world. He is also an important artist."

In the sixties, as Betty's reputation as the most daring art dealer in the post-World War Two era spread, word got around, too, that Betty Parsons had been collecting art all the years that she was running one of the most interesting galleries in New York. In interviews and in social situations, Betty began to talk about "my collection." Indeed, she owned many works, some of them by major artists; but for a variety of reasons, she had never exercised the avidity or discipline that propels many collectors.

Between 1942 and 1968, she bought a few works from shows she sponsored, occasionally bought something directly from an artist she knew, and even bought (rarely) a piece from another dealer. She amassed her large collection of paintings, drawings, and sculpture less through her modest purchases, however, than from gifts from or trades with artists.

In March 1968, Finch College mounted an exhibition of Betty's collection and her friend Rosalind Constable reviewed it for *Art News*. Summarizing the already well-rehearsed details of Betty's life in that article, Rosalind Constable catalogued critically the major holdings in the collection: an untitled Gottlieb collage that she bought from that artist's first show at the Wakefield Gallery; two watercolor paintings by Wols from the same period, acquired for $55; paintings by Hans Hofmann, Mark Rothko, Clyfford Still, and Jackson Pollock given to Betty by the artists; a few pictures that she accepted as payment for artists' debts owed to the gallery; some parting gifts from

Saint-Jean-Cap-Ferrat, 1968

artists leaving the gallery (Hofmann, Kelly); some pieces that she bought in unusual circumstances—de Kooning's *Still Life* purchased for "under $100" from his dealer, Charles Egan; Robert Motherwell's *Western Figure* bought from a client for $200 in 1950; and a Cornell box that she bought in 1956 from a visitor off the street who asked $150 for it.

Betty tried several times to interest The Katinkas in staking her to some purchases; she succeeded once, in 1952, when both Mark Rothko and Clyfford Still needed cash, and she managed to borrow $5,000 from Dumpy with which to purchase works from them. She bought a large Barnett Newman in 1959, paying more for it than she had paid for any other single work of art in her collection—$1,500, according to Rosalind Constable but, according to a letter to *Art News* from Barnett Newman, Betty paid $3,000. Newman added, "In 1959, $3,000 was, to coin a phrase, a lot of coin or as they say today, a lot of bread. However, had the painting been bought in 1949 when it was first shown, it could have been bought for a song."[6]

Bradley Walker Tomlin, Ad Reinhardt, and Kenzo Okada gave major works to Betty. Other gifts, however, were not of the same caliber. As Betty traveled about the country judging exhibitions, attending openings of exhibitions of her own or her artists' works, she attracted gifts ranging from first-rate works by first-rate but unknown artists to ill-made and thuggishly conceived junk. She kept it all, hanging the important beside the trivial in the same style that she listed in her travel logs insignificant information beside passionately felt observations.

When hard up for money to pay the gallery's bills or to maintain her studio, she sold a few of the appreciated works and they fetched prices that astonished her. "Just think," she mused, "how rich I would be if I could have bought out the shows of those early artists in my gallery. Nobody wanted them. Nobody appreciated their work. I tried like hell to get everybody I knew to buy Pollock and Still and Barney. And I wanted to buy them. And if I had bought them, they would have stayed in my gallery. But I never had any money and they needed money."

After the initial showing at Finch College of the entire unedited Betty Parsons collection in 1968, portions of it would be shown in other museums and galleries, contributing to Betty's reputation as a passionate and important collector. So what if the collection, looked at critically, was uneven? Rosalind Constable met the critics head on at the conclusion of her article:

The Betty Parsons Gallery is largely an anthology of all the artists she has ever shown. It is also a survey of 25 years of contemporary art. Like all anthologies, it can be faulted by critics inclined to look for mediocrities and to take the presence of masterpieces for granted. Like all anthologists, Betty Parsons reserves the right of personal taste—and it is precisely in the personal taste of the anthologist that the main interest lies. Above all, she has had the courage (although she does not think of it as courage) to show her entire collection—marvels and mediocrities, oddities and all.[7]

Betty, now in her late sixties, continued to travel in the summers and to see friends throughout the year in New York and on Long Island. Each summer she visited Adge Baker; often she went on to the Continent to see William Congdon or other friends. In 1968, while attending the Biennale in Venice, a cablegram from Jock shattered her festive mode with the "terrible news of Paul Feeley's death on Sunday, June 12." Feeley, an artist who taught at Bennington College and who had shown with Betty for several years, delighted her, as Barney had, with his work and with his talk. Never comfortable with writing, Betty drafted a condolence letter to Feeley's wife, Helen, in her journal:

Dear Helen,
What can I say? All of my sympathy. He carried a torch that helped us; it will last and last. I will always miss him and his extraordinary creative affirmations. Hope to see you soon. Will be back in New York July 7 or 8. My love to your children—Betty.

Immediately upon her return to New York, Betty had dinner with the Alloways and Bill Rayner, reported on her travels and, after a few days in the city, fled to her studio on Long Island to work on her own paintings and wooden sculpture. After a week's rest there, Betty and Jock Truman (who had bought a summer house near Betty's on Long Island) caught the ferry to New London, lunched in Hartford, and then drove to Bennington to visit Helen Feeley and the Alloways, who were also there.

Over the next few days, Betty and Jock examined Paul Feeley's paintings, making an inventory, assessing value, and documenting dimensions and conditions for the settlement of his estate. "It was sad work," Betty declared, "because he was really on to something. He was such a great artist and I never was able to really put him over. If he had lived longer, I think he would have been understood better."

The next fall, after a visit to Russia with Aline Porter, Betty resumed her New York schedule. She and Agnes Martin visited Bennington early in November for a party with Helen Feeley and an exhibition of Paul Feeley's work at Bennington College. On the following day, Betty attended the opening of the Tony Smith exhibition at the Wadsworth Atheneum in Hartford. She wrote in her journal:

"Tony Smith show is terrific. Monumental. Very serious with reach to the forces. Angels and demons keep the peace. May it see the sun."

The following day, looking again at Smith's works, Betty called them "Giants in the light of day," and wrote of them:

Photograph of Paul Feeley, 1960s

The sky looked down
and all around
The earth was under
Something grand
it was not rocks
It was not sand,
it was the scale
Upon the land,
That reached the summit
Of the light
And tossed the day
Upon the night.

In December, Betty returned to Bennington College for the opening of a show of her work. The students "loved my work," Betty boasted, "and asked me every kind of question about the creative, the cosmic forces, the expanding universe." She added, "I think I told them some things they wouldn't hear from professors."

If Betty loved her own work, she also loved that of other artists. At a December exhibition of Ad Reinhardt's work, Betty wrote:

The rooms opened to another shore
between the waves of night,
where darkness ever folds itself
within the waves of light

Betty, at sixty-eight, scoffed at any suggestion—generally tendered timidly—that she retire or turn the major management of her gallery over to Jock Truman. The Betty Parsons Gallery, whether intended or not, was an extension of herself. She had not achieved sufficient recognition as an artist, however, to satisfy her ambition in that arena. Did she resent the time that she had given to other artists, the energies that she had invested in establishing other careers and building other reputations, the time she had taken away from her own painting and sculpture to attend to the needs of other artists? Perhaps. She admitted in retrospect: "I've never had enough time, you see, to paint. And I think I turned to painting—I was a sculptor first—because it took less time."

If Betty now pressed her case as an artist with increasing urgency and effectiveness, Jock Truman openly functioned in the Betty Parsons Gallery as a special agent for Betty Parsons as an artist. He directed attention toward her work in a way that she could not do for herself, responding to clients' inquiries about gallery artists and, simultaneously, mentioning Betty's new work or providing opportunity for examples of Betty's work—now often in the gallery and easily visible—to be seen in passing. As curators and museum directors visited the gallery to select works for shows, they might conclude in the course of a conversation with Jock that an exhibition of work by Betty Parsons would adorn handsomely an exhibition schedule in the making.

Jack Tilton,[8] a gallery busboy who became Betty's assistant when Jock Truman left, believes that, in the late sixties and through the seventies, Betty only wanted to handle young, unknown artists—"discoveries"—and, when they were established, she wanted them to move on to other galleries. She wanted no possibility of being overshadowed by giants; she no longer accepted the eclipse as an artist that she had suffered during the years that The Four Horsemen (as she often called Pollock, Still, Newman, and Rothko) galloped free.

After twenty years of being known primarily as a dealer, Betty wanted to keep that crown and gain recognition as an artist in her own right. She was delighted, therefore, when, in the catalogue for her 1968 exhibition at the Whitechapel Gallery in London, Brian Robertson and Lawrence Alloway praised her as both dealer and artist. Robertson, observing that the sixty-eight-year-old Betty had been working as an artist for forty years, reminded readers that, since 1941, she had also run a gallery in New York, "giving up the greater part of her energy and certainly the whole of her time to the demands of other artists ... [for whom she has been] a benevolent Robin Hood going through the thinly disguised motions of a dealer on behalf of her fellow artists."

In the same catalogue, Lawrence Alloway contributed an essay, "The Art of Betty Parsons," in which he referred to her sketchbooks, which mingled drawings with diary entries

> *and aphorisms and quotations in ways that give insight into her temperament and way of working... [her] verbal bits occur among pencil and pen sketches of people, pets, and gardens, among watercolors of flowers and architecture... [and] warm-tinted crayon and watercolor drawings, which have a tendency towards wild linear ripples...."*
>
> *Most of Betty's paintings, extended from such sketches, carry references to season, climate, time, local color.... The subjects of her earlier works, which Betty retains, are basically landscape.... She has always drawn the figure and, frequently, she allows curves and sudden notches of line to translate vivid poses into Zadkinesque forms.*

The Whitechapel Gallery exhibition fixed her fame, Betty thought, as both dealer and artist; her two lives were no longer separated in the public mind. She agreed with Jock: she was a star.

"Yes," Betty mused, "I think the sixties gave me a lot. I lost friends. I had troubles. I didn't have enough time for my own work. But, finally, it seemed that I was showing my work. And, you know, they were all liking it very much. I sold some pieces—quite a few, really—and a lot of people knew that I was an artist. A serious one."

Calvert Coggeshall, Betty, and Jack Tilton, Newcastle, Maine, 1977

THE GALLERY IN THE SEVENTIES

Barnett Newman's death on July 4, 1970, robbed Betty of a major confidant, a source of inspiration and cheer, and an intellectual anchor for the gallery. Although Barney's influence with Betty and on the gallery's roster had diminished in recent years, as Betty had gained confidence in herself, Barney had advised and influenced Betty more than any other individual on matters pertaining to the gallery—its operation, artists to be shown, trends and attitudes to be anticipated or pursued and shaped. Moreover, Barney had been Betty's friend and ally. "You know how much I loved Barney and how important he was," she exclaimed, grief still apparent in her face and voice ten years after his death. "Barney was a complete artist, a complete individual. He was a Renaissance man. He could do anything, think anything. God, what a force he was. A true friend."

In the seventies, the Betty Parsons Gallery, institutionalized in the legends of the contemporary art world, occupied the center of a magnetic field; the epicenter, Betty herself. If the gallery had a cohering factor, it may have been simply friendship: by the seventies, many of the artists were friends with each other; virtually all of the artists in Betty's gallery considered her a friend.

Betty, beyond the age of retirement for regular people in regular jobs, faced the seventies with absolute trust in her vision and her skills in operating the gallery. If the art world had changed—and all evidence suggests that it had done so on a dramatic scale—Betty took little heed of the forces changing the business of art dealing; she continued to select artists, hang exhibitions, and generally run the gallery to suit her own largely unexamined tastes and inclinations.

In her later years, two factors influenced the way in which Betty looked at paintings, looked for art: first, with the deaths of the original Katinkas, she was lonely and turned in part for friendship to artists and hangers-on who glimpsed her fame and identified themselves, in whatever manner available and to whatever public gave credence, with Betty; second, she came to believe that objects which elicited outrage and shock from a viewer had intrinsic merit. As a consequence, the gallery was increasingly influenced by these two forces. Her friends became her artists too often, though, perhaps as a result of the energy generated earlier, artists of major talent still sought her out and worked to become her friends. And as the audience for contemporary art became more sophisticated and larger, she took an increasingly antiestablishment stance.

In 1971, *Arts Magazine* invited her to make a statement about her gallery; she responded:

> *I opened a gallery with my name in 1946. The first exhibition was of Northwest Coast Indian art and the announcement had a foreword written by Barnett Newman.*

Betty having tea at the edge of Long Island Sound, 1978

I was trying to convey the freedom of the creative world by showing some of the great innovators of our period. Creative freedom has given my gallery its continuity. . . .

The critics were very antagonistic and it was the '60s before their receptivity began to change. A few enlightened collectors and the Museum of Modern Art in particular gave us tremendous support. But it was the artists who believed in and helped one another. They helped one another hang shows. . . .

From the first, I was captivated by the expanding world these painters were concerned with, so different from the world-within-walls that concerned the European artists. What these painters really had was a cosmic sense of the integrity and bigness of life.

Gradually, the artists began to be seduced by money and were more interested in values other than the ones for which they had been fighting. In that connection, I always think of what Barnett Newman said to me: "It is most important to struggle to dignify the work."

As a dealer, I have never been interested in trends, fashions, or styles. As I begin the third decade of my gallery, I realize that I have always used my intuition rather than my judgment.

The gallery has survived because there was a gradual realization in America on the part of the museums and collectors of the artist's importance. . . . I feel the purpose of the gallery was always to find a fresh outlook on the world. I tried to make the space as pure as possible so only the picture dominated. The gallery was the first to be painted white and the first to show really big pictures when Pollock broke away from easel painting. The importance of the gallery was the importance of its artists.

My aim was always to find the most creative spirit of the period. I don't care whether I have babies or giants but there has to be a creative note. I want to follow what each man has to say on his own. I am not looking for the one artist of the one painting or the one style.

The future of the creative galleries looks very dim as the hardboiled, well-endowed galleries are taking over, turning art into merchandise. But I hope there will always be a place for the creative artist.[1]

Certain artists gave the gallery continuity over a period of years and affirmed for Betty that she—and, thus, the gallery—had a point of view. Other artists furthered the reputation of the gallery as experimental, daring.

Minoru Kawabata belonged to the long-lived segment of the roster. Although he was never highly acclaimed by critics or widely appreciated by the public, Betty believed Kawabata possessed unusual vision and vigor. Her conversations with Minoru Kawabata consisted of brief and simple phrases, occasional sentences, and much near-to-dancing physical language. Before his work, as before that by Okada, Betty often smiled extravagantly—a child's drawing of a lipsticked smile cutting across her face—and nodded approval; she swayed, hugging herself or throwing her arms wide apart as if to embrace the universe. "Yes, yes, yes," she muttered. Both Okada and Kawabata responded with sinewy bows and broad smiles, with head-nodding and handshakes. English—or a combination of English and whatever other language (in Betty's case, it was sometimes French) came to tongue—served to fix a workable communication between East and West.

Once asked if she had a particular predilection for Oriental artists—after all, she showed Okada, Kawabata, and Shinoda—Betty thought about it as if for the first time, "Art has no country," she replied. "Of course, the Orient is more attuned to things of the spirit than we are. And these artists all have that in common. They are all artists of the spirit." Pointing to Kawabata's paintings, she said, "What can you say about these pictures? There's nothing to say. They say it all. I hear the winds of the spirit in my eyes."

Henry Pearson, in a thoroughly Western manner, also provided continuity in the gallery's roster. He came to Betty's gallery through her friend Muriel Oaks in California. As a young serviceman stationed in California in the forties, Pearson knew Muriel Oaks, one of the original Katinkas, who took Pearson into her life, fed him quantities of precious rationed red meat, included him in parties with her famous and near-famous Hollywood friends, and organized his life to the degree that he would allow it. "She was a dish," he recalled, "a really gorgeous woman. And she was warm and kind and knew everybody. Her house was open to anyone—to Angela Lansbury dashing in wearing blue jeans or to a more established star who wanted to discuss marital problems; she gave lavish and wonderfully easy parties. And I went to them often. When she found out that I was an artist," he continued, "and on my way to New York as soon as the war ended, she said, 'You must look up my good friend Betty Parsons.'" Pearson had read about the American Abstract Expressionists and about the Betty Parsons Gallery; from a distance, he admired Betty Parsons and knew more than Muriel about the magnitude of her influence. But he thought it unlikely that he would ever have the courage to approach Betty in her gallery and ask that she look at his paintings.

In time, however, he found himself in New York and established in a midtown studio. While making his regular reconnaissance of the galleries, he went to the Betty Parsons Gallery where Betty was sitting behind her makeshift desk reading. She looked up and smiled; he identified himself. "Oh," she said, "I've been expecting you. What took you so long? Muriel said you would be here much earlier."

With that, a friendship began, and shortly after that meeting, Henry Pearson began to show with the gallery and to invite Betty regularly to dinner at his studio.

Pearson's highly competent, often quiet work aroused no great enmity from viewers. Those who liked it, liked it precisely for its subtle and gentle mien. "His work," Betty observed, "is free as air, full of despair. Everywhere, everywhere and very bare: it cares. Why stare?" As she chanted her spontaneous verse about Pearson, she smiled and punctuated the rhymes by slicing the air with her hand; finishing, she made a mock bow and laughed. "These are wonderful, wonderful pieces," she said.

During the seventies, Cleve Gray also figured prominently in the gallery's schedule of exhibitions. By the seventies, known both as a writer and as an artist, Cleve undertook a series of sculptures that, for Betty, disclosed another dimension of his protean talents. "Cleve is very, very intelligent. In fact," Betty confided, "he is *too* intelligent. For a long time he wanted to show with me and I wouldn't show him because I thought his paintings were too intellectual, too much about the past. Then when he caught on to the life of the abstract world and his paintings became powerful and free, I thought he had his own voice. And I showed him."

Cleve developed his paintings in series—all variations of an image or an idea, not an uncommon practice among post–World War Two American painters. For Cleve, this convention provided an exercise ring for his considerable analytical intelligence: each painting took a position, and next to it, another painting refined or contradicted or explicated the essential ingredient. In the seventies, he worked with vertical "figures" against or within bands of color, at once a play on the tensions of horizontal-vertical juxtapositions and on the concept of figure-field in the psychology of perception.

"Look, just look at these things," Betty exclaimed, "They're mysterious and powerful. This is Cleve's best work." It was work that made Betty happy enough to dance, and indeed, she jigged around the gallery, moving her body to the imagined music of the works. "You know, I've never been able to put Cleve over," she whispered conspiratorially—despite evidence that, in fact, Cleve Gray was well recognized as an artist and that his works resided in major collections as a result, at least in part, of having been associated with the Betty Parsons Gallery.

She continued, "God knows I've tried. I think there is a lot of prejudice against him in the art world because he's rich and he went to Princeton and he writes books. He's not the way artists are supposed to be. And in this world you cannot be different. But because he's different doesn't mean that he isn't good. He *is* good; look at this work." And she spun round looking at the work before adding, "Museum directors don't know anything about art at all and they don't care. They are only interested in raising money and in getting grants. They aren't interested in art at all. The only ones who ever cared a damn about art—Sweeney and Barr and Goodrich[2]—but, I didn't often agree with Goodrich, I just knew that he cared about art. He cared about art of the past and of the academy. But Sweeney and Barr, both of them, they had their eyes on the future. Such brilliant men. And they liked artists. That's the key, you see. You have to like artists. I've always been mad for artists. I don't give a damn for bankers and businessmen. But, hell, I *am* an artist."

In her blind-to-evidence damnation of the system, Betty insisted that Paul Feeley was another artist whose work had not gained proper appreciation. In an effort to put his achievement in the context of twentieth-century American art, Betty assembled a collection of watercolor paintings done by Feeley in the ten years before his death. While Feeley was known for his cloverleaf or club-motif and for his symmetrical repetition of this image, his watercolors revealed a questing, uncertain side. Whether in response to the spontaneous nature of the watercolor paint or as a consequence of a conscious decision, Feeley's watercolors derived from a freer fashion of working and an avoidance of his characteristic serial use of his motif. Instead, he played with imagery, incorporating bits of observed nature—lobster claws or leaves—with notations about geometry.

Cleve Gray, *Hawaii #1*, 1970

"You see," Betty explained, "everyone thinks Paul Feeley did just one or two things. They say he lacks range. That's not true. He had great discipline and he included his whole world of ideas in these very disciplined paintings. The watercolors, you see, show his mind working. He was always involved with painting—the way that I am always involved in painting—even when he wasn't thinking. He was an artist and everything he saw or thought became art. This show proves that."

Betty also thought Calvert Coggeshall—"Coggie"—underappreciated—due to her shortcomings. He began showing with her in 1951; he helped her construct the interior for her gallery on West Fifty-seventh Street; she visited him often in Maine. Coggie, like Okada, had not received the recognition from museums that Betty felt he deserved.

"They think he's like Rothko and they think only one artist can paint one thing," Betty explained. "But a lot of artists can paint simple shapes and they can all be different. Art is big enough for many artists. Art is as big as the universe. And Coggie paints about the universe. That's why he reminds people of Rothko. Both of them, I always say, paint light and air, paint above the horizon."

Betty's loyalty to friends extended, in at least one instance, to their children as well. Stephen Porter, Aline's son, showed his very playful sculpture at the Betty Parsons Gallery. Young, well-educated, and intelligent, Stephen Porter produced sculpture reflecting his considerable knowledge of structure and of basic physical principles, but overall, he showed sculpture that made play an essential ingredient of its production and its apprehension. Working with modules, exploring the relationships of sides to sides, edges to edges, he allowed a variety of sequences to alter the rhythm and overall disposition of the works. Apparently enchanted with the myriad transmutations of form possible, Stephen Porter played with both the simple and the complicated; with the yields of both analysis-deduction and synthesis-comprehension: he used sculptural elements to win a private game of possibility, chance, and inevitability. Betty quickly shared his fascination for the mutability of form and for the richness of textural surfaces possible within the confines of metal.

Often working with very simple shapes, fat horseshoes or U shapes, Porter suggested the particular pattern for deployment of the several pieces comprising a work. Viewers were encouraged to alter, to rearrange, and to witness the role of change in the extending pageant of possibilities. Whether moving the U's about or regrouping a series of triangular forms, the viewer thus engaged with the physical being of the work and therefore in collaboration with the artist, and sensed the power of possibility, of organization, and of system and sequence.

Porter's work fueled Betty's view of order. "Nothing is accidental. Look at these. They're like the basic atoms—the first grains—of the universe. From these pieces you could build a whole new universe." She expected evidence of awe from visitors and became exasperated if, as was sometimes the case, someone shrugged off the work as mere examples taken from the pages of a loopy geometry book.

"This is serious work," she said, "These are like the great primitive pieces. These pieces know everything about order. And," she pressed her point, "all art is playful. Play is the doorway to art. Creativity is play. Play is seriousness let free."

If artists who were old friends provided coherence for one aspect of the gallery, Betty's determination to extend her reputation as a discoverer furnished another ongoing theme. She discovered Allan Hacklin, whose earlier shows had consisted of paintings that were mostly all white or white only slightly broken by hints of other colors. With those works Hacklin had convinced Betty of his ability to push the limits of perception, to preempt attention with modest, highly controlled modulations of color. Now, conversely, he showed the opposite side of the same imagery: his new paintings were mostly black or, if not completely black, of deeply saturated and close-keyed hues as dark as night; at the edges of these canvases—their surfaces sprayed with mat paint—he caused small patches of color to intrude, rather the way a photographer's color scale is sometimes included in the photograph as a measure of color balance. The result, built on clear knowledge of color theory and technical sophistication in painting, gratified Betty's belief that paintings should require concentration from the viewer. "Look at these," she exclaimed, pointing to Hacklin's paintings. "Aren't they amazing? He knows everything there is to know about color. Like Ad Reinhardt." The comparison to Reinhardt was high praise from Betty for, next to Barney Newman, he remained her example of the most intellectual and most learned artist. Hacklin's work, however, won little response either from critics or from the gallery-going public.

She tested Jan Groth to see if his work could carry the freight of avant-gardism, a decision that seemed out of character to those friends who had heard her denigrate crafts. For Betty, however, it was simple: she saw Groth as an artist. The Norwegian-born artist—aided by Benedicte, his wife and a weaver of obvious skill—worked in tapestry. He drew simple black lines on white paper which she, reversing his patterns, translated into black tapestries cut by white lines which, rendered in fabric, took on a softness that opposed the hard lines of the drawings. Similarly, the drawings were free of any suggestion of actual or implied texture while the tapestries incorporated the natural textures of the fabric in the overall design.

Above, left: Stephen Porter, *Square Post Large*, 1970

Above, right: Allan Hacklin, *My Old Flame*, 1968

Betty, touching gently the surface of a tapestry, swayed as she made a verse chant about the work:

Great Danes dance in the night
Their lines sing a song of sight
The dark clouds listen to the song
Not a chime, not a gong.

Groth's drawings often consisted of one extended and languorous line that might loop back on itself to enclose a little arbitrary shape, might bifurcate into thinner and frailer lines. The tapestries, composed of a black field of richly textured fibers with a white line, provided an appeal to the hand, a suggestion of sensuality. Still, the sparsity of identifiable elements as well as the meticulous use of black and white invited skepticism from a few visitors who threw down before Betty the challenge she loved best: Is it art? Betty welcomed the skeptics for they, far more than the admirers, confirmed her image of herself as a brave discoverer of talent, and further, the existence of scoffers proved that her work was not finished: so long as anyone dared to doubt the power of art, the potency of things of the spirit, Betty had psyches to convert or conquer.

"They came to the gallery," she reported incredulously, "looking for *rugs*. These aren't rugs; these are works of art. They aren't for the feet, they're for the eyes."

Betty had long voiced hostility toward crafts, a category in her thinking that embraced the activities and products of both the loving-hands-at-home amateur as well as the glib and skillful manipulator of material toward function, the human hand

Betty and Jan Groth in Denmark, ca. 1977

and mind doing the work of a machine. While she wore a number of rings at all times, loved beads—especially those that she found in her travels in Africa and the Orient—used almost ceremoniously the pottery that she had acquired for her studio, and tossed across her beds in New York and on Long Island various woven and stitched throws, she dismissed objects of craft as lesser items in the galaxy of things. "Fine arts. Pure arts. That's what I've always believed in. You see, in craft, someone must make something and is not free to explore the realm of the spirit," she insisted.

By the time Betty was extolling the virtues of Jan Groth as an artist, craftsworkers—whether in clay, metal, fiber, glass, wood, or other materials—had begun their assault on the temple of art. Objects that had once been identified by their material as craft, and had been further confined by function, were now treated by craftsworker-artists as the vocabulary with which to address issues at the core of art: the role of material in determining form, the expressive essence of an object, the symbolic portent of things made by human beings, the requirement that fine art be nonfunctional (something to enrich leisure, something of value for those with the wherewithal to acquire valuable goods). The American Craft Museum, an institution on West Fifty-third Street that Betty occasionally visited, through its exhibitions had urged craft continually toward the realm of pure beauty, of pure expression, and of pure craft—in the sense of skill with material—free of the need to produce function.

Betty, however, did not see herself as supporting the movement of craft-into-art, and despite her own fascination with hand-produced objects from all cultures and times as well as her passionate conviction that Jan Groth produced art, she never yielded on the issue of craft. It was, she had learned in the ateliers of Paris, inferior to art, and so far as she was concerned, it should remain forever in its place: it could live in a lean-to attached to the rear of art's temple and its inhabitants, provided they acknowledged their betters, could produce goods which she would happily buy and incorporate into her life.

Groth's work, whether craft or art, did not prompt the scorn that Richard Tuttle's shows elicited among those Betty enjoyed irritating. Tuttle's first show in the gallery, shaped wooden painted wall objects, excited enough outrage to persuade Betty her judgment was right. His second show consisted of works in metal and it, too, inspired scorn from a number of visitors to the gallery; his third show, consisting of shapes in rags, brought forth profane anger—to Betty's delight; his fourth show, of paper shapes glued to the wall (the collector purchased the pattern, and the artist took charge of the installation at an agreed-upon site), inspired howls of outrage which came as music to Betty's self-consciously radical ears. In the early seventies, Tuttle's fifth show in the Betty Parsons Gallery consisted of "works"—not objects—that were small pencil lines drawn on the wall alongside of a fine wire which cast a shadow, this part of the work being left to chance. For Betty, this work was a deeply spiritual summation of the distinctions among drawing, painting, and sculpture, and between two- and three-dimensional existence.

Betty invited Annie Laurie Witzel, among others, to the gallery with mischievous anticipation of horrified response. Annie Laurie fulfilled Betty's hopes. "I was," she said, "just amazed that Betty had put these things in her gallery. I said to her, 'Betty, I need a drink and I think you should never drink again.' Then I went home and I called Hope Williams. 'Listen,' I said to Hope, 'you're not going to believe what Betty has done this time.' "

Visitors to the gallery tended to joke about the work: "Oh, wow, less is less is less." Or, "What are these anyway, the hooks for the paintings you're about to hang?" Or, "Where's the show?" The resistance and disapproval pleased Betty in a way that no amount of praise could have done. She was at bat again and prepared to hit a soaring homer. She was eager to do battle, to tilt in a public arena with anyone who would challenge the validity of Tuttle's work. He was a discovery; she was the discoverer. It was that simple.

Two visitors to the gallery toured a Tuttle exhibition smirking and mocking, making sure that Betty and the people working in the gallery heard their clever remarks. Betty, glowering, rose from her desk and stomped into the gallery. "Do you have questions about this show?" she demanded.

"Well, yes," replied one of the visitors. "Is this what you call Minimalism?"

"To hell with *isms*," Betty roared back. "Richard Tuttle is a great artist. He's in love with the new." She turned on her heel, abruptly lifted a shoulder to dismiss the visitor, and stalked toward her office.

There, furiously frowning and shifting papers on her desk, she continued her diatribe: "Will they never learn? I work like hell to find and put over great art. Why do they come to this gallery? Don't they know that I *never* show the old? I don't give a damn about the past. Everyone looks to the past, the past, the past. The past is dead. Now is alive. Now is tomorrow. I live in tomorrow." As her fury peaked and receded, she relaxed, flopped back against her chair, and said, "It's time for lunch." The storm was over; a triumph recorded.

Betty's combative tone on behalf of Tuttle's work suggested to some of her friends that she had heard the gossip about her failing eye, her slipping prestige. This

Saul Steinberg, *Hard and Soft Figures*, 1952. Private collection, New York

show and this artist, they speculated, provided her with the means once again to assert the gallery's significance and her own radical vision.

For Betty, the seventies brought no challenges to her basic concepts about art. Those concepts, and their attendant values, however, admitted even in her later years a wide range of objects and efforts. Play, for instance, might appear under a variety of guises, but play, Betty insisted, had a dominant position in the creative personality.

Another playful artist, Richard Francisco, had followed Tuttle into the role of "busboy" in the gallery and, moreover, had followed Tuttle as an artist and into the stable of the Betty Parsons Gallery. Francisco crafted small eccentric and whimsical objects out of a wide range of materials. Some of his constructions suggested children's toys or, perhaps, small-scale private jokes about larger constructions. Francisco's work, delicate to the edge of frailty, nonetheless seemed to Betty to be "powerful and mysterious. Just look! He made these up. He uses all of these things to make new things. Poetry of things, that's what Richard Francisco is about."

Playfulness and whimsy marked many of the exhibitions in the Betty Parsons Gallery in the seventies. One of the first artists associated with Betty, and also one of her dearest and oldest friends, was also the dean of playfulness and whimsy in art, Saul Steinberg. In 1977, as was his diplomatic custom, Saul Steinberg showed simultaneously at Parsons and at Janis, thus enforcing an alliance between the two dealers that would otherwise have been impossible. Betty's love for Steinberg and his work far outweighed her enmity toward Janis; she was, as a friend once observed, a much better friend than enemy for she could sustain friendship but, with rare exceptions, she lost interest in enmity.

Steinberg's black and white drawings, inflected with a few daubs, brushstrokes, and byplays of watercolor, evoked mirth in virtually everyone who came into the gallery. And Betty led the claque in joyous response to the artist's linear reconnaissance of the line between absurdity and actuality. "Saul can make a line dance and sing all at once," Betty liked to preach to visitors. "He's an absolute master of the line. And a great, great wit, too." If the visitor evinced interest—and who did not?—she showed off the "diploma" that Saul Steinberg had made for her, an elaborate mock-dignified certificate of passage that she kept on her office wall. "For my birthday, Saul made me this perfectly wonderful wooden birthday cake. He cut it out and painted it and it looked just like a cake but it was wooden." The mental image of the cake elicited her throaty chortling laugh.

As Betty Parsons approached her eightieth birthday, she laughed a lot. But above all, she continued to fight her particular battles for "The New Spirit."

Over the years, dealing with artist-friends, Betty developed little traditions or conventions for showing their work. For instance, she liked to show Kenzo Okada's work in the spring—especially in May. His works, she insisted, "should come out with the spring flowers. With the cherry blossoms. With spring itself. He is very close to nature." Okada joined the gallery in the fifties and over the twenty years that he remained (almost exclusively) in the Betty Parsons Gallery, his work had sold steadily. There were years, indeed, in which sales from his paintings supported the gallery. "Okada," Betty gauged, "often paid my rent. When nothing else was happening and I was broke, broke, broke, someone—usually David Rockefeller—would come into the gallery and just buy up the Okadas. That's the way it is with Okada. The critics hate him. But collectors—certain collectors who have what I think of as a spiritual eye—they *love* Okada and, for them, no one else will do."

In fact, Okada enjoyed continuous popularity among major collectors: "David Rockefeller owns many paintings by Okada; collectors in the Midwest and the West; collectors everywhere are crazy about Okada," Betty often told visitors to the gallery. "But," she added angrily, "the damn museums think he is too beautiful and they hate, hate, hate beauty. They just don't understand Okada's work. On the surface it's beautiful but it's not decorative, it's not pretty, it's powerful and *spiritual.* Just because he doesn't shout and scream, just because his work is quiet and serene—did you ever see such subtlety?—all the museum directors think he is weak and unimportant. I've tried and tried and tried to put him over with the museums and I've never been able to get a single museum show for this great, great artist. It's a shame."

In the spring of 1979, Okada installed in the gallery his large, mistily painted abstract references to perfectly imagined formations of land in a fanciful Zen garden.

"Damn it," Betty said as she stood in the gallery surrounded by Okada's works, "who could not love these paintings?" Then, with a grin, she answered, "Tom Armstrong, that's who." This remark resulted from her repeated efforts to persuade Armstrong, then director of the Whitney Museum, to mount a major Okada show. "He always says," Betty explained, "that he doesn't make any decisions about art, that he leaves that to the curators and that they don't like Okada because they think he's too beautiful, too pretty." She closed the subject with a frown and a shake of her head.

She still had work to do.

Turkish Church, July 23, 1971

Betty in Wyoming, 1974

Betty and Zero Mostel, May 5, 1976, at the Skowhegan Awards dinner

THE LAST YEARS

•

1970-82

In the last decade of her life, Betty was visibly old and tired, though still beautiful. As the doyenne of American modern art, Betty was courted for attention and favors, invited to dinners and events, photographed, interviewed, and honored. Mount Holyoke College gave her an honorary degree, as did Southampton College. Other institutions—the Rhode Island School of Design, the Parsons School of Design, the National Arts Club—feted and decorated her. She received a special award from Mayor Edward Koch of New York. She brandished the scrolls and medals and commendatory letters as well as news clippings before admiring friends. "I don't know why everyone is making such a fuss over me," she offered, coyly and unconvincingly. "All those years when nobody, nobody cared at all what I did or what the gallery did or what the artists did. Now," she said grinning, "they all give me these awards. And everyone wants to show my work. I just don't understand it all."

Betty rejected age; she rejected death. "I hate negative talk and negative people," she emphasized, meaning that she wanted no talk of death in her presence. Her diaries and notebooks contain no indications of dates of death or funerals for even her closest family members—mother, father, sister Emily; the one exception to the rule occurred on the occasion of Jackson Pollock's death, when she inscribed, "a terrible waste." When she discussed death, always euphemistically as "passing over" or "crossing," she recognized it as a way station in a long series of reincarnations. She discussed freely, and less whimsically than listeners often thought, her previous lives: "I was a little dog once.... When I cross into the next state, I may return as a little black cat.... I once lived a long time ago in Egypt and had an interesting life there.... In another life, I walked through this little town [in France] and had a delicious dinner with some little peasants nearby. I was a noble lady and traveled with a whole lot of other noble people, all dressed up." Her friends received these confidences with indulgent smiles or eyes glazed, according to their own persuasions in such matters.

Adge Baker, Betty told friends, had died and come back. Seriously ill, Adge had "crossed over" through a tunnel of light, had experienced great peace, had thought of Betty; but something brought her back. Later, Betty reported, the doctors told Adge that for a while she had "actually been dead." Adge's experience corroborated Betty's belief.

For all of her belief in the spiritual realm, however, Betty did not reject her body. She had regular appointments with the hairdresser in Southold who, she explained, "can really cut my hair and besides is cheaper than anyone else, even with a tip." She visited dentists and doctors on schedule. She took pills for high blood pressure, she took vitamins that she ordered from a special doctor in Arizona, and she took an assortment of other prescribed medicines. At breakfast, lunch, teatime, or dinner as well as other specified times, she rummaged in her pillbox, dug out a green or red or

Jeanette Young, Hope Williams, and Betty, who was awarded an honorary degree from Southampton College on May 30, 1976

Betty, unidentified man, H. H. Arnason, Nancy Hanks, Perry Rathbone

Jacquelyn Mattfeld, president of Barnard College, Betty, Maud Cabot Morgan, a Boston artist, and Barbara Novak, professor of art history at Barnard, late 1970s

Betty and Esteban Vicente, 1972, judging Maryland Annual Exhibition, Baltimore Museum of Art

Betty with Susan Sollins, Guest Curator, Maryland Annual Exhibition, Baltimore Museum of Art

Left to right: Missy, Amanda, and Betty on the beach on Long Island, 1972

Church at Izmir, Turkey, from a sketchbook, 1970

yellow pill, which she swallowed with the liquid of the moment. She ate sparingly, and save for a devotion to the richest French vanilla ice cream and sweet butter, she ate sensibly. She exercised regularly; drank moderately; did not smoke. She amazed everyone—her artists and friends, her assistants in the gallery, journalists and critics who interviewed her, casual acquaintances—with her energy; she boasted of that energy and performed feats calculated to win applause for energy. "I am," she said, "always energetic. I work, work, work. God knows I work. No one knows how I do it. But," she added, "I believe energy comes from the creative and I have always believed in the creative."

But physical being as well as spiritual force succumbs to governing laws. In the last decade of Betty's life, she seemed to accelerate all her activities: she ran the gallery at a frantic pace; she whirled through a daunting social life; and she labored continually on her celebrity by showing her work at every invitation, through interviews with the press, and through public appearances at every opportunity.

In the last years, she entrusted very little introspective writing to the journals; the subject and substance of the journals became the drawings, the observations, the plans for larger work. No longer her private confidant, the recipient of her worries and fears and searches, the journals carried the freight of her art and of her identity as an artist; and they held the currency that she accrued to spend on grander creative acts. She might have to defer working in her studio as she traveled or attended to gallery business, but as long as she had the journals at hand and a clutter of colored pencils and magic markers, she could plan, dream, think about painting and sculpture. She could affirm herself as an artist, however privately. And, all the while, she sought public attention as an artist.

In 1973, Kathryn Gamble, director of The Montclair Art Museum, offered Betty a retrospective exhibition. Betty invited Kathryn to the Long Island studio, took her to warehouses where older works were stored and, with Kathryn at her side, dug through closets and dark corners of her Manhattan apartment. Betty was, Gamble believed, unique: a dealer of historic significance and an artist with a highly personal voice, an appreciation for offbeat ideas and materials, and a naive approach to technique that provided energy to her work. Kathryn especially loved Betty's little journal drawings, watercolor sketches of animals seen on an African safari, boats swung about by stiff sails in the Mediterranean, flower petals and fragments of leaves, churches and beaches and a few figures. They resonated with the artist's singular personality, Kathryn observed.

Soon after the exhibition opened at The Montclair Art Museum, Piri Halasz, *The New York Times* reviewer, identified Betty as "one of the more celebrated of Manhattan's art dealers...known less as a painter and sculptor in her own right." Halasz reiterated the Parsons legend and, pointing to her more recent batting average, noted Betty's role in bringing renown to Ellsworth Kelly and Jack Youngerman; moreover, Betty was continuing to explore new frontiers with the work of such younger "conceptual artists" as Richard Tuttle. No wonder, observed the critic, that "Mrs. Parsons's own paintings are also in the abstract vein. But it would be a mistake to assume that they borrow directly from the efforts of the artists she has shown."

Reviewing Betty's work from the past, including "a terracotta head and a bronze cat and dog done in the thirties" as well as "watercolors of a Norman cathedral and a Brittany landscape," the critic gave highest marks to Betty's recent work. Betty might employ "many bright, gay, simple colors, built into small, distinct images" in the building of a painting; she might use circles within circles or lozenges within lozenges, and bold, sticklike forms as the major elements; or in such paintings as *Moth,* she might narrow her palette to a few colors to show "a single, floating scrap of red on an otherwise all blue field." Finally, Halasz identified a series of abstract paintings which relied on thinly brushed semitransparent paint—works that Betty identified as "more gestural technique" and which showed more of the artist's participation in the act of applying paint.[1]

The Montclair Art Museum exhibition occasioned a handsome catalogue that was widely distributed. Artists and critics from New York visited the show; The Montclair Art Museum purchased Betty's painting *Clocks of Time,* and students from neighboring colleges as well as museum members attended the opening and lectures connected with the successful exhibition. But, Betty muttered, The Montclair Art Museum was small; her work deserved a still larger audience.

But it was Betty, not her work, that seemed destined to reach the larger audience. Reporting on a surprise seventy-fifth birthday party for Betty, arranged by friends in January of 1975, *The New York Times* critic Grace Glueck called Betty a "Monument," and reported that Betty danced until two in the morning and that she was preparing for two shows of her own work in the spring. Betty told Glueck: "I couldn't care less about trends. I'm just as interested today in finding the artist with the individual note as I was in the early years." Finally, Glueck noted, Betty would soon celebrate her thirtieth anniversary as a dealer with an exhibition of artists she had discovered and promoted.[2]

As she prepared for the exhibition in celebration of her gallery's thirtieth year, Betty admitted her pride in her accomplishments. "I had no help," she said, "no help. And the critics all hated me and my artists. But," she stressed, "I had an eye for the creative, for innovation, and I stuck it out." When John Russell reviewed the thirtieth anniversary show for *The New York Times,* he remarked Betty's early and more

Saul Steinberg's contribution to Betty's seventy-fifth birthday book

turbulent days, the early years of the gallery's existence, when very few people claimed a serious interest in serious art. Thirty years later, Russell observed, matters had changed and, in large measure, as a result of Betty's pioneering efforts, her successes as a discoverer. "Characteristically," he added, "she does not keep to the famous names, though the famous names are there in abundance.... Each [artist] gets equal time. It is her private sensibility that dictates, and not the state of the market."[3]

Triumphant, her ears ringing with applause for her thirty years of successful art dealing, Betty flew to Europe for the summer. There, too, her fame caught up with her and, in August, she was featured in *The International Herald Tribune,* where Mary Blume identified her gallery as "the only survivor among the handful of galleries that dared to bring the New York School to the public's eye in the late '40s and '50s."

Describing Betty as "finely drawn, proud, wry, in constant and imperceptible motion, rather like a hummingbird," Mary Blume quoted Betty: "Change is the answer. Security is another value that's crazy. The only time we're secure is when we realize we're not."

Betty told Mary Blume that "love" made the best collectors and that the art prices of the day made her dizzy and a bit queasy. "That Pollock that just sold for $2 million. $2 million!" she exclaimed. "I had it on my wall. It cost $3,000. I feel like Mrs. Rip van Winkle going back not 30 years but 200 when I look at my books."

Owning up to the artists listed as her discoveries, Betty told Mary Blume, "The kind of energy that they were producing got to me—that energy and force and conviction...[because] I'm always looking for the creative note—the guy who has found something he loves and is saying something about it.... Feeling is the content of art. People are scared to death of the word feeling, but there are higher dimensions. People think you're crazy if you see visions. You're not crazy, you're seeing something."[4]

The once shy Betty now fed greedily on celebrity. Indeed, her appetite for public acclaim whetted, she sought to exhibit her art and to preach her lessons anywhere and everywhere that she might. The art public, finally aware of Betty Parsons, had a living legend, a heroine. The accolades continued; she feigned protest in the face of praise;

Constructions on the porch of Betty's studio, Southold, Long Island, ca. 1975

she cited her shyness; and, a product of her upbringing, she tried to affect a modest mien. "I don't know why they are all so interested in me," she told a friend. "God knows they used to hate me. And now, suddenly, everybody is interested in the gallery and all the artists I made famous and in me and in my work, too. They want me to talk. I'm no good at talking. They want me to make *speeches* and I tell them that I never do that. But, sometimes," she added a trifle coyly, "I *do* talk. I never know what I'll say; I just get up and tell them how I see things."

On one occasion when she "just got up and told them how she saw things" in a seminar at the Radcliffe Institute for Women's Studies, she turned the ingredients for academic disaster into a moment of personal triumph. The audience, mostly women prepared to hear the fiery rhetoric of a fierce feminist, received Betty enthusiastically. When she rose to speak, she mumbled that, having not prepared a talk, she would like to answer questions. Silence. Then the shuffling of feet and rearrangement of nervous bodies. A woman stood and asked a question; Betty's garbled "answer" was without reference to the question. After several such fumbles, the audience became aware that, in addition to not having prepared remarks on the topic of the seminar session, Betty was not hearing the questions asked. A few disgruntled women left; others, however, began to rise, one by one, and make mini-speeches about art, with or without reference to Betty and her gallery.

At the dictation of whim, Betty interjected remarks from what had become her "stump speech," saying, "I never cared for fashion.... I've never been interested in *isms*.... I'm interested in the individual voice.... I have no use for the past; the past is dead; I'm interested in the future.... I never cared a damn for what other people thought or for making money...." For the most part, Betty's utterances, mostly about herself and delivered in her brusque growl, did little to further rigorous intellectual inquiry.

When the seminar ended, however, Betty smiled as the group thronged around her to give her slips of paper with their addresses, to invite her to visit their studios, to

Above, left: *Foot*, date unknown

Above, right: Betty in the late 1970s, working

ask to visit her in New York. Betty smiled, nodded, and collected the proffered pieces of paper, which she inserted in her black notebook.

Settled later into the front seat of an automobile for the drive back to New York, she boasted to the driver, "I really told them a few things, didn't I? I shook them up. They never hear *that* kind of talk from professors, do they?" Remembering the virtues of modesty after a pause, she added, "Well, I never went to college and I hate making speeches. And I don't believe in art history. And I don't believe in criticism. But I got through. They understood. The young always do." She settled against the car seat, smiled, and dozed peacefully.

Jock Truman had established a gallery under his own name but loyally continued to work as Betty's agent. He arranged with fellow dealer Jill Kornblee to offer a joint show of Betty's work. "Yes, yes, yes," Betty agreed. And in 1976, during the last part of the summer, through autumn and into the winter, Betty worked steadily on her wooden sculpture and new paintings in anticipation of the show at the two galleries. Kornblee, an affable and hearty woman who unabashedly adored Betty, shared Jock's opinion that Betty's reputation as a dealer, while fitting, had too long overshadowed her work as an artist; and they intended to reveal Betty's overlooked talent both to the public that respected her as a dealer and to an audience not yet familiar with her as an artist.

Betty talked continually of the coming exhibition. "Critics have never liked me, you know; they've never understood what I'm about. I'm always looking to the future, and critics look at the past. They want to compare me with something they know and I want to work with the unknown," Betty insisted. When reminded that past reviews

Above, left: Betty composing a sculpture

Above, right: Betty working at Lee Hall's house, 1972

Betty working at Lee Hall's house, 1972

Betty going down stairs to the beach, 1978

had often been quite favorable and sometimes insightful, Betty responded, "Well, sometimes I'm lucky."

Betty prowled the beach below her studio to collect the components of her wooden sculpture. She had her requirements; she let her sight run before her like a playful freed creature, to sniff out quarry, to identify and claim the wooden components that would become her constructions. "I never use driftwood," she explained. "All of my wooden pieces were shaped by the hand of man. They were pieces of houses or docks or boats or signs. And something happened and they were lost. They tossed about in the sea for I don't know how long. And then they washed ashore, broken and changed, and I find them." She believed that each piece of wood chosen had a rightful, ordained, place in a sculpture that also *was meant to be.* Betty's job, as she had always known, was to mediate, to be the instrument through which perfection found shape. The mystery of creation—big concepts thrilled her—opened to her, she felt, as she selected pieces of weathered wood, hauled them up the cliff that separated the beach from her studio-house. She dumped them clattering onto the studio floor. Seated on an Early American stool, she sorted through her hoard of wood fragments. Rounds with chipped edges. Almost squares with pocked surfaces. Pieces of wood with attached nails or canvas or rope. A broken piece of balustrade. A portion of a boat with black lettering over chipped white paint.

As she laid out the wood collected from the beach, she turned each piece in her hand, felt its edges and heft, recognized it as a phrase in a total statement or composition. Walking among the fragments, toeing one this way or that into proximity and possible configuration with another, she began to combine and recombine personages. She didn't hurry. She let the personages take their own order, let them become the correct who and what that she would recognize as rightness. Pointing to

Betty and Kenzo Okada at the opening of Betty's work at the Jill Kornblee Gallery, New York, January 1977. Jeanne Miles is at the lower right.

first one and then another, she let her imagination find identities to be formed, to be given expression in the context of a construction. "Oh, look at him. What a funny hat he wants to wear.... This one, look at him smiling.... And here's a pirate.... But the owl, over there, is watching, watching, watching. He sees everything. Hoo, hoo, hoo.... A prince, a dancer, a king.... This mad priest, probably from Russia.... And here comes a strong little boat chugging against the waves.... This one, standing up, will be a terrific African warrior...." She applied little stripes and daubs of acrylic color straight from the jar to each piece; sometimes she painted a plane of the fragment a solid color and then adorned it with further colors. Her selection of colors was straightforward: blues, reds, yellows predominated; then a few oranges, ochres, and greens; and, finally, a bit of white or black. Only occasionally would she mix colors or tone down a pure color.

Thus Betty amalgamated the images of travel and childhood storybook with those of her own imagination and store of stock characters. With semiliquid acrylic paint straight from the jars, she dabbed, spotted, and painted the individual wooden pieces. She brushed onto the wood fragments stripes and circles, dots and dashes, vertical or horizontal panels of color.

When convinced that the fragments had found a home in combination with other fragments, she would fix the pieces together: hammering, gluing, wiring, and doweling the pieces, she paused to look incredulously at the work evolving. She was a child among toys, a great empress among her treasures; she exercised total power, final authority.

On leaving the studio briefly to tend chores, she looked back at the collection on the floor and remarked, "Now they'll talk about *us* while we're away."

Betty often invited younger people, friends and associates, to join her on Long Island specifically to help her put the work together. "My wrist was broken, you know, and I have no strength," she would murmur, as if sharing a secret.

Indeed, her wrist, broken in a fall, was weak and her hands were gnarled with arthritis. Physically wiry and resilient as an athlete, she yet lacked the sheer strength needed to put power behind the hammer, to drive nails or set screws into weather-cured wood or wood so fragile that any penetration of its surface might cause cracking, splitting, or crumbling. She gave no heed to the physical characteristics that wood brought to the problem of constructing her sculpture but chose pieces of wood because of shape, texture, and color. If, in addition to providing the appearance she sought, the chosen piece was toughened oak encased in brittle tar or was cork-soft and crumbly from repeated soaking and sun bleaching, she discounted those qualities; all pieces were treated as if they possessed the same physical properties. In this respect, Betty's wooden sculpture grew from the same casual and careless techniques that prompted her painting; she worked in pursuit of control and in the belief that order inevitably issued from accident, that higher spiritual pursuits allowed total disregard for the traditionally defined *facts* of materials. She believed she could and did capture pure spirit; what place had physical limitations in this quest? None for Betty.

She directed guests to cut pieces of lathe or quarter-inch plywood to nail to the backs of constructions, like tape, to hold the components together. Sometimes Betty wanted Elmer's glue applied, "in case the nails pull out. Nails are not very good in some of this wood. It's because of the sea," she explained. If a guest suggested a more sophisticated method for joining pieces of wood, Betty listened and appropriated the proffered technology: dowels, thus, join some of the pieces. "Be sure," she cautioned, "that you put Elmer's glue in those holes. Otherwise those sticks will pull out of the wood. It's the ocean that does it."

As Betty glued and nailed together her odd bits of retrieved-from-the-weather-and-sea wood or as she harnessed the energies and skills of younger friends to drive the nails, set the screws, dowel reluctant shapes into alliance, her powers–magical, she thought, and mysterious–amazed her. "I don't know where it comes from. I lose myself in the work and it takes over and then everything is just right. And I know it."

In the magic of her imagination, she called into being personae reminiscent of pirates and warriors, architectural configurations suggesting medieval or classical structures. These evocative pieces, further emboldened to dwell in the land of fantasy by the names Betty gave the works, nonetheless remained largely abstract—rhythmic and pleasing patterns of shapes configured, quickened, by a sophisticated eye. Despite the often primitive appearance of her pieces, they were, at the end, constructions that lacked both the repetitive patterns and the predictable components of primitive work.

In 1977, the sculpture filled the Kornblee and Truman galleries with whimsy, an air of playfulness, and currents of witty energy. A piece resembling an African shield was named "George"; he goofily stood guard over asymmetrical sailing vessels, lopsided castles, a mock-Parthenon set on circus stilts, leering totem poles, drunken birds and beasts of uncertain parentage. Modestly priced—Betty liked to sell her own works but drove no better bargain for herself than she did for her artists—the sculpture attracted attention from collectors, especially younger collectors, who sought the piece of work as well as a piece of the legend of Betty Parsons.

The festive opening and following celebration tickled Betty. "Oh yes, they loved my work. They came and came. Everyone said perfectly wonderful things. I think they understood what I was getting at—the unknown, the new." Remembering that good manners required tempering of the boast, she added, "Well, I don't understand it at all but they liked it. Why I'll never know, but I'm very pleased that they got it." Betty's "they" included critics, other dealers, and artists, friends, and anyone else who saw the show. In part, she was indeed surprised by the response to her work; but her "I told you so" remained unspoken for she knew and had always known that she was an artist.

Betty in her studio, 1974

As she neared eighty years, Betty Parsons held court in her office, a cove in front of large dirty casement windows in her gallery at 24 West Fifty-seventh Street, littered with the leavings of tides of art that had washed through the gallery. Picture postcards lived chockablock with artists' sketches; the distorted faces of African masks glared over elegant geometric sculpture by Ruth Vollmer; the gray-yellow dirty windows filtered the light that fell on serene paintings by Okada; and, casually, paintings and sculptures by artists famous and unknown littered the office and adjacent storerooms, falling over one another in energetic disarray. Betty's desk, in keeping with the larger theme of the office, was a jumble of calendars, checks, unanswered mail, trinkets from her travels, and her own sketchbooks. Animal sculpture by Marie Taylor peered from under a pile of art magazines and a small bronze by Cleve Gray held down another stack of paper. As Betty talked with visitors or answered the telephone, she would hand over a small stone figure and watch fondly as a stranger enjoyed its contours and volumes.

"This looks just like Barney." She would add her characteristic "hee-hee-hee" laugh, delivered as if she read each *hee* from a script, giving each syllable perfect attention to enunciation if not to generating mirth.

"Barney was a genius. He knew everything. He once ran for mayor of this city. Ran on something like the Artists and Writers ticket. He lost, of course. He would have been a terrific mayor. All that energy. All those ideas. And he knew everything."

The younger artists of the sixties and seventies, she thought, might talk as much as Barney but they didn't say as much. She was on the lookout for conversation. Her intellectual stimulation came from people and not from abstract ideas or from books; her spiritual well-being from art, not from a church.

Visitors to the gallery, whether collectors or poor students who came to look at shows and catch a glimpse of the now legendary Betty Parsons, might bring little gifts of conversation, news from distant camps of intellectual fervor. She received visitors according to the mood of her inner day; gray spirits set before the visitor an impenetrable and icy wall with Betty, scowling, refusing to acknowledge the visitor's presence: let him stand and shift from foot to foot; let the more foolish or insensitive blather and try to wedge himself or herself into the cluttered office corner of the

Betty at the National Gallery of Art, Washington, D.C., for the opening of "American Art at Mid-Century," October 1973

gallery. Ignore the cheeky pup. Betty excused herself as she turned to her desk and fiddled deliberately with the accumulated mess. On a day blessed by a sunny mood, Betty smiled and chortled, talking and gesticulating merrily with visitors.

Certain guests, regardless of the day's spirits, were greeted with Betty's whoops of recognition, with name-chants and smiles. "Oh, Hopey, Hopey," Betty would chant as she greeted Hope Williams, one of her oldest and closest friends. "How are you? How are you?" Perhaps it was a requirement for symmetry that compelled Betty to repeat words, phrases, sentences. Perhaps it was a shy person stalling for time: she didn't smoke a professor's pipe, after all, and couldn't dally with the ritual emptying and filling and packing of a pipe before conversation. She had to buy those precious minutes for sizing up the visitor (all visitors to an artist are potential intruders), for setting the barricade in place, and for adjusting the persona necessary for the occasion as if she harbored a computer that would show on its screen: *Please wait.* Betty ordered her data behind the ritual of greeting.

When asked a question, or called upon to respond to a situation, Betty didn't merely nod her head or utter an affirmative word or so. She chanted "yes." *Art News* editor Tom Hess, amused by the punctuation of conversation with "yeses," deciphered the code in an essay he wrote on the occasion of the exhibition of Betty's work at The Montclair Museum. One or two "yeses," he declared, could as easily mean *no;* three or more "yeses" meant, definitely, *yes.*

Any visitor in serious conversation with Betty elicited the yes-yes-yes motif, an expression of both agreement and encouragement. It meant, "I am with you; I know what you are saying: I want you to continue talking in this vein."

Conversation with Betty followed the loops and swirls of her patterns of attention, shifting from topic to topic; any subject could be stalled by her frantic search through the desk-midden to produce an example, a postcard on a related matter or from a country under discussion, or a clipping from a newspaper or magazine. Visitors waited or discreetly left the office-cove as telephone calls came through.

One day in the spring of 1973, the telephone on Betty's desk rings piercingly (its sound had been turned high by Jack Tilton, her assistant, who knew that her hearing had lost an edge and that she was not recognizing or admitting the impairment). As she picks up the receiver, her several heavy rings flash light borrowed from the large casement windows behind her desk. She brushes her hair behind her ear, shifts in her seat, scowls slightly, and acknowledges the call: "Hello," in a deep voice, slightly drawled. A pause.

"Oh, Bunny. Bunny. How *are* you? How I *long* to see you!" A pause: the scowl deepens. She looks at the visitor who rises from the chair beside Betty's desk to leave and provide privacy for her conversation; Betty motions the visitor to stay and, covering the mouthpiece of the telephone, says in a throaty whisper: "This is Mrs. Mellon. Mrs. Mellon. She needs my advice. I'll just be a minute. A minute. Stay. Stay."

Betty listens intently. She folds and refolds the scarf around her neck. She grins, peers over her glasses at her visitor.

"Yes, yes, yes. I'm so honored. I'll do my best. Of course. Of course. Yes, yes, yes."

She covers the mouthpiece and leans toward the visitor; she stage whispers: "Mrs. Mellon wants my work for the National Gallery in Washington. It's the *most* famous museum in *all* of America."

She adjusts her glasses and scribbles dates and notes on the back of a drawing she made earlier on Long Island. She completes the telephone call with, "Good-bye and much love to you."

"Jack. Gwyn." She summons her assistants as she begins to move toward the outer office where the two are stationed to greet visitors, pass out information on exhibitions, and answer the telephone.

"The most amazing and terrific thing. Mrs. Mellon. Bunny. A *great* gardener. You should see what she has done with her house in Virginia. And a *great, great* patron of the arts. She knows everything. She has everything. All the best artists. She bought from me for years. And she's married to this perfect genius who is also very, very rich."

She pauses for breath; the best is yet to come. Jack and Gwyn smile. Whatever the message, they know that it is good news.

"Mrs. Mellon. My friend, Bunny Mellon. She just asked me to—she *commissioned* me to—make sculptures for the opening of the National Gallery's new show. It's in Washington, you know. It is an honor, a great, great honor."

Ironically, the National Gallery, which Betty had earlier regarded as the bastion of reactionary attitudes, was to call attention in the United States (as the Whitechapel show had in England) to Betty's dual role as artist and dealer and, as a result of the circumstances, to give her considerable attention as an artist. The exhibition about which Mrs. Paul Mellon called Betty—"American Art at Mid-Century"—did just that.

Mrs. Mellon, in preparing for the opening, looked at the several pieces of Betty's sculpture that she owned—and invited Betty to construct one for each table at the opening dinner party.

During the months following the invitation, a seventy-three-year-old Betty spent her summer on Long Island largely working to fulfill Mrs. Mellon's commission. She worked steadily to make the sculptures, speculating all the while on the likely reception. "They'll hate my work. They always hate my work." The lamentation was punctuated with a sharp bash of the hammer that missed the intended nail, leaving the imprint of the hammerhead on the sea-softened, grainy gray wood.

Throughout the summer and into the cool days of early fall, Betty and her troops worked. Her excitement bubbled and sparkled. She told everyone she met, all of her friends who telephoned, of her commission. "It's a great honor," she repeated in her deep voice, "a very great honor. Mrs. Mellon has perfect taste, you know."

The National Gallery exhibition of modern American art opened with a series of private viewings late in October 1973. Mr. and Mrs. Paul Mellon invited guests to a formal dinner in the museum bringing together leading figures from the philanthropic, social, and creative worlds in the United States.

When the big day arrived, Betty took the train to Washington. For weeks, as she worked on the sculptures, she planned what she would wear. She dreamed of how her little wooden sculptures would look on each table and wondered if the guests would like them.

Visitors arriving at Betty's gallery during the next several weeks heard, and heard again, the stories of the evening. Everyone loved the sculpture, Betty reported incredulously, and at the end of the festivities, all the sculptures were bought on the spot—a sellout. The people there loved art; they knew about art. And, said Betty beaming, they loved her sculptures.

Five years later, the National Gallery was again the site of a triumph for Betty. This time the occasion was the opening of the new East Wing, designed by I. M. Pei. Again the Mellons gave a dinner, and again the outstanding people in the arts, society, business, and philanthropy were guests.

John Canaday, reviewing the exhibition and its glamorous opening for *The New York Times,* observed:

> *The exhibition took on a secondary character as a tribute to Betty Parsons, New York art dealer, when someone counted up that 10 of the 23 artists represented had been given their first one-man show in her gallery. In addition to Pollock and Gottlieb, there were Mark Rothko, Clyfford Still, Barnett Newman, Hans Hofmann, Ad Reinhardt, Richard Pousette-Dart, Joseph Cornell, and Bradley Walker Tomlin.*[5]

Waving Canaday's review, she smiled. She had been recognized both as dealer and as artist. She had been celebrated along with the artists she made famous, the artists she stitched into the fabric of American art history. Never mind that, strictly speaking, she had not given first one-man shows to all of those artists. They were her artists, inexorably linked in history to her gallery and to herself as a discoverer. She was ecstatic. She was famous.

Fame brought both rewards and problems to Betty. Whether she sought the mantle or squirmed uncomfortably beneath its weight, her achievements and her style of behavior guaranteed that she would be identified as a *feminist* and that she would be sought often by women's groups, as well as by individual women, to share her wisdom and to serve as a symbol of change. She found it an agreeable enough adjunct to her more general fame and, soon, she recounted her difficulties: "Yes," she explained, "I was always interested in what happened to the women. I had to do unpleasant things, had to miss out on things, because I was a woman. I couldn't even go to college and I wanted to go to Bryn Mawr. But my family thought college would make me unfeminine. Imagine! And that's why I believe in feminism now. I believe in women being able to do whatever they *can* do, just as men do whatever they *can* do."

By now, Betty was not only accustomed to being interviewed, she relished the opportunity to have her say, to reinforce the legend and—with a nudge of the truth here and there—to extend it a bit. Earlier, she had been meticulous in pointing out that

Betty on the beach in Southold, fall 1974

Peggy Guggenheim gave *first* shows to the giants of Abstract Expressionism; now, when an interviewer assumed that the first shows had been in the Betty Parsons Gallery, Betty let the assumption go unchallenged. Earlier, too, Betty often credited Barnett Newman with advising her during the infancy of the gallery; now, however, she promoted the image—the legend—of herself as a lone operator.

In 1978, *L'Officiel/USA* published a lengthy article in which, again, Betty's legend was paraded for general readers, her discoveries listed, and she was quoted extensively:

> *I was born with a gift for falling in love with the unfamiliar.... I have never made money because I saw things too far in advance. Actually, being an artist gave me the jump on other dealers—I saw things before they did.... I have always been lucky enough to be in the right place at the right time.... Most dealers love the money. I love the paintings.... I have a gift for friendship, my friends don't forget me.... Painting is a compulsive thing with me; it's a way of keeping alive.... I have lived many lives and have enjoyed all of them.... The world stinks, but life is marvelous! When you look at a tree, a pebble, a sunset... that's life, when you look at people, they depress you....*[6]

In 1979, Betty was pictured on the cover of *Art News;* Grace Lichtenstein wrote the cover story, identified Betty as "the den mother of Abstract Expressionism," and reported on Betty's hyperkinetic visit to portions of her collection stored in a Long Island City warehouse, where, accompanied by Jack Tilton, Betty rediscovered objects with exclamations of proprietary delight: Murch, Pollock, Hedda Sterne, Youngerman, Agnes Martin, and Coggeshall.

"In a black beret and black shoes, sensible-length skirt and simple blue cloth coat, Parsons, at 79, [rummaged] through these treasures like a bargain-minded antiques hunter at a weekend flea market," wrote Lichtenstein.[7]

By the time Betty might have retired from a conventional business, her celebrity as a dealer had extended and, to her unabashed delight, included the fact that she was an artist. Her work was shown widely and attracted attention. In 1980, Joan Mondale, wife of then Vice President Walter Mondale, visited New York where she afforded the press "photo opportunities" in Jill Kornblee's gallery. The resulting picture of "Joan Mondale views paintings at the Kornblee Gallery" shows Mrs. Mondale holding and looking at a gouache by Betty Parsons.[8]

During the last decade of Betty's life, after the public appearances, after the exhibitions, after the interviews and the jumble of social activities, she returned to her studio. "My studio on Long Island. I must go there, you see," Betty would say, "because that's where I am able to work. That's where I do most of my work. I put aside the gallery—I don't even think about it when I'm out there. I just work, work, work. Like a Trojan horse [*sic*]. I *must* work every weekend," she explained, "That's the only time I have. I have to be in the gallery. I have to talk on the telephone. I have to write letters. God, those letters. How I hate all those letters. Everyone wants something," she intoned, her voice thickening with irritation until she finally growled: "No one makes it easy. No one."

She often invited friends to spend weekends on Long Island. One frequent guest, Gwyn Metz, Betty's gallery assistant and frequent traveling companion on automobile journeys to the West or to New England, recalls those weekends as rituals of unvarying routine, comprising set social and professional ingredients. Gwyn enumerated the intricacies of the weekend routine, beginning with Betty's determination to leave New York City before three o'clock on Friday afternoons, in order to "beat the traffic" on Long Island. Gwyn, like many of Betty's other friends with a will to survive, insisted on driving. While Gwyn pressed Betty's station wagon through Manhattan's crosstown streets, across bridges or through tunnels, and onto the densely trafficked highways of Long Island, Betty dozed or sketched in her black notebooks. But, as they neared Southold, driving on less traveled and smaller roads, Betty put aside the sketchbooks and magic markers, combed her hair and painted lipstick across her mouth. Her conversation sped up, her gestures keeping pace. Watching for familiar landmarks, she commented on people and buildings and natural aspects of Southold that signaled her approach to her studio. Child-happy, unable to sit totally still, Betty rehearsed the house rules and the schedule for every guest, including Gwyn, who visited often and who could recite the weekend's schedule as handily as could Betty. "We'll go out to dinner. The Barge, I think. They have the best fish," she instructed her friend behind the wheel. "But first, we must go home and open the windows and let the air in. And we'll freshen up a bit."

Assured that the plans were accepted, Betty continued, "Now, tomorrow we'll get up early and have breakfast. I'll cook. Boiled eggs. Then I'll work. We can go to Greenport for lunch and shopping."

After unloading the car and opening the studio, Betty and Gwyn drove to The Barge, where Betty ordered her usual weekend drink: "A little Manhattan. Very cold. But straight up." Dinner usually consisted of fresh fish, vegetables, and salad; vanilla ice cream—one scoop, perhaps a dollop of chocolate sauce—closed the meal.

In view of Long Island Sound, Betty ate her dinner and talked about travels and people, about politics or conversations with friends. The coffee cups emptied (Betty insisted upon a demitasse of American coffee: "Oh, my god. If I even drank one drop of Italian coffee, I'd never, never sleep.") As the summer night pressed against the restaurant windows, shutting out the view of the Sound, Betty anticipated the next day. "I'll get up early and we'll have breakfast about eight." Then she softened the command with a question: "Is that all right?"

Back at the studio, Betty read a while before sleeping in her large bed butting the window; all night, the sound of the gentle or fierce surf on the shore below rolled against her slumber. "Sometimes, the waves roll into my dreams and take me away to make me a pirate," she remarked.

As she had said, Betty rose shortly after sunrise. In fine weather, she left the studio and sat seminude atop her cliff where she performed her exercises, a blend of Subud, yoga picked up from friends, and stretching prescribed by doctors to thwart arthritis. Following her morning shower, she dressed in blue jeans—"dun-ga-rees," she said—and a French sailor jersey, her uniform for work.

Betty's weekend guest, appearing at eight o'clock as instructed, might lay the table and chat with Betty about the identity of the crockery: "the little brown bear bowls" must be set out for the boiled eggs at breakfast, for the pasta or rice at lunch. Betty made coffee in an old-fashioned Silex percolator, a two-part affair that produced strong and fragrant coffee. She burned the toast. Almost always. And each time smoke and the smell of charred bread filled the morning air, Betty said, "Damn. I don't know why that toaster burns the bread. He's just terrible that way. But you can't get toasters like this one anymore. This is a good toaster. Tom Eastman gave him to me and I could never replace it. It must have cost a fortune."

After breakfast, Betty often gazed across Long Island Sound. "Over there," she said, pointing toward Connecticut on the other side of the glistening water, "directly over there is where my great friend, my dear friend, Min Luddington lived. When she died—and she's buried exactly across from this very spot—I went to her funeral. A thousand black birds swooped down into the cemetery. Isn't that amazing? A thousand. Maybe more. They all came in a flock—I don't know from where—to say farewell to Min. Maybe they came to take her spirit off to another world. I'll never forget that. All those birds."

Betty worked in the studio for about an hour, stopped for a snack, a stroll among the works on the floor and a few minutes of watching boats or weather. Then, more work. By lunchtime, a few constructions firmly joined and stacked about the studio for viewing, Betty, as often as not, would abandon her plan for lunch in Greenport and cook rice or pasta while her guest made a salad. Conversation flowed easily; life seemed good. After "a little rest," Betty wanted to walk on the beach to collect another trove of wooden fragments.

At eighty-one, Betty was remarkable in energy and zeal, though vulnerable and increasingly frail, more forgetful, more vague, more childish, and more vain. She wanted her way—as she had always wanted her way—but now exercised little subterfuge in demanding it. Often imperious, sometimes rude, she could nonetheless fold into childlike limpness, accept a hug with a grin, and prattle on about an adventure, a treasure found in an unlikely place, an article or book just read, or an award won. If Betty believed herself immortal, as she professed, those close to her worried about her growing frailty but hesitated to suggest to her that the time had come for a more prudent pace.

The gallery, under the steady daily hand of Jack Tilton, continued to show artists who, some felt, comprised an embarrassingly mixed stable. Perhaps people visited the Betty Parsons Gallery to see Betty Parsons as much as to see shows of work by her various artists.

In November 1981, Betty prepared for the opening of an exhibition and for the party to follow. As was her custom., she supervised the hanging of the show and then took the artist to lunch at her favorite restaurant, Le Champignon, around the block

Betty and her nephew William Rayner at an opening in her gallery, January 1977

from the gallery. There, after effusive greetings from the aging French couple who ran the dark little restaurant with its predictable French menu, Betty took her pills and made a toast in red wine to the artist.

"Wine of the wind, wine of the sea
Art of the mind, art of the heart
Here's to you and here's to me
You're a bird, I'm a bee."

After lunch, she checked the hanging of the paintings and barked orders to Jack Tilton. "Jack," she demanded, "where did you get that hammer? Is it new?"

"I bought it," Tilton told her, "with money from petty cash."

"Why, why, why," she scolded, "did you buy a new hammer? This gallery is not made of money. I've been in this business for forty years and I never needed *two* hammers."

Betty stomped into her den at the rear of the gallery, snapping damnation on hammers and on the "young pup" who had purchased a second (and needed) hammer for the gallery. "They know nothing. *Nothing* about running a gallery. They think money grows on trees. I taught him everything. Everything. His grandmother was my friend. He wanted to be a dealer and I said, 'All right, you can come work for me and I'll teach you.' I called him my puppy." Betty's incensed conjuration of Jack Tilton as her puppy dispelled the anger; she smiled.

Betty returned to her apartment to dress for the opening and the party. When she appeared in the gallery again, she was scrubbed and her hair was still wet from a schoolgirl combing; her slash of lipstick fresh. She wore a full-sleeved white silk blouse tucked into black velvet knickers; she wore red stockings and low black patent leather pumps. "Look at me," she invited. "I look like a page in King Arthur's court. I think I was once in King Arthur's court. I was many things before. A friend who knows about

Betty's apartment 1970-80

such things—Adge Baker—told me that I was once an Egyptian cat and that I was in King Arthur's court. I think I was a page at the Round Table and tonight I'm that page again."

As visitors to the opening came into the gallery, Betty met them with enthusiastic remarks about the paintings displayed and with encouragements to consider her costume and her previous life as a page in King Arthur's court. Smiling and chatting, she offered little bows to people she especially liked or valued as potential clients. She introduced friends to other friends. She received adulation from young admirers who came to the show as much to see—perhaps to meet—the famous dealer as to look at the paintings on view.

Following the opening, Betty hailed a cab, arrived at the SoHo address, and climbed four long flights of candle-flanked stairs to the already festive party. "No, no, I'm not tired," she insisted, "I have lots of energy. I can dance all night." But she did not dance; rather, she sat, a tiny ancient child enthroned, and tapped her feet to the music. She received visitors; she accepted wine and food. Straining to hear conversation, answering often in non sequiturs, which, in turn, were not heard in the din, she smiled and nodded at admirers. Left alone, she slumped in her chair, her fatigue as evident as her rejection of it was vehement. "No, I'm not tired. It's this damn noise. I can't hear a thing. Wonderful party. Wonderful!" she shouted.

Shortly before midnight, she took leave of the artist and the hostess and returned to her uptown apartment. That was a Tuesday night. Betty arrived later than usual at the gallery the next day, grumbled about too much work to do, and went home earlier than usual. On Thursday, she again observed a shortened schedule punctuated by irritability. On Friday morning, sometime before dawn, a massive stroke pounded her brain, obliterating her ability to speak, paralyzing one side of her body.

Billy Rayner telephoned Betty's close friends with the news: she seems out of danger; we must wait to see if the paralysis leaves her in the next few days; we don't know what to expect. Slowly, the paralysis ebbed; Betty moved both legs and arms; she clenched and unclenched both hands; she smiled symmetrically. But speech did not return. Nodding in understanding of a question put to her, she responded in squeaks and gibberish. She tried to write notes but produced childish scrawls. She mimed. Friends applauded the recognizable words that pushed through her babble and told each other that, "Betty is just as she always was. She's fine. She's well. She's going to be all right." They reassured one another with joking and loving recollections of Betty's *ordinary* speech: "She never speaks in sentences. She always speaks in poetry. Betty doesn't talk the way other people do."

Throughout the months that followed, Betty had continuous and loving care. Friends visited. Chessy and Billy Rayner watched over her. Renata and Tom McCarter worried about doctors and therapists. Nurses and therapists attended her in her sunny Beresford apartment overlooking Central Park West and The Museum of Natural History.

There, Betty was surrounded by thriving house plants, assorted works of art—paintings by Okada, Tomlin, Newman; prints by Jasper Johns, Kelly, Robert Rauschenberg; watercolors and drawings by artists from the gallery and beyond. The apartment, despite its treasure of art works, suffered from Betty's age and from her neglect: faucets dripped, long-burned-out light bulbs refused to shine, the bathtub drained sluggishly, and tiles in the bathroom were loosening from their cement. The apartment needed paint and cleaning but it received only passing care.

Betty played with her collection of little animals and dolls in her bedroom; she leafed through the accumulation of her journals that she kept on the lower shelves of her living-room bookcases. In her bedroom, she slept on a narrow bed that she had pushed into a corner to keep space for a work table on which she laid out watercolors for completion. Collections of scarves and strings of beads hung on doorknobs, over chair backs, around bed posts. On her dresser, she arranged and rearranged her dolls and animals, careful always to put a picture postcard or small painting before them so that "they will have something to look at and think about. When I'm not here, they need amusement."[9]

By Christmas of 1981, following her stroke in November, Betty had recovered sufficiently to want a Christmas tree, which she decorated all in red. Billy Rayner arranged Christmas dinner for her in a hotel in New York—one of the few good restaurants open on that holiday. In preparation for the party, Betty dressed festively and greeted her guests with hugs. As she led them to her Christmas tree, pointing out the red bow and red cardinals that she had attached, she smiled and chortled. As she unwrapped her gifts, she grinned and mimed her gratitude and her plans for each gift. A roll of primed canvas would, she acted out, be subjected to sweeping brushstrokes and picador-dabbing; before it she would stagger, bedazzled, and throw open her arms to receive its full impact.

Bowing, she offered her arms to her companions who helped her into her coat and handed her her ubiquitous beret, who watched her smear on her brilliant red lipstick, and who took her to dinner. She toyed with the menu, accepted assistance in selecting roast chicken, rice, green beans, and ice cream with chocolate sauce. She ate eagerly, drank red wine, and smiled as Billy Rayner smoked an after-dinner cigar.

During the months that followed, Billy Rayner, assisted by the gallery staff, tried to keep Betty calm, tried to anticipate her needs and to take care of her; he made certain that she was not alone and that she kept doctors' appointments and received medication and therapy on schedule. She came to the gallery and met visitors, who came in

Betty walking along Long Island Sound

scores, often bringing little gifts. Through slightly improved speech, scribbling on note pads, and miming, Betty made herself understood. To those who knew her.

Strangers, however, did not understand her garbled and shattered speech any more than they read her miming. Slipping away from her daily nurse one morning, she managed to hail a cab, which the doorman of her apartment building reported, and drove off downtown, toward the gallery. But she did not reach the gallery, and for three hours, while Jack Tilton and Billy Rayner telephoned everyone they could imagine she might have visited, she was missing. Finally, she appeared at the gallery, angry and waving her fists, spouting confused invective. The magnitude and itinerary of her adventure remained locked in Betty's mind.

As summer neared, Billy Rayner arranged for Betty to spend several months at her studio in Southold. Wendy Peters, a gentle young woman who worked in the gallery, would stay with Betty. Neighbors and friends in the Southold area would visit; Chessy and Billy Rayner would look in on weekends. Betty would be in the place she most loved and would work as much as she could.

On the morning of her death, Betty rose early, dressed, and began her breakfast ritual. She laid her solitary place at the table, filled a "little brown bear bowl" with blueberries; she made coffee in her glass coffee pot. As she carried the coffee the few steps from her kitchen to her white formica-topped table, a stroke cracked through her brain. Losing consciousness, she fell so gently to the floor that she set the pot beside her without spilling a drop.

Betty Parsons died on the morning of July 23, 1982.

NOTES

•

An American Girlhood · *1900–15*

1. Paul Cummings, Interview for The Archives of American Art of the Smithsonian Institution, June 4, 1969.

2. The family fortune came primarily from the Ramapo Iron Works, which had begun in 1794 with the establishment of a partnership between Josiah G. and Isaac Pierson, John Friederich's great uncles. Initially, the firm, in New York, produced nails and other iron commodities for the growing country. Three years after the founding of the partnership, the brothers moved their equipment and machinery to Ramapo, New Jersey, where they expanded their manufacturing. In 1822, the firm was incorporated as Ramapo Manufacturing Company with a capitalization of $345,000, including thirty-six hundred acres of land. Operations soon expanded to include cotton mills, saw mills, granite quarries, and a larger production of nails, hoops, and files.

The first cotton mill in the Northeast was probably built at Ramapo under the auspices of the Pierson family. The family business grew to include a water company as well as a number of iron plants, rolling mills, and cotton mills. Later still, the holdings included Ramapo Car Works, which produced the railway cars that traveled the nation's newly laid tracks; the Ramapo Wheel and Foundry, which furnished other necessities for railroading and shipping, and the Ramapo Land Company.

3. Susie, supported initially by her family's fortune, built houses in both Newport and Palm Beach. Both, according to Betty, burned down. "I don't know why Mother's houses always burned down; they just did. But she rebuilt them." William Rayner recalled:

[There are] two houses that I've actually seen that belonged to Gram (Betty's mother). There's one that still exists in Palm Beach.... And there's another charming house in Newport.... It's an old house, a tiny old house. It was built before the great mansions were built. Near Bailey's Beach... [at the end of] Bellmont Drive. Everything was tiny: a little tiny ballroom, a tiny little poolroom; everything was Victorian and tiny. Great enormous charm.

4. Betty typically discussed her mother in terms of taste: "My mother had good taste, beautiful taste. She loved beautiful things—crystal, china, textiles, furniture—but she didn't know a damn thing about art and she didn't care. Everything was always very special, but there was never any mention of art." As if to stress her mother's most applauded characteristic, Betty often added, "Everything was very elegantly done." Thus, "good taste," an accolade to Susie, was often a pejorative term in Betty's personal lexicon.

Courtship, Wedding, Marriage · *1915–23*

1. Helene Aylon, "Interview with Betty Parsons," *Womanart,* Fall 1977. p. 10ff.

2. William Rayner (Lee Hall: interview. Henceforth referred to as LH:int.):

It was an odd match. It was probably family pressure—both families. They probably also—well, Schuyler had an artistic bent and I think they had some things in common. He loved pretty things—silver, objects, decorative arts, and that kind of thing.

3. Schuyler Livingston Parsons, *Untold Friendships* (Boston; Houghton, Mifflin, 1954). He never mentions Betty by name in this autobiography.

4. Hope Williams (LH:int.):

Betty was a bartered bride. Her family thought it a brilliant social match. After all, Schuyler had so much money it seemed impossible that he'd someday be a shopkeeper in Palm Beach, a failed antiques dealer, and interior decorator in Charleston and New Orleans. He was in the Social Register and related to several other chapters. He was a playboy, a drunkard, and a homosexual. And Betty, whatever else, was giddy, determined to win from life the pleasures available to her and, at the same time, to be superficially a good girl. The rebel had not been fully born when she married Schuyler.

5. With careful guidance from their attorneys, the couple filed a document of divorce in Paris; the hearing was held on May 19, 1923. In the document, Betty, as plaintiff, alleged that no marriage contract preceded the ceremony and that, therefore, the couple were in regard to property under the system in force in the State of New York. That is, they maintained separate property.

She assured the authorities that no child had been born in the marriage, that at first the couple had lived in New York, harmoniously enough, but after some time, Mr. Parsons manifested the greatest coldness and the most complete indifference toward his wife; that having decided to live in France, the couple took an apartment in Paris at no. 60 rue Boissière. In the month of March 1923, Mr. Parsons left and took up residence in the Hotel Berkeley. When the plaintiff asked for an explanation of his strange conduct, Mr. Parsons replied that he had had enough of her and wished to regain his liberty.

According to the document of divorce, Betty then summoned her husband to come back to her. He repeated his refusal, saying that life with her had become too intolerable and that he absolutely refused to receive her again.

These facts, according to the document, constituted cruelty and, therefore, grounds for divorce under French law.

Schuyler was summoned to appear before the tribunal one week later, represented by his solicitor, to "hear pronounced upon the pleading of a divorce between Mr. Schuyler Livingston Parsons and Mrs. Betty Bierne Pierson, his wife, on the application and in favor of the latter."

Freedom and Paris · *1924–33*

1. Resoundingly corroborated by Hope Williams:

Betty hadn't really grown up. She was a giddy good-time girl. Of course she had a lot to say about art but I never thought she knew what she was talking about at that time. She thought that art *would give her a good time, a good life; a lot of fun without too much responsibility. It was later—and partly as a result of her years in Paris—that she grew up and became an important person.*

2. Despite the General's disinheritance of her as a result of her divorce, Betty was not estranged from her family. Her mother lived in Paris and Betty saw her on holidays ("especially Thanksgiving... a sort of American holiday, you know") (LH:int.). She and Emily wrote often; both Emily and their other sister, Sukes, visited Betty in Paris.

3. In 1977, Betty told Helene Aylon (*op. cit.* p. 12.):

I have many close friends... a very close friend in England, Adge Baker.... I went over there to get a divorce. She was ten years older than I was. I met her through friends. She took an interest in me and I was flattered. Ten years older—that was quite old then. It's nothing now! And really, I was very pleased. Very extraordinary Englishwoman. And she gave me hell all the time; she was extremely critical. She never let me do anything but the best. She had quite an influence on me to keep my feet and not be dominated by the male. In fact, I don't think I would be alive today if I never met this Englishwoman. She was an artist. She saw so clearly, she was so wise. She saw through the male at a very early age. She had nearly always lived alone....

4. Betty said (LH:int.):

Well, when I bought this house and decided to live in it with Adge Baker, I could see my mother casing the joint. I told her that she absolutely could not live there. It was my life and my life was bohemian. Her life was conventional. "Stay where you are," I told her, "and we'll visit on holidays." She didn't like that very much but she stayed where she was and I lived the way I wanted to.

5. According to Rosalind Constable (LH:int.).

6. "Marriage Announced," *The New York Times,* January 25, 1926, p. 25, col. 2.

7. Betty Parsons's journals (Henceforth referred to as BPJ).

8. BPJ.

9. William Rayner (LH:int.):

My father and Betty did not get along at all. They were really at odds. To be perfectly honest, I never heard Betty say anything about Father but I know perfectly well that my father just didn't approve of Betty. Didn't approve of her life. You know. Probably didn't approve of art per se. He really wasn't at all interested in it. And they had absolutely nothing in common whatsoever. Well, me and my mother. But nothing in common in terms of their own interests.

10. BPJ.

11. BPJ.

12. Aylon, *op. cit.*

Unsettled Homecoming · *1933–35*

1. LH:int.

2. Hope Williams made mirth among her friends in amateur theatrics, married a socially prominent doctor, R. Bartow Read, and, with his blessing and after a series of amateur triumphs in Junior League productions, was chosen by Philip Barry for a professional role. An immediate success, a natural comic with a goofy walk and an upper-class style, an impeccable delivery and a confiding manner of overacting, Hope Williams served as a model for Katharine Hepburn's public persona. Hope's bobbed hair, trim boyish body, and merry air of impudence delighted audiences for decades. She was especially successful in early Cole Porter productions. Along with the British entertainer Bea Lillie, she set the standard for female comics in the decades between the world wars.

3. Cummings, *op. cit.* Betty Parsons summarized her life in California:

I went out to California and spent four years there. I worked at sculpture. I also taught sculpture and drawing. And I did a few portraits. I taught privately. I had my own studio in Hollywood. And then I moved to Santa Barbara. I had a studio in Santa Barbara where I used to teach drawing and sculpture. And I had quite a few students too, there.

4. Cromwell, according to his obituary in the October 13, 1960, *The New York Times,* was fifty at his death. *The Times* identified him as an artist who had attended the Chouinard Art School but who gained his first recognition in the 1931 movie *Tol'able David.* Under his real name (Roy Radebaugh), he won a following for his portrait masks and oil portraits of motion picture personalities and for a few short stories and a novel. Cromwell then played a series of supporting roles, including Lee Austin in *Life Begins at Forty,* which starred Will Rogers (1935); he played Matt Clay in *Young Mr. Lincoln,* in support of Henry Fonda's Lincoln; Lieutenant Stone in *Lives of a Bengal Lancer* (1935), in which Gary Cooper played the leading role; and, in 1939, he joined W. C. Fields in *Poppy.*

Cromwell, in addition to his screen career, decorated the houses of screen personality Colleen Moore and the composer Cole Porter. In 1945, he was married for eight months to the actress Angela Lansbury.

5. BPJ.

6. In conversation with Betty about Garbo, it was clear that she was confused about the actress's nationality.

7. Aylon, *op. cit.*

8. Betty's friends and family who outlived her did not meet Stuart Davis but knew of him through Betty's talk about him and about her plans to marry him. Both Hope Williams and Rosalind Constable recalled Betty's complaints about his heavy drinking; William Rayner, through his mother, knew that Stuart Davis had existed but knew no details of the affair.

9. Betty spent a lot of time with Min Ludington, which was reflected in the many references to her in the journals:

Min is a yellow crocus with brown wings.

Much magic has Min!

Happy heavenly day went swimming with Min....

Bathing, tennis, lunch. I poured all day—took on a heavy load of alcohol. Min.

Min's beach house
The clouds before the islands
whispering to the sea
No wind, no rain just
laughter and tranquility

10. Cummings, *op. cit.* Betty Parsons, explaining her decision to return to New York, said:

So I had four years in California and I was very glad to leave. I'd had it. That was enough. There is some private stuff in there but I don't suppose I want to talk about it. There was a man I came back with that I thought I was going to marry. But I don't want to talk about it. But there it was. Four years. Just too much drink. I've always liked people that drink. My husband had the same problem.

A Dealer's Apprenticeship · *1935–45*

1. BPJ.

2. Betty remembered, "I didn't want to talk to anyone. Not even Dumpy. And I didn't want to be with Stuart. I wanted to be by myself so I went to this friend's house and slept in the guest room."

3. References to Tim's illness and death are taken from BPJ, November 15–25, 1935.

4. In this manner, she gained new clients for the Midtown Galleries and made friends with decorators who, in addition to The Katinkas, would subsequently join the list of early and regular clients at her own gallery.

5. Betty, in interviews and conversations for this book, agreed to (and did) talk freely about her friends and lovers, usually loyally emphasizing their talents and graces. "Gina" was another matter, however; she wanted to protect her identity and, therefore, I have honored her concern and have used a fictitious name.

6. BPJ.

7. Betty was uncertain about the sequence of meeting Gertrude Macy and Gina. She thought, at first, that she had met Gina first but, later, wondered if Gertrude Macy had introduced her to Gina.

8. Eastman, an amateur pilot (or, as Betty noted in her journal, *pilote*) enjoyed buying gifts for Betty and added both necessary and luxurious items to her life until his death. "This freezer and this radio and this stove," she said, pointing to objects in her Southold studio in 1978, "were all given to me by Tom Eastman. He gave me presents all the time. I don't know why. I think he liked to give presents."

9. Betty attended figure drawing sessions at the League on and off throughout her life. In the sixties, she persuaded William Rayner, her nephew, to join her in these informal but intense classes on Saturday mornings when she did not go to the country.

10. BPJ. This was the first of many visits to college art departments. During the early

exposure to art on college campuses, not surprisingly, Betty found both faculty members and students unendingly dull and reactionary. "They just didn't appreciate new art. They were still looking at the old," she said.

11. LH:int.

12. BPJ.

13. Doris Brian, *Art News,* vol. 41, no. 7, May 14–31, 1942, p. 22.

14. Letter from Hedda Sterne to Betty Parsons, undated.

15. LH:int.

16. Billie Clarke, writer and photographer, lived near Betty Parsons on Long Island, and in Betty's later years, Billie Clarke volunteered to do chores, run errands, and help Betty with home maintenance.

The Betty Parsons Gallery · *1946–51*

1. Elsa Maxwell, "Elsa Maxwell's Party Line," December 20, 1946, *The New York Post.*

2. Elaine de Kooning devoted many hours to recollection and conversation about the early years of the Betty Parsons Gallery. In the same spirit of concern for the artists of the gallery, she read the manuscript, added details to anecdotes, and provided valuable advice.

3. In one instance, at least, the understanding was less than perfect. Robert Motherwell indicates (and Marie Hartley, Betty's assistant in the gallery, corroborates) that he left the Betty Parsons Gallery both because he felt that Betty failed to represent his work vigorously enough and because he found himself in competition with Betty for the attention of Natika Waterbury, who worked as Betty's assistant in the gallery.

4. The exhibition contained (according to *Art News,* vol. 46, no. 1, March, 1947, pp. 15ff.) thirty-six paintings by Constable, thirteen by Turner, and twelve by Hogarth.

5. Emily Genauer, *New York World Telegram,* June 8, 1948.

6. *The New York Times,* June 4, 1950.

Betty Parsons Sets the Pace · *1951–56*

1. LH:int.

2. *Art News,* vol. 53, no. 2, April, 1954.

3. "Betty Parsons Visits Two of Her Artists," *Memphis Commercial Appeal,* September 12, 1954.

4. Paul Mocsanyi, United Press feature, October 8, 1954.

5. *The New York Times,* December 1954.

6. *Art News,* vol. 54, no. 2, April 1955.

The Second Decade of the Gallery · *1956–66*

1. *Art News,* vol. 55, no. 9, January 1957.

2. According to Kelly, Betty actually discovered him in New York, and he urged Youngerman to return from Paris and see Betty. (LH: int.)

3. This comment could be an allusion to Jackson Pollock's often quoted remark about himself, "I am nature"—an idea that charmed Betty and that she repeated over decades as she had occasion to describe Pollock.

4. Gerald Silk, interview for the Archives of American Art of the Smithsonian Institution, June 11, 1981.

5. BPJ.

6. BPJ.

7. BPJ. In passages dealing with foreign travel, perhaps more than in other situations, Betty derived her eccentric spelling from hearing, not reading.

8. BPJ.

9. BPJ.

10. *Art News,* vol. 58, no. 3, May 1959.

11. (LH:int.) A frequent and characteristic remark.

Fame · *1962–69*

1. LH:int.

2. LH:int.

3. "Best Show in Town," *Time,* November 16, 1962.

4. LH:int.

5. LH: interview with Lawrence Alloway.

6. Barnett Newman, letter to *Art News,* vol. 67, no. 3, May 1968, p. 6.

7. Rosalind Constable, "The Betty Parsons Collection," *Art News,* vol. 67, no. 1, March 1968, pp. 48.

8. LH:int.

The Gallery in the Seventies

1. Betty Parsons, *Art News,* vol. 70, no. 2, April 1971.

2. James Johnson Sweeney headed the Solomon R. Guggenheim Museum from 1952 to 1960; Alfred H. Barr, Jr., headed The Museum of Modern Art from 1929 to 1967; and Lloyd Goodrich directed the Whitney Museum of American Art from 1958 to 1968.

The Last Years · *1970–82*

1. Piri Halasz, "Betty Parsons Exhibits in Montclair," *The New York Times,* Sunday, March 31, 1974, p. 14.

2. Grace Glueck, "Art Notes: The Last of the Big-Time Internationals," *The New York Times,* Sunday, March 23, 1975, p. 31.

3. John Russell, "Betty Parsons Gallery Marks Anniversary," *The New York Times,* Saturday, April 3, 1976, p. 20.

4. Mary Blume, "Changing Art Game Rules," *The International Herald Tribune,* August 21–22, 1976.

5. John Canaday, *The New York Times,* Friday, November 1, 1978.

6. Phyllis Linn, "Betty Parsons, Artist and Dealer Extraordinaire," *L'Officiel/USA,* October 1978.

7. Grace Lichtenstein, "The Remarkable Betty Parsons," *Art News,* March 1979, pp. 52-56.

8. *The New York Times,* Friday, March 14, 1980.

9. Billie Clarke, among other friends, remembered Betty's habit of changing the little animals' picture each day; always with the remark, "They will have something to look at...."

EXHIBITIONS OF BETTY PARSONS'S WORK*

Solo Exhibitions

Galerie des Quatre Chemins, 1933

Stendhal Gallery, Los Angeles, 1934

Midtown Galleries, New York City, ten exhibitions, 1936–57

University Gallery of Minnesota, 1937

Pensacola Art Center, 1958

Georgia Museum of Art, 1958

Latow Gallery, 1960

Sydney Wolfson Gallery, 1962

Miami Museum of Modern Art, 1963

New Arts Gallery, Atlanta, 1963

Bennington College, 1966

Gallery Sever, Boston, 1967

Grand Central Moderns, New York City, 1967

Whitechapel Gallery, London, 1968

Studio Gallery, Washington, D.C., 1971, 1973, 1975

Sachs Gallery, New York City, 1972

The Montclair Art Museum, "Retrospective of 50 Years," 1974

Benson Gallery, East Hampton, New York, 1975

Jill Kornblee/Jock Truman, New York City, 1977

Group Exhibitions

The New Chenil Gallery, London, 1927

Barbarie Gallery, Hollywood, 1937

The Price Gallery, Hollywood, 1937

Midtown's Christmas Exhibition, 1945

Dayton Art Institute, 1952–53

Midtown, "The Nude Traveling Show," 1952–53

John Herron Art Institute, Indianapolis, Indiana, 1954

"Midtown's Season's Retrospective," 1954, 1957–59

"Midtown's Watercolor Group," 1956–58

Art Barn, Southampton, New York, 1956

Memphis Museum, 1956

Madison Square Garden, New York City, 1956

Columbus Gallery of Fine Arts, 1957–58

Midtown's Opening Group Show, 1957, 1959

Midtown's Anniversary Shows, 1957–59

Pennsylvania Academy of the Fine Arts, Jury Meeting, 1957

Summit Art Association, 1958

Miami Beach Art Center, 1959

National Council of Women of the United States, 1959

American Abstract Artists, 1962

Society of the Four Arts, 1964

American Abstract Exhibition, 1964

Arts and Crafts Center, 1964

The Museum of Modern Art, New York City, "Penthouse Exhibition," 1964, 1966

The Heckscher Museum, Huntington, New York, 1964

Riverside Museum, New York City, 1966

Southold Gallery, New York, 1966

The Heckscher Museum, "Artists of Suffolk County, Part II—Abstract Tradition," 1970

Hurlbutt Gallery, Greenwich, Connecticut, "Mr. and Mrs. Joseph H. Hirshhorn Select...," 1970

*From the gallery archives.

EXHIBITIONS AT THE BETTY PARSONS GALLERY*

1946–47

September 30–October 19 · Northwest Coast Indian Art

October 22–November 9 · Ad Reinhardt

November 12–November 30 · Pietro Lazzari

December 2–December 30 · Christmas Group Show

January 2, 1947–January 18 · Walter Murch

January 20–February 8 · Ideographic Painters

February 10–March 1 · Theodoros Stamos

March 3–March 22 · Mark Rothko

March 24–April 12 · Hans Hofmann

April 14–April 26 · Clyfford Still

April 28–May 10 · Charles Owens

May 12–May 31 · Mortimer Brandt Group

June 7–June 28 · Boris Margo

1947–48

September 23–October 11 · John Stephan

October 13–November 1 · Boris Margo

November 3–November 22 · Hedda Sterne

November 24–December 13 · Ad Reinhardt

December 15–January 3, 1948 · Herbert Ferber

January 5–January 23 · Jackson Pollock

January 26–February 14 · Theodoros Stamos

February 16–March 6 · Gerome Kamrowski

March 8–March 27 · Mark Rothko

March 29–April 17 · Richard Pousette-Dart

April 19–May 8 · Seymour Lipton

May 10–May 28 · Sonia Sekula

*From the Gallery archives.

1948–49

September 27–October 16 · John Little

October 18–November 6 · Ad Reinhardt

November 8–November 27 · Maud Morgan

November 15–December 4 · Richard Pousette-Dart (brasses and photographs)

November 29–December 18 · Hedda Sterne

December 20–January 1, 1949 · Giglio Dante

January 3–January 22 · Walter Murch

January 24–February 12 · Jackson Pollock

February 1–February 19 · Jurgen Jacobsen ("8 Gouaches")

February 14–March 5 · John Stephan

February 21–March 12 · Sonia Sekula

March 7–March 26 · Richard Pousette-Dart

March 28–April 16 · Mark Rothko

April 18–May 7 · Theodoros Stamos/ Ernst Geitlinger

May 9–May 28 · William Congdon—"Paintings 1948–49"/Adaline Kent

1949–50

September 19–October 8 · Pietro Lazzari

October 10–October 29 · Group Show

October 31–November 19 · Ad Reinhardt/ Marie Menken

November 21–December 10 · Jackson Pollock/ William Gear

December 12–December 31 · Guitou Knoop/ Theodoros Stamos

January 3, 1950–January 21 · Mark Rothko

January 23–February 11 · Barnett Newman/ Amy Friedman Lee

February 13–March 4 · Hedda Sterne

March 6–March 25 · Herbert Ferber

March 27–April 15 · Richard Pousette-Dart/ Buffie Johnson

April 17–May 6 · Clyfford Still/ William Congdon

May 8–May 27 · Bradley Walker Tomlin/ Jeanne Miles

May 31–June 18 · Group Show—1949–50/Perle Fine

Perle Fine, *Bicycle Forms*, date unknown

1950–51

September 26–October 14 · John Stephan/ Anne Ryan (collages)

October 27–November 4 · Seymour Lipton

November 6–November 25 · Boris Margo/ Sari Dienes

November 28–December 16 · Jackson Pollock

December 18–January 6, 1951 · Forrest Bess/ Hedda Sterne

January 8–January 27 · Theodoros Stamos

January 15–February 3 · Richard Pousette-Dart (watercolors)

January 29–February 17 · Clyfford Still

February 5–February 17 · Marie Menken (watercolor, stone and string paintings)

Theodoros Stamos, *Red Sea Terrace No. 2,* 1952. Oil on canvas, 92 x 70¼". Marion Koogler McNay Art Museum, San Antonio, Texas. Purchase 1960.1

February 19–March 10 · Perle Fine

March 13–March 31 · Day Schnabel

April 2–April 21 · Mark Rothko/Sonia Sekula

April 23–May 12 · Barnett Newman/ Marie Taylor

May 14–June 2 · Walter Murch/ Robert Rauschenberg

June 4–June 23 · Ad Reinhardt

1951–52

September 24–October 13 · Richard Pousette-Dart

October 15–November 3 · Lee Krasner/ Anne Ryan

November 5–November 24 · Alfonso Ossorio

November 26–December 15 · Jackson Pollock

December 17–January 5, 1952 · Calvert Coggeshall

December 18–January 6, 1952 · Forrest Bess

January 7–January 26 · Ad Reinhardt/ Marjorie Liebman

January 28–February 16 · Saul Steinberg

February 18–March 8 · Theodoros Stamos

March 10–March 29 · Sonia Sekula/Emil Hess

April 1–April 19 · William Congdon/Ahmed

April 21–May 10 · Maud Morgan

May 12–June 14 · Group Show—1952

1952–53

September 29–October 11 · Recent Paintings—Group Show

October 14–November 1 · Seymour Lipton

November 3–November 22 · Jeanne Miles

November 24–December 13 · Calvert Coggeshall

December 15–January 3, 1953 · Perle Fine

January 5–January 24 · Theodoros Stamos

January 27–February 14 · William Congdon

February 16–March 7 · Hedda Sterne

March 9–March 28 · Richard Pousette-Dart

March 30–April 18 · Bradley Walker Tomlin

April 20–May 9 · Herbert Ferber

May 11–May 30 · Boris Margo

June 1–June 20 · Ethel Schwabacher

1953–54

October 5–October 24 · Kenzo Okada

October 26–November 14 · Adaline Kent/ E. Box

November 16–December 5 · Ad Reinhardt

December 7–January 2, 1954 · Alfonso Ossorio

January 4–January 23 · Anne Ryan

January 25–February 13 · Richard Lindner

February 15–March 6 · Enrico Donati

March 8–March 27 · Walter Murch

March 29–April 17 · Marjorie Liebman

April 20–May 8 · Sari Dienes/Marie Taylor

May 13–June 5 · Hugo Weber

1954–55

September 27–October 16 · José Guerrero

October 18–November 6 · Hedda Sterne

November 8–November 27 · Seymour Lipton

November 29–December 18 · William Congdon/Lyman Kipp, Jr.

December 21–January 8, 1955 · Group Show—Drawing/Dorothy Sturm

January 10–January 29 · Boris Margo

January 31–February 19 · Ad Reinhardt

February 21–March 12 · Calvert Coggeshall/ Pietro Lazzari

March 14–April 2 · Kenzo Okada

April 4–April 23 · Anne Ryan—Memorial Show

April 25–May 14 · Maud Morgan

1955–56

September 25–October 15 · Hugo Weber

October 17–November 5 · Enrico Donati

November 7–November 26 · Richard Pousette-Dart

November 28–December 17 · Sari Dienes

December 19–January 14, 1956 · Group Show—1946-56

January 16–February 4 · Theodoros Stamos

February 6–February 25 · Richard Lindner/ Lyman Kipp, Jr.

February 27–March 17 · Ethel Schwabacher

March 19–April 7 · Alfonso Ossorio

April 9–April 28 · Adaline Kent/Jeanne Miles

April 30–May 19 · Dusti Bongé

May 21–June 9 · Ellsworth Kelly

Enrico Donati, *Gore et Mandra,* 1957. Oil on canvas, 60 x 60". Collection of Whitney Museum of American Art, New York. Purchase 58.9

1956–57

September 24–October 13 · Elizabeth McFadden/Marjorie Liebman

October 15–November 3 · Kenzo Okada

November 5–November 24 · Ad Reinhardt

November 26–December 15 · William Congdon

December 17–January 5, 1957 · Group Show

January 7–January 26 · José Guerrero

January 28–February 16 · Thomas Sills

February 18–March 9 · Hedda Sterne

March 11–March 30 · Walter Murch

April 2–April 20 · Day Schnabel

April 22–May 11 · Dorothy Sturm/ Marie Taylor

May 13–June 1 · Maud Morgan/ Theora Hamblett

1957–58

September 23–October 12 · Ellsworth Kelly

October 14–November 2 · Calvert Coggeshall/E. Box

November 4–November 23 · Enrico Donati/ Forrest Bess

November 25–December 14 · Ethel Schwabacher

December 16–January 4, 1958 · Group Show

January 6–January 25 · Boris Margo

January 28–February 15 · Seymour Lipton

February 17–March 8 · Richard Pousette-Dart

March 10–March 28 · Jack Youngerman

March 31–April 19 · Lyman Kipp, Jr./ Jesse Reichek

April 21–May 10 · Dusti Bongé/ Elizabeth McFadden (collages)

May 12–May 31 · Pietro Lazzari/ Theora Hamblett

Alfonso Ossorio, *Blood Wedding*, 1958

1958–59

September 22–October 11 · Adaline Kent—Memorial Show

October 13–November 1 · Hedda Sterne

November 3–November 22 · Alfonso Ossorio

November 25–December 13 · José Guerrero

December 15–January 3, 1959 · Group Show—"Paintings for Unlimited Space"

January 5–January 24 · Ad Reinhardt

January 26–February 14 · Thomas Sills

February 16–March 7 · Richard Lindner

March 9–March 28 · Enrico Donati/ Hugo Weber

March 30–April 18 · Richard Pousette-Dart

April 20–May 9 · Walter Murch/Forrest Bess

May 12–May 30 · William Congdon/ Jesse Reichek (drawings)

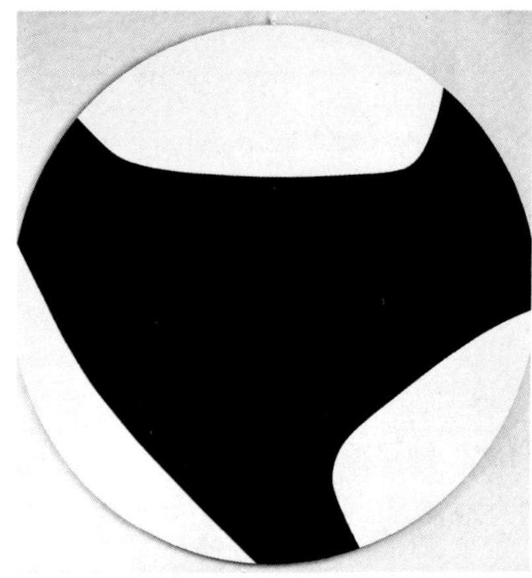

Leon Polk Smith, *Anitou*, 1958. Oil on canvas, 56⅝" diameter. Collection, The Museum of Modern Art, New York. Gift of Dr. and Mrs. Arthur Lejwa

1959–60

September 28–October 17 · Sari Dienes

October 19–November 7 · Ellsworth Kelly

November 9–November 28 · Kenzo Okada

November 30–December 19 · Alfonso Ossorio

December 21–January 9, 1960 · Group Show—"Paintings for Limited Space"

January 11–January 30 · Jack Youngerman

February 1–February 20 · Ethel Schwabacher/ Marie Taylor

February 23–March 12 · Boris Margo

March 14–April 2 · Eduardo Paolozzi

April 4–April 23 · Alexander Liberman

April 25–May 14 · Lyman Kipp, Jr.

May 16–June 4 · Paul Feeley

Sidney Wolfson, *Swept*, 1959

SECTION II: 1959–60

October 6–October 24 · Jeanne Reynal

October 27–November 14 · Marjorie Liebman

November 17–December 5 · Thomas George

December 7–December 24 · Paul Bodin

December 29–January 16, 1960 · Agnes Martin

January 19–February 16 · Wallace Putnam

February 9–February 27 · Leon Polk Smith

March 1–March 19 · David Budd

March 22–April 9 · Minoru Kawabata

April 12–April 30 · Yehiel Shemi

May 3–May 21 · Judith Godwin

May 24–June 11 · Ruth Vollmer

1960–61

September 26–October 15 · Dusti Bongé

October 17–November 5 · Ad Reinhardt—"25 Years of Abstract Painting"

November 7–November 26 · José Guerrero

November 28–December 17 · Enrico Donati

December 19–January 8, 1961 · Group Show

January 10–January 28 · Chryssa

January 30–February 18 · Thomas Sills

February 20–March 11 · Alfonso Ossorio

March 14–April 8 · Seymour Lipton

April 10–April 29 · Richard Pousette-Dart

May 1–May 20 · Calvert Coggeshall/ Guido Somaré

May 22–June 10 · Minoru Kawabata

1961–62

September 25–October 14 · Agnes Martin

October 16–November 4 · Ellsworth Kelly

November 6–November 25 · Hedda Sterne

November 27–December 16 · Jack Youngerman

December 18–January 6, 1962 · Group Show

January 8–January 27 · Forrest Bess

January 29–February 17 · Alexander Liberman

February 20–March 10 · William Congdon

March 12–March 31 · Kenzo Okada

April 2–April 21 · Lyman Kipp, Jr.

April 23–May 12 · Eduardo Paolozzi

May 14–June 2 · Paul Feeley

Sven Lukin, *Maleus Malleficarum*, date unknown

SECTION II: 1961–62

December 20–January 7, 1962 · New Names (Guest Show)

January 9–January 28 · Sven Lukin

January 31–February 18 · Sidney Wolfson

February 21–March 11 · Sasson Soffer

March 13–April 1 · Paul Bodin

April 4–April 22 · Wallace Putnam

April 25–May 13 · Aline Porter

1962–63

October 1–October 20 · Boris Margo

October 22–November 10 · Ethel Schwabacher

November 12–December 1 · Dusti Bongé

December 3–December 22 · Walter Murch

December 26–January 5, 1963 · Group Show

January 7–January 26 · José Guerrero

January 28–February 16 · Thomas George

February 18–March 9 · Minoru Kawabata

José Guerrero, *Light Around Darkness*, 1962

March 11–March 30 · Sasson Soffer/Ruth Vollmer

April 1–April 20 · Jesse Reichek

April 22–May 10 · Alexander Liberman

May 13–May 31 · Marie Taylor/Paul Feeley

1963–64

September 23–October 26 · Amlash

October 29–November 23 · Ellsworth Kelly

November 26–December 14 · Hedda Sterne

December 17–January 4, 1964 · Group Show—"Toys by Artists"

January 7–February 1 · Kenzo Okada

February 4–February 29 · Lyman Kipp, Jr.

March 3–March 28 · "The Painter's Eye"

March 31–April 25 · Jack Youngerman

April 28–May 23 · "10 Artists of the World's Fair"

Eduardo Paolozzi, *Icarus II*, ca. 1963

1964–65

September 29–October 24 · Alexander Liberman

October 27–November 21 · Paul Feeley

Toko Shinoda, *#10*, ca. 1963

November 24–December 19 · Richard Pousette-Dart

December 21–January 22, 1965 · Drawings

January 5–January 30 · Toko Shinoda

February 2–February 27 · Minoru Kawabata

March 2–March 27 · Ad Reinhardt (3 galleries)

March 30–April 17 · Robert Murray (first one-man show in U.S.)

April 13–May 8 · Jesse Reichek (drawings)

April 20–May 8 · Luigi Parzini (first one-man show in U.S.)

May 11–June 5 · Andrea Cascella (first one-man show in U.S.)

1965–66

September 7–September 25 · Richard Tuttle (first one-man show in U.S.)

September 28–October 23 · Jack Youngerman

October 26–November 13 · Thomas George

November 16–December 4 · Lyman Kipp, Jr.

December 7–December 31 · Paul Feeley

January 4, 1966–January 22 · Walter Murch

January 25–February 12 · Ruth Vollmer

February 15–March 5 · Hedda Sterne (portraits)

March 8–April 2 · Alexander Liberman

April 5–April 23 · V. V. Rankine

April 25–May 14 · Enrico Castellani (first one-man show in U.S.)

May 17–June 11 · Timothy Hennessy

Robert Murray, *Track,* 1966

1966–67

September 13–October 1 · Walter Barker/ Marie Taylor

October 4–October 21 · "Constructed Works": Lyman Kipp, Jr., Alexander Liberman, Jack Youngerman, Ruth Vollmer, Robert Murray, Paul Tuttle, Enrico Castellani, Robert Smithson, Paul Feeley

October 6–October 21 · Russia

October 25–November 12 · Kenzo Okada

November 15–December 10 · Saul Steinberg

December 13–December 31 · George Murray (drawings)

January 3, 1967–January 21 · Jesse Reichek

January 24–February 11 · Minoru Kawabata

February 14–March 4 · Cohen

March 7–April 1 · Alexander Liberman

April 3–April 22 · Calvert Coggeshall

April 25–May 13 · Paul Feeley

Walter Barker, *Paradox Series No. VII*

1967–68

October 3–October 21 · "4 British Painters": Michael Kidner, Bruce Tippett, Michael Tyzack, John Walker

October 24–November 11 · Jack Youngerman

November 14–December 2 · Richard Pousette-Dart

December 5–December 30 · William Congdon

January 2, 1968–January 20 · Richard Tuttle/ Jean Jones Jackson

January 23–February 10 · Hedda Sterne

February 13–March 2 · Lyman Kipp, Jr.

March 5–March 30 · Andrea Cascella

April 2–April 20 · Thomas George

April 23–May 11 · Thomas Stokes

April 24–May 11 · Emil Hess

May 14–June 7 · Toko Shinoda

Jean Jones Jackson, *Siesta,* 1966. Maynard Walker Gallery, New York

1968–69

September 17–October 5 · Jesse Reichek

October 8–October 26 · Robert Murray (sculpture)

October 29–November 16 · Jack Youngerman (watercolors, drawings)

November 19–December 7 · Ruth Vollmer (sculpture)

December 10–January 4, 1969 · Calvert Coggeshall

January 7–January 25 · Minoru Kawabata

January 21–February 3 · "Animals"— Adge Baker, Marie Taylor, Kathleen Cooke

January 28–February 15 · V. V. Rankine— "Plastic Constructions"

February 18–March 8 · Alexander Liberman

March 11–March 29 · Kenzo Okada

April 1–April 19 · Group Show—"Reductive Vision": Cleve Gray, Enrico Castellani, [Jesse] Reichek, [Allan] Hacklin, [Bruce] Tippett

April 22–Mary 10 · Stephen Porter (sculpture, first one-man show in U.S.)

May 13–June 6 · Walter Barker

1969–70

September 15–October 4 · Thomas Stokes/ Theora Hamblett

October 7–November 1 · Allan Hacklin

November 5–November 29 · Saul Steinberg (drawings)

December 2–December 20 · Bruce Tippett/ Gregory Masurovsky

January 6, 1970–January 24 · Cleve Gray— "Paintings and Painted Forms"

January 27–February 14 · Paul Feeley

February 17–March 7 · Richard Tuttle/ Anne Ryan

March 10–March 28 · Hedda Sterne

March 31–April 18 · Timothy Hennessy

April 21–May 9 · Calvert Coggeshall

May 12–May 30 · Jesse Reichek

June 2–June 20 · Emil Hess/[Kathleen] Cooke

1970–71

September 22–October 10 · Brian O'Doherty/James Rosen

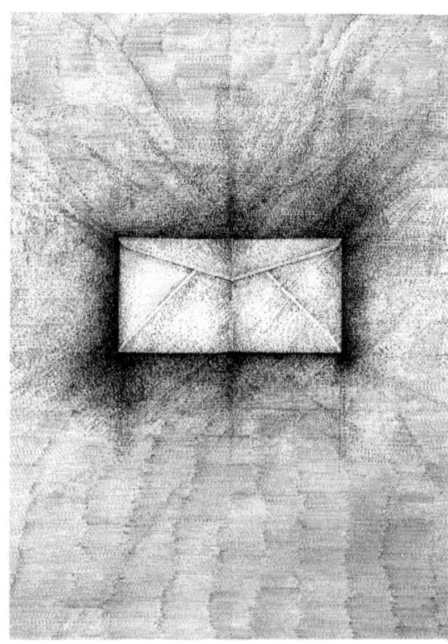

Gregory Masurovsky, *The Letter,* 1970

October 13–October 31 · Thomas George

November 3–November 14 · Ruth Vollmer

November 24–December 12 · V. V. Rankine

December 15–January 2, 1971 · Group Show—Sculpture

January 5–January 23 · [Minoru] Kawabata/ [Marie] Taylor

January 23–February 13 · Jack Youngerman

February 16–March 7 · Andrea Cascella

March 9–April 3 · Kenzo Okada

April 6–April 24 · Allan Hacklin/ William Taggart

April 27–May 15 · [Toko] Shinoda

May 18–June 5 · Thomas Stokes

1971–72

January 12–January 30 · Minoru Kawabata

February 2–February 20 · Henry Pearson/ Jeanne Reynal

February 23–March Nuaga/ Gregory Masurovsky

March 16–April 10 · Kenzo Okada

April 13–May 1 · Allan Hacklin/Gego

May 4–May 22 · Toko Shinoda/ Kathleen Taylor

May 25–June 12 · Thomas Stokes

January 4, 1972–January 22 · Timothy Hennessy

January 25–February 12 · Mark Lancaster

February 15–March 4 · Barbara Chase-Riboud

March 7–March 25 · Hedda Sterne

March 28–April 15 · Cleve Gray

April 18–May 6 · Calvert Coggeshall

May 9–May 27 · Calvert Coggeshall

May 30–June 16 · Calvert Coggeshall

1972–73

September 19–October 7 · Edward Zutrau

October 11–October 28 · Dorothy Heller

October 31–November 25 · Andrea Cascella

November 28–December 16 · Thomas Stokes/ Kathleen Cooke

January 9, 1973–February 3 · Ray Johnson

February 7–March 3 · Saul Steinberg

March 6–March 31 · Kenzo Okada

April 3–April 21 · Ruth Vollmer

April 24–May 12 · Cleve Gray

May 15–June 15 · "Sources of Inspiration": Barbara Chase-Riboud, *Hop Scotch*; Minoru [Kawabata], *Envelopes*; Koehler, *Artichokes*; Greg Otto, *T.V. Color Amplitude Correction*; V. V. Rankine, *Monuments at Night*; Risa, *Water Towers*; Henry Pearson, *Topography Maps*

"New Talent": John Thomas, Richard Francisco, Eve Clandentin, James Rosen, Candido, Fernandez, Sam Russo, William Taggart, William Hopper, Thomas Noskowski, Chris Parker, Liz Kossoff

1973–74

September 4–September 22 · Richard Francisco

September 25–October 13 · Zuka

October 16–November 8 · Yehiel Shemi

October 23–November 10 · Ed Baynard

November 13–December 1 · Hans Richter

December 4–December 21 · Jan Groth/ "Very Small Paintings by Five Painters": Fanny Brennan, Lee Hall, Jean Jones Jackson, Jean Hugo,Walter Murch

January 8, 1974–January 26 · Patrick Ireland/James Rosen

January 29–February 16 · Calvert Coggeshall

February 19–March 9 · Hedda Sterne

March 12–March 30 · Richard Tuttle

April 2–April 20 · Stephen Porter

April 23–May 11 · Thomas George

May 14–May 31 · Cleve Gray

June 4–June 15 · New Talent Show (drawings)

1974–75

September 10–September 28 · William Taggart

September 24–October 19 · Walter Murch

October 1–October 19 · Mark Lancaster/ Walter Murch

October 22–November 9 · Henry Pearson/ Susan Eisler

November 12–November 30 · Minoru Kawabata/Gregory Masurovsky

December 3–December 21 · Mario Ceroli

February 18, 1975–March 8 · Risa/Greg Otto

March 4–March 22 · Aline Porter

March 11–March 29 · Thomas Stokes/ Allan Hacklin

April 2–April 19 · Richard Francisco/ Michael Robbins

April 22–May 16 · Lee Hall/Richard Tuttle

May 20–June 6 · "Only Large Paintings": Calvert Coggeshall, Cleve Gray, Minoru Kawabata, Kenzo Okada, Eliza Moore, Patrick Ireland, William Taggart, Bob Yasuda, Yardley, Edward Zutrau

1975–76

September 9–September 27 · Helen Aylon

October 7–October 25 · Dusti Bongé

October 14–November 8 · Hedda Sterne

November 4–November 26 · Group Show (Collage): [Susan] Eisler, Allan Hacklin, [Mario] Ceroli, Sybyl Weil, Ed Baynard, Arthur Pierson, Risa, [Yehiel] Shemi, William Taggart, [Dorothy] Sturm, A. Shields, Richard Francisco, Cleve Gray, Saul Steinberg, [Vita] Petersen, Hans Richter, Anne Ryan, Esteban Vicente, Michael Gitlin, E. Moore, Sue Howard

December 2–December 20 · [Yehiel] Shemi

January 6, 1976–January 24 · Zuka

February 3–February 21 · Dorothy Heller

March 2–March 27 · Kenzo Okada

March 30–April 24 · 30th Anniversary Show: William Congdon, Calvert Coggeshall, Hans Hofmann, Boris Margo, [Jeanne] Miles, [Maud] Morgan, Walter Murch, Barnett Newman, Alfonso Ossorio, Jackson Pollock, Richard Pousette-Dart, Ad Reinhardt, Mark Rothko, [Anne] Ryan, Sonia Sekula, Theodoros Stamos, Saul Steinberg, Hedda Sterne, Clyfford Still, Bradley Walker Tomlin

April 27–May 15 · Thomas George

May 18–June 11 · New Talent Show: Sylvia Guirey, Eliza Moore, Jonathan Thomas

1976–77

September 21–October 9 · William Taggart

October 12–November 6 · Cleve Gray

November 17–December 4 · Saul Steinberg

December 7–December 31 · Jan Groth

January 4, 1977–January 22 · Lee Hall

January 25–February 12 · Richard Francisco

February 15–March 5 · Thomas Stokes/ John Goodwin

March 8–March 26 · Bob Yasuda

March 29–April 16 · Ruth Vollmer/ Jeanne Miles

April 19–May 7 · Toko Shinoda/Marie Taylor

May 10–May 28 · Eliza Moore

May 31–June 18 · Arthur Pierson

INDEX

Pages on which illustrations appear are in *italics*

PHOTOGRAPH CREDITS

•

The majority of the photographs, documentary and otherwise, were provided by the Estate of Betty Parsons. Photographs not obtained from museums are as follows (numbers refer to page on which illustration appears):

Baker, Oliver, New York: 80, 120; Brenwasser, New York: 57, 58 below; Burckhardt, Rudolph, New York: 185 center column; Clements, Geoffrey, New York: 87; Cseh, Bela, New York: 156 center; Eddowes Co., Inc., New York: 71; Ferrari, John A.: 133; Hall, Lee, New York: 163 above right, below; Juley, Peter A. and Son, New York: 73; Landshoff, Herman, New York: 135; Leen, Nina, *Life* magazine, © Time, Inc.: 98; Liberman, Alexander, New York: 12; Metz, Gwyn, New York: 76, 142, 144, 154 center, 156 above, 164, 165, 167, 171, 174; Moriwaki, A., New York: 86; Naar, Jon, New York: 126; Namuth, Hans, New York: 102; Piaget, St. Louis: 112 above; Pocock, Philip, New York: 72, 118, 128, 160; Pollitzer, Eric, New York: 149 right; Rabin, Nathan, New York: 52, 112 below; Rancon, Stephanie, New York: 154 below; Robb Studio, Salem, Mass.: 119; Savio, Oscar, Rome: 111; Seligson, Stanley, New York: 156 below; Suter, Dennis, Baltimore: 156 above, center; Suttle, William, New York: 134, 149 left, 185 right column; Ward, Cora, New York: 140.